Pearl and Bessie

A baby abandoned on a rubbish dump,

and the woman who saved her

JULIA BISHOP

with

ANDY BULL

DEDICATION

To the late Revd Keith Parsons, without whose generosity with his time and knowledge this book would not have been begun; to my husband Hugh, without whose support and encouragement it would not have been continued for so long; to my cousin and 'ghost' Andy Bull, without whose patience and expertise it would not have been completed.

ACKNOWLEDGEMENTS

I am very grateful both to the Bodleian Library, University of Oxford and to the Methodist Missionary Archives at the School of Oriental and African Studies, University of London for permission to consult their collections. I am also grateful to Friends of the Church in China for their contacts and helpful advice.

I owe a special debt of gratitude to the late Revd Keith Parsons and his brother the late Revd Kenneth Parsons, and their respective children, Helen Parsons and John Parsons, for their help and permission to use the extensive Parsons Family papers. Special thanks also go to Arnold Pacey for his kindness in showing me his mother's letters and his helpful comments on them and to Dan Lu for information about Pearl's later life.

Many other people were also very helpful and I hope this list is complete:
The Revd Peter and Betty Brooks; Peter Forsaith of the Westminster Institute; Revd J. Michael Franklin, Margaret Gardner, Revd Ted Harrison, Revd George Hood, Revd Edgar and Mrs Margeret Hopkins; Mrs Isobel Hurst, Revd Paul and Stella Jeffries, Revd Geoffrey Jones, the late Alison Lewis (daughter of Elliott Kendall), Revd Li-Ping Kwong, President of the Methodist Church in Hong Kong; the late Geoff Mauldon, Margaret Patton; Geoffrey Senior, James Savin; John and Patricia Savin; Roger Thorne, David Van Meter; The Revd Bob and Maggi Whyte; the late Professor Henry Wu (Wu Hsin-Fu); John (Alfred and Bessie's adopted son) and his son; Zhu Aiguang.

A NOTE ON PLACE NAMES

The names of many of the places in this story have changed over time. I have used the name as it was at the time I am writing about, but note at the first mention where that name later changed. Chaotung became Zhaotong and Tung Chuan became Hweitze. However, in the case of the capital of Yunnan province, which was Yunnan fu but became Kunming in the 1920s, I have used both throughout, as the two names seem to have been used interchangeably over a long period.

CHARACTERS

Arnold, Roger, runs the Young Men's Christian Association in Kunming, gives Mildred Button away at her wedding to Leslie Pacey

Bryant, Nancy, (see Parsons, Nancy)

Bryant, Phil, Nancy Parson's brother, to whom she often writes

Bull, Bessie, engaged to and later marries Alfred Evans

Button, Mildred marries Leslie Pacey, close friend of Pearl Evans

Chang-ru-ih Chang rebel general opposed to Long Yuin, the ruling warlord in Yunnan

Chiang Kai Shek, leader of the nationalist Kuomintang during the fight with the Communist forces of Mao Tse-tung

Chu Huang Chang, Chinese pastor and leader of the Miao at Stone Gateway. Commits suicide after Communist takeover

Chu Shui Kwang, senior Chinese pastor at Chaotung. Commits suicide after Communist takeover

Constantine, Leonard, missionary dean of Hua Chung University and author of *The Bitter Years*

Dingle, Edwin, travel writer who is nursed for months by Alf and Bessie Evans. Writes about them in *Across China on Foot*

Dymond, Frank lifelong friend of Sam Pollard who came to China with him in 1886. Wife Maud, son George and daughter Cathie. Cathie marries Kenneth May. They take in John (Alf and Bessie Evans' adopted son) for a year (1935-6) when he is schooled at Chaotong, and Alf and Bessie go on furlough

Evans, Alfred, engaged to and later marries Bessie Bull

Evans, Bessie (nee Bull), wife of Alfred Evans

Evans, John, adopted Chinese son of Alf and Bessie Evans, moved to America in 1944

Evans, Pearl, adopted Chinese daughter of Alf and Bessie Evans

Fung, Jennie and **Fung, Jane,** sisters who share a home with Alf Evans and look after him in his final years in Hong Kong

Goldsworthy, Heber, married to Ida, missionary murdered at Stone Gateway in 1938

Grandin, Dr Lilian, comes to China along with Alf Evans. Marries Edwin Dingle, but they soon divorce

Grist, William (W. A.) author of books on Sam Pollard and the Chinese missions

Harrison, Edward missionary, and wife **Harrison, Isobel,** missionary and nurse. When their house near the Evanses is bombed they move across the lake to Alf and Bessie's retirement home

Hicks, Charles, missionary, wife Maria, son Charlie. Travel to China with Alfred Evans.

Hudspeth, Will missionary, worked with Sam Parsons on developing a written language for the Miao

Kendall, Elliott, last missionary to leave Kunming in 1951 after being tried as a suspected spy alongside Vernon Stones, author of *Beyond the Clouds, the story of Samuel Pollard in South West China*

Li Shuang-mei, Chinese teacher companion of Lettie Squire.

Li, John preacher and brother of Stephen Li, dies in prison after being arrested during the Communist takeover.

Li, Norah, Pearl Evans's long-term companion. A close friend from 1936 until Pearl's death in 1994

Li, Stephen a Chinese member of missionary team, brother of John Li

Long, Yuin Warlord who ruled in Yunnan in defiance of Chiang Kai Shek

May, Kenneth, marries Cathie Dymond (daughter of Frank Dymond), close friends of Muriel and Leslie Pacey.

Mao Tse-tung, later Mao Ze Dong, leader of the Communist forces that defeated the nationalist Kuomintang, later chairman of the Communist Party 1943-76

Moody, Henry, missionary, wife Beatrice a nurse. They survive the attack on Stone Gateway in which Heber Goldsworthy is murdered

Moody, Edward, known as Ted, missionary committee's representative at Kunming in the years just before foreigners were ejected from China

Pacey, Mildred, nee Button, (close friend of Pearl Evans) marries Leslie Pacey.

Pacey, Leslie marries Mildred Button

Parsons, Harry comes to China as a new recruit with Bessie Bull. Marries **Annie**, known as Nancy or Nance née Bryant. Twin sons Philip Kenneth and Richard Keith born Chaotung. Both become missionaries.

Parsons, Keith (see Parsons, Harry)

Parsons, Ken (see Parsons, Harry)

Pollard, Sam, wife **Emmie**, sons Bertram, Walter, Ernest. Creator of the Miao's written language

Pu Yi, Henry, last emperor of China. When they invaded Manchuria, the Japanese imposed him as ruler of the puppet state of Manchukuo

Rattenbury, Harold, mission secretary at Mission House in London, tours Kunming and clashes repeatedly with Alfred Evans over his lateness in filing accounts and acting without authority

Savin, Dr Lewis, with his wife Kate and their baby son, return to China on same boat as Bessie Bull. Three children are Kitty, Agnes and David

Squire, Lettie, teacher and missionary, companion of Li Shuang-mei

Stedeford, Charles, Foreign Secretary of the Missionary Society

Stephenson, Gladys, Pearl Evans's supervisor at Hankow hospital

Tremberth, William, missionary, with his wife Emily and their three children, return to China on same boat as Bessie

Stones, Vernon arrested as a spy in Chaotung during the Communist takeover. Held in solitary confinement in Kunming before being tried along with Elliott Kendall, then deported from China.

Thexton, Hilda, offers Pearl Evans a home in England in the 1960s.

CONTENTS

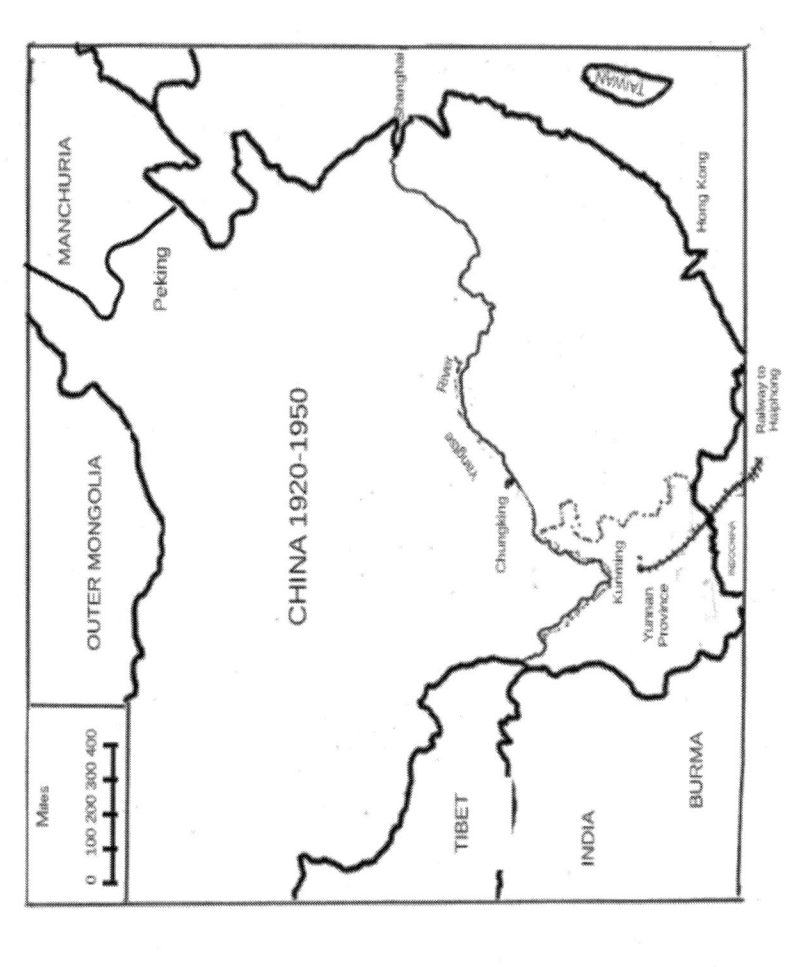

The Gopu and Miao areas of North East Yunnan around 1950

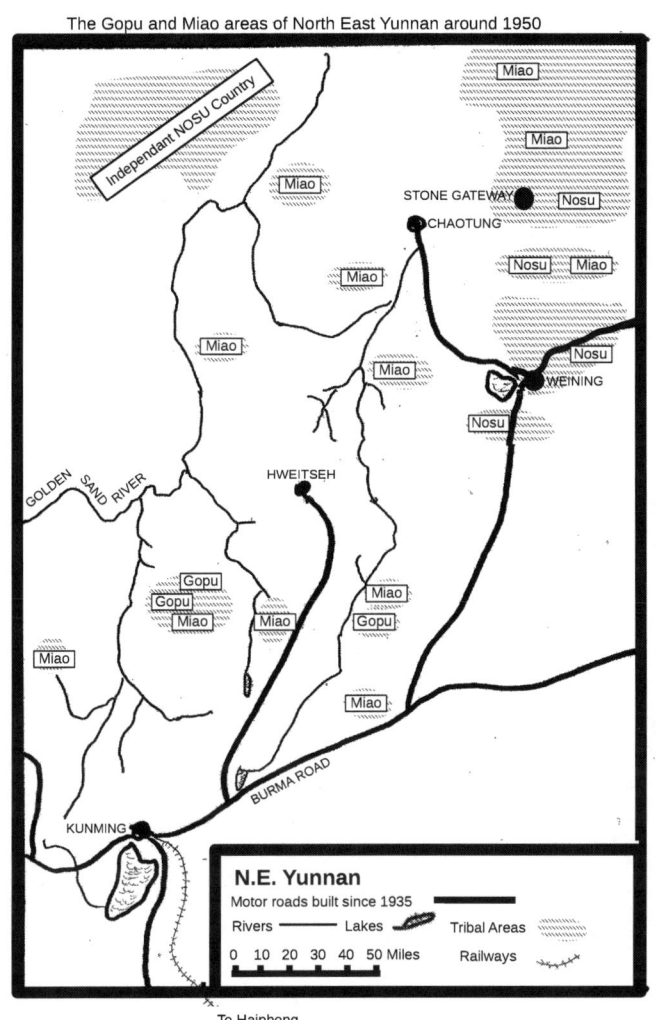

1 PEARL

On the rubbish dump, a baby cried.

The cry was weak, and fading. The wild dogs had picked up the sound and the scent, and were circling, closing in.

Bessie left the trail, walked towards the sound, stepping over the filth and the tangled vegetation. She picked up a rock and hurled it at the closest dog. It gave a snap of displeasure, lowered its head and slunk away, but not very far away. The dog was hungry, and its fear of being hit by a rock only just outweighed its desire to feed.

Bessie thought she knew why the baby was here and, when she reached it, lying naked in the long grass, her suspicion was confirmed. This was a little girl. She had been abandoned because of her sex. It happened often here, in China.

The thought of a child left to die hit Bessie like a stab to the heart. Back home in England her nine-year-old sister Gladys had died, just after Bessie's arrival in China. She could not forget Gladys's ghostly look; a knowledge and fear of death in her poor, pale face as she approached the end of her short life. Gladys had been loved, and Bessie's parents had done everything they could to keep her alive. This baby was unloved, unwanted by those who ought to have been protecting her.

Bessie had learned very quickly after her arrival in the province of Yunnan in south west China why girl babies were left to die, or sold into slavery, or sexual serfdom. In the city of Chaotung, mothers threw unwanted girls into a baby tower, where they were left to starve to death. Elsewhere, they might be strangled and thrown over the city wall, to be devoured by dogs or wolves.

Just a year before she found herself standing here, over this crying baby, Bessie had been faced with two other deaths. Her baby brother George had died, aged four. When she received that news, Bessie had a baby girl in her care. The mother had died seven days after giving birth.

Bessie had been powerless to help her own little sister, or her brother. So, here, now, how could she let this little life slip away, when she had the power to save it? This baby would be torn apart by dogs if she didn't pick it up. There was no time to think what she would do with her. If she hesitated there would

1

be no baby to think about. There were plenty of reasons to walk away. This was not her country, nor her culture. And she was thirty years old and single. Her fiancé was a week's journey away, and there was no way to get word to him, to ask his opinion before acting. How would he feel when she presented a child to him before they were even married?

Bessie drew close, and crouched down.

Parting the long grass in which the baby lay, she saw that her scalp was cut and bleeding in several places. Birds had found her before the dogs, and had been picking at her soft head. But they had not, thank God, plucked out her eyes, which was often the first point of attack. Bessie unwrapped the scarf from her head and spread it on the ground. She lifted the baby gently onto it and wrapped the ends around her, swaddling her. Then she slipped her hands beneath and lifted this little bundle, now almost too weak to cry, and cradled her in her arms.

Did this baby girl mean nothing to her mother? Maybe the woman had no choice. Perhaps poverty had forced her to abandon this baby, not just the fact that she was a girl. In which case she might not be just worthless, but a threat to the survival of other children.

Bessie carried her back to the group she was with, handed the bundle to one of the men, got back into her sedan chair and then took the baby in her arms once more. As she did so, a parable came to mind. Bessie knew her Bible, and thought of the words of Matthew:

'The kingdom of heaven is like unto a merchant man, seeking goodly pearls: Who, when he had found one pearl of great price, went and sold all that he had, and bought it.'

— *Matthew 13:45-46*

So, Pearl would be the baby's name. But how much would Bessie have to give up in rescuing Pearl? How much would this baby change her life? And what of Pearl herself, as she grew up? Bessie was giving Pearl a life, but it would be a life profoundly different from that she had been born into.

I have a personal connection with this story. Bessie was my great aunt. I never met her, but when I was a little girl I remember my grandfather talking about his elder sister; about Alf, the man Bessie would marry; and about Pearl. But they were just names, and they merged into a long list of great uncles, great aunts and cousins with names like Flo, Charlie and Ethel, most of whom were already dead. So I didn't take much notice. I knew little of my exotic Great Aunt Bessie, who travelled to China, on the far side of the world, lived a life of unimaginable adventure and drama, fighting for her life, conquering wild country, saving souls.

And I doubt whether, as an adult, I would have thought much more about Bessie if my father hadn't challenged me, over forty years later, to find out about her. He wanted her story explored and told, and for Kate Winslet to play her in the film version of that story. He was quite convinced she would. So I had to bring Bessie to life. But this story began over a century before. Would I find that the trail had gone cold, that there was nothing to explore? Would Bessie ever amount to more than a faded memory? A ghost?

My quest for Bessie led inevitably to a quest for Pearl. Because it seemed to me that rescuing Pearl was one of the bravest, most significant things Bessie did in her remarkable life.

I wanted to know this baby as Bessie had, to trace her story, to find out how her life played out. And as I learned more and more about Pearl, and the life she led, it became impossible to let the story go.

I soon began to realise that Bessie and Alfred had lived through extraordinary events in China, spanning sixty-five years. They lived lives of great struggle, great achievement, great hardship, great danger, against the backdrop of epoch-shifting events: the overthrow of the ruling Manchu dynasty; a civil war; battles between competing warlords; an invasion by the Japanese; the long struggle between Chiang Kai Shek and Mao Tse Tung; and the subsequent Communist revolution and takeover. These seismic political and cultural shifts would shatter the lives of Bessie and Alf, and send Pearl afloat like the flimsiest of boats on the roughest of seas.

By the time I began my quest, both of my grandparents, all of that generation and many of their children were dead. Sadly, the mysterious Pearl had died in 1994, only a few years before I started my researches into her life.

It has taken me twenty years to piece this story together, during which time I have found out who Pearl loved and who she lost; what she achieved and what was taken from her; about her happiness and her suffering; the particular forms of psychological cruelty and mental torture that were practised upon her, and how she was forbidden to be with the adopted father she loved as his life ebbed away. As I learned more about her, and how her life played out, an awful question grew in my mind: did Bessie's rescue of Pearl turn out to be a blessing or a curse?

Bessie and Pearl would gradually take shape before me, until I felt I knew them almost as well as if I had lived alongside them. But that was at the end. Now, let me go back to the beginning of Bessie's great adventure.

2 RIDING THE RIVER DRAGON

The smell of boiled turnips and pork frying in garlic drifted over the wooden houseboat as it slid between the dark walls of the ravine. The cook was hard at work in the galley. The small army of trackers on the towpath, who were hauling the boat up-stream, would soon come on board for their evening meal, hungry after a day spent pulling the plaited bamboo ropes against the strong currents and rapids of the Yangtse river.

On deck, the six adult passengers and four children could see the last rays of the sun strike the farmsteads at the top of the cliffs, nearly a thousand feet above. Their voyage had already taken many weeks; long days at sea from Southampton to Shanghai and then onto the steamer which had brought them a thousand miles up the river to Yichang.

On a wintry afternoon in February, the hills still covered in snow, they had boarded this houseboat for the journey through the rapids and gorges of the Yangtse. Although the boat was quite small – just 50ft long and 12ft wide – it had a crew of thirty-five: eight onboard to row, steer and manage the ropes, twenty-two to haul it along from the towpath which was high above the water level, and five others to assist wherever they were needed.

For the rapids, which were particularly dangerous, local people would add their labour to that of the trackers, sometimes as many as 200 at a time. Where the cliffs were too steep for the trackers to find a path from which to pull the craft along, sailors worked oars positioned at the front of the boat. There was a space at the back where the steersman stood. When the current was not too strong and the wind was favourable, they hoisted a sail and tacked slowly upstream.

The boat set off accompanied by a volley of fire crackers to scare off evil spirits, and with clouds of incense spiralling to the sky to awaken the smile of heaven. On the prow, a patch of still-warm, congealing blood stained the spot where the captain had sacrificed a hen, to atone for any sins committed by the travellers and appease the river gods.

The year was 1903, and the two married couples – members of the Bible Christian Church, an offshoot of Methodism – were returning to their mission in the province of Yunnan, south-west China, after home leave: Dr Lewis Savin with his wife Kate and their baby son; and the Revd William Tremberth, with his wife Emily and their three children. With them were two young missionaries on their first journey to China: Bessie Bull and Harry Parsons.

The ancient-looking boat was cramped. The passengers' accommodation was amidships, a 24ft long space divided by thin partitions into four narrow rooms, with one window each. One apartment was occupied by Bessie and Ruth, the Tremberths' eldest child, another by the Savins, a third by the Tremberths and their other two children; the fourth, towards the prow, by Harry Parsons. By day, Harry's quarters became the dining room. Towards the stern there was a kitchen, screened off from the rooms by just a string of rugs, nailed up as dividers.

The captain, Huang Hong-shuen, with his wife and two children – a girl of 13 and a boy of 11 – occupied a tiny room built right over the stern of the boat. Then there was the cook, busy preparing that great basin of fat pork fried in garlic, bowls of turnip in smoking hot liquor, and rice to the ever-hungry crew and more restrained passengers.

The missionaries had not expected to go far on the first day and, when the boat tied up at the far end of the city, they were pleased that this part of the journey had started at last.

Then some well-dressed Chinese men came aboard asking for donations for a society which gathered up the bodies of shipwrecked passengers from the banks of the Yangtse and gave them a decent burial. This seemed to be a worthy cause, so the missionaries made a donation, although they were surprised that none of them had heard of the society before. Their contribution was graciously received and the Chinese left, wishing them a safe journey.

But all was not as it seemed. While the visitors distracted the missionaries, there was a lot of activity among the crew. Belatedly, they realised that more cargo was being carried on board, although all their own luggage was already stowed in the hold. Dr Savin went to challenge the captain, and was soon engaged in an angry conversation in Chinese.

The captain eventually admitted that his men were involved in smuggling; they had just brought their contraband on board, stuffing forged bank notes and sacks of cotton wool into the dark recesses of the boat. Dr Savin protested in the strongest terms that the missionaries had hired the boat for their exclusive use; they would take no responsibility for any of the crew's illegal activities if the contraband was found when the boat reached the customs barrier. The captain insisted that the contraband would come up-river with them: smuggling was a normal part of the crew's way of life.

Next morning the customs officers came aboard, examined their papers, chatted pleasantly with the captain for a few minutes and then left, without looking into the hold. Dr Savin gave the order to move on; the captain smiled and obeyed. Shortly after passing the customs barrier, the boat entered the Yangtse Gorges, where huge cliffs, shaped like ruined fortresses and gigantic pipe organs covered with moss and lichen, rose a thousand feet. At regular intervals, the mountains were bisected by deep gullies and, peering from the windows, the travellers could look up between those dark walls to the bright sunshine above, and catch glimpses of picturesque homesteads standing on natural terraces planted with cereal crops, surrounded by ferns and palms.

Elsewhere, the sides were too steep for agriculture, and there was little wild life other than the occasional hawk silently circling the heights as it watched for prey, far below. The only sound, apart from the water slapping against the side of the boat, was the muttering and cursing of the trackers, and the occasional song as they hauled on the ropes.

The voyagers found this wonderful panorama overwhelming: a landscape so weird and melancholy that they likened it to a fairyland. At times, when they looked ahead, the river seemed to end in a wall of sheer rock but, as they approached, a sudden angle revealed a long vista of enchanting gorge, and they saw that there was a narrow way through the mountains.

For six days a week the missionaries were busy reading and studying; Bessie and Harry worked hard at their lessons in Mandarin Chinese, with the help of the older missionaries. On Sundays they all rested from their labours and Dr Savin paid the captain extra to allow the crew a rest day.

This new weekly holiday caused astonishment among the crew: usually, their only time off was during the Chinese New Year, when they would spend three days gambling and drinking. On their first free Sunday they hung around awkwardly, wondering what to do with themselves, until one started a fight, which kept them busy for a while. Later, a number watched with interest as William Tremberth held a service in Chinese. As the day wore on, some of the men gathered sticks and lit a fire on shore to warm themselves, others wandered off to a nearby village to tell all they knew about the foreigners on their boat, and be envied for their privilege of making so close a study of these barbarians' ways.

When the young missionaries' day's studying was over, they would listen with some disquiet as the Savins talked about the alarming events in Yunnan which had forced them to leave China during the Boxer Rising in 1900, nearly three years before. The Boxers, called Righteous and Harmonious Fists in Chinese, were at the forefront of a wave of resentment against foreigners, who were blamed for many of China's ills, including a terrible drought.

The Boxers believed that the spires of Christian churches pierced the sky and prevented the rains from falling. They wandered the country, attacking foreign missionaries and Chinese Christian converts, emboldened by the belief that the exercises they practised, called spirit boxing, would make them invulnerable to bullets.

In Kunming, also known as Yunnan Fu, the capital of Yunnan province, they attacked the Savins' house and that of another missionary, Frank Dymond, destroying everything. Their lives were saved only because another missionary group took them into their compound, protected by a garrison of eighty Chinese soldiers. At night as they lay in bed they heard children in the street playing at rioting, and shouting as they marched past: 'Beat, beat, kill, kill!' Finally, the missionaries fled back to England.

All of which left Harry and Bessie wondering what would face them when they arrived. They were assured that public opinion had swung in favour of the 'foreign devils' again.

Three days out of Yichang, as they were sailing in quiet water, they heard the distant sound of the first set of rapids, then noticed a number of wrecked boats along the banks, their crews trying to salvage the cargoes. The roar of the rapids grew louder and the missionaries held on tight to the children as the water rushed them along between rocks like giant sharks' teeth.

This was just a taster for the terrors that were to come.

On the sixth day they crossed the K'in-t'an, notorious in Bible Christian history as the point where four missionaries had almost lost their lives. They had been thrown into the water, but rescued by Chinese lifeboats. This time, the missionaries' boat anchored for the night just before this point. The monotonous roar of the rapids they must brave in the morning kept them awake all night.

Next morning, they nervously ate their porridge standing, while the crew prepared to shoot the rapids. Boats sometimes waited two days before conditions were considered favourable to tackle K'in-t'an. Today they were to wait five or six hours, during which time junks carrying salt and fruit came down. None were wrecked, but several almost capsized, and the missionaries turned away from the terrifying sight of a boat apparently about to founder. Finally, their boat was readied to tackle the rapids. Four stout ropes were attached to it, dozens of hired men prepared to haul on them under the instruction of special pilots. The boat survived, thanks, according to a young Buddhist priest, to his burning incense in a nearby temple in order to appease the river gods.

The next day, at Kwan-tie-ko, another set of rapids, there were further heart-stopping challenges. Two boats that went before them both broke their ropes and were hurled back in a great fury onto their own boat. But the worst was yet to come.

As William Tremberth later wrote: 'The narrowest escape was on the eighth day, when we were within an ace of being capsized... The boat was being brought up to the rapids, the pilot who ought to have been watching for the cross currents was off his guard, and the prow – instead of cutting into the swift waters – fell foul and went across the stream and got the full force against our side.'

The boat was carrying almost a full sail at the time, making it heel over. 'The trackers clung desperately on to the ropes fastened half-way up the mast, hoping to pull her around, but that only increased the danger. The children all rolled to the side with their elders, followed by the cups and saucers and boxes, and pans of water fell upon the beds in great confusion.'

The captain was at the stern, smoking opium, and only realised the danger they were in at the last moment. He rushed to the prow and ordered the sail to be lowered, just saving them from a horrific wreck.

When they were not deep in their studies, or clinging to the side of the boat as it shot the rapids, Bessie and Harry talked about their families; hers in Southampton and his in Plymouth. Bessie was the eldest of ten children born to Jabez and Alice Bull. Just before she set off for China in 1902, the family gathered together in the back garden to have their photograph taken.

I am looking at that photograph now.

Bessie with her family, just before leaving for China

They are all wearing their best clothes: Jabez, a commercial traveller, watch chain across his waistcoat and a greying goatee beard, looking more prosperous than he actually was at the time, with his sons and daughters around him. His plump wife Alice sits comfortably, holding her baby son Leslie, a worried smile on her face. Nearby is one source of her anxiety: her youngest daughter, Gladys, a pale girl of nine in a white frilly dress which does not disguise her sickly appearance. Gladys died a few months later. Alice was not to know that the baby, too, would die before she saw Bessie again. Bessie was another cause of worry. The prospect of sending her eldest daughter to the other side of the world gave Alice much heartache.

Bessie is standing straight-backed, wearing a dark silk dress with a high collar and a tight waist, her brown hair piled on top of her head. She is of medium height, has a determined chin and is looking the photographer in the eye, unsmiling, as if daring him to make a mistake. She has a triumphant air: this gathering celebrates the achievement of her long-standing ambition. No matter that she was only accepted by the China mission of the Bible Christian church at her third attempt, and had had to earn her living as a milliner until then, working in the Southampton chapel in her spare time. The earlier disappointments are behind her and she is on the threshold of a glorious adventure.

In turn, Harry told Bessie about his family, who ran a grocery in Plymouth. Like Bessie, he had left school at 12. His first job was to drive a horse and cart, delivering groceries. In his spare time he studied for the ministry, and was accepted.

The Bible Christian church had split away from the Methodists in 1815 in an attempt to get closer to the original teachings of the Bible, and its members set great store by long services and rousing sermons, designed to stir up the congregation. The church had started in Devon and spread along the south coast of England at about the same time as the Primitive Methodists were active in the north. Bible Christian missionaries had been working in South West China since 1885; Bessie and Harry were among the second generation to go there.

Fear was not the only emotion evoked during this journey up-river. The landscape could also conjure awe and wonder. The most remarkable sight was the Dragon Rapid, a newly-formed torrent alongside which a village had quickly grown up to serve river travellers. They reached the village at sunset, the brilliant array of colours on the water making them think of St John's description: 'A sea of glass mingled with fire.' This new rapid had been formed six years before, when a huge rock landslip had forced the Yangtze's waters to split into a V, 'with a terrible vortex at the point'. There was also a separate, calmer sub-channel to one side.

Most up-river boats unloaded their cargo, leaving the boat much lighter and more manoeuvrable as it was hauled up the torrent. Their captain decided not to unload, and to make the attempt first thing in the morning by the side channel. After breakfast, while the missionaries took their money, study books and lunch and stepped onto *terra firma*, dozens of trackers were harnessed into the hauling ropes, not just men but women and even children, some no more than four or five years old. As the travellers walked up the river bank, they witnessed a terrifying sight.

Just as their boat was facing the torrent, a small boat shot down the course they were to take and was forced to enter the main current at the point of the treacherous V. Will Tremberth gave a dramatic account of what happened: 'It looked as if they would be swallowed up by the boiling surf, but the five brave fellows nobly battled with the unruly elements and got at last into a more hopeful situation. Alas, however, when we hoped they were safe, a whirlpool of malicious intent capsized their boat, throwing them all into the surging gulf.

A breathless silence fell upon the eager crowd that looked on. Half a dozen lifeboats pushed off at once to the rescue.

'Three of the men crawled onto the bottom of the inverted boat before help reached them. But we saw nothing of the other two. Everyone said they were drowned.'

Meanwhile, the missionaries' boat was making progress: 'Quite 200 persons were upon the ropes, the ends of which were wound around stone pillars to prevent a relapse if the trackers failed. Gradually, yet surely, our little craft came up the steep ascent. It was with a great sense of relief that we saw her sail into quiet waters.'

During their six weeks on the river, the missionaries had plenty of time to observe the men who were risking their lives getting them to their destination. William Tremberth wrote: 'All day long, they are kept at the towline, like a team of horses, under a driver who addresses them in the vilest language, and who never hesitates to use the lash in his hand, whenever he thinks it necessary.' At night, utterly exhausted, their clothes soaked, they slept on the wet deck, their only bedding a few bamboo mats. To haul the boat they had to navigate rough paths, scramble over huge boulders and sharp rocks. They sang as they worked: 'One man leads in a highly pitched, falsetto voice, singing a couple of bars, then all join in the refrain. For variation, they sometimes grunt in unison.'

The missionaries observed the trackers' faith and religious observance, which they compared unfavourably with their own: 'Religion hardly enters into life. The rites of the same, however, are generally attended to by the cook, it being part of his duties. Morning and night, incense is offered to the god of the boats – Chen-kiang-wan – and the patrons of wind and tide.' Twice, they made offerings at riverbank temples, sounding gongs and letting off fire crackers.

After six weeks on the houseboat, the party disembarked at Chongqing, where the Savin family would stay for a while.

Bessie and Harry, the two young missionaries, had much to think about: the strangeness of everything they had seen on their journey and the demands of the work which lay before them. They both had another anxiety: before leaving England they had each become engaged: Bessie to Alfred Evans and Harry to Annie Bryant, known as Nancy or Nance. Neither knew when their prospective partners would also be accepted as missionaries and could come out to join them. A long separation seemed inevitable for both couples.

They would have been more worried if they had heard the comments passed by some senior members of the church hierarchy: 'It would be more convenient and more economical for the church if Harry and Bessie had been engaged to each other, so that both their partners could be left at home!'

3 MY SOUL, MY LIFE, MY ALL

The one thing missing from this account of Bessie's river trip, though so full of detail and drama, is her voice. I knew she was present in the scenes that Will Tremberth's account brought so vividly to life for me, but she remains a shadowy, almost silent figure in the stories of the others. I needed to hear her speak. If she wrote letters home from that river trip they have not survived, but one piece of her writing has. Before she left for China, Bessie wrote an article for the Bible Christian magazine and, in it, I heard her voice for the first time.

I heard an idealistic, passionately committed young woman. Brave. Determined. Good. Devout. With the very best of intentions, and a burning mission to serve the people of China. The sort of young woman who could never leave a baby to die on a rubbish tip.

This is what Bessie wrote: 'As the time draws nearer for my departure for distant China, my heart is filled with mingled emotions – feelings of praise and thanksgiving – that though all unworthy, He has called me to leave all and follow Him. Gladly I go forth, "For His name's sake," knowing that He who has called me will not permit me to go alone, but will Himself walk with me, and freely give me all things; He is my sufficiency.

'It is only this assurance that makes me ready and willing for such an undertaking. When I look back over the past years, and think how the desire to tell the Chinese of the love of Jesus has been fostered in my heart and strengthened year after year, until it has become quite a burden, I can see the Hand of God gently guiding and preparing the way for my work.'

It had taken three years before she was accepted for the China mission, during which time she began to wonder whether God intended her for another path. 'He knew the yearnings of my heart towards the Chinese especially, and if China were not the place where He required me to be, I was willing to stay at home, and work and pray.'

Bessie is also conscious that few who could make a commitment such as hers actually do so, and she is pretty direct in calling them out: 'If every one of our

11

Church members at home, had the burden of souls laid on them... there would be no lack of offers for China, as there is now. Surely there are among our active young men and women those to whom the voice of the Master has come, saying, "The harvest truly is great, come ye and work in my vineyard?" In China today, souls are groping in the dark, for they know not what, and there is no one to give them the light; shall they miss the way, and perish, because *you* are not willing to obey the voice. Is the sacrifice too great?'

She quotes a couple of lines from the hymn, *When I Survey the Wondrous Cross*:

'Love so amazing, so Divine,
Demands my soul, my life, my all.'

She gives thanks for 'a happy Christian home and praying parents, who have so willingly given me up to God's service,' but makes it clear that she has not found it easy to leave her family, her home and the life that she knows for utter uncertainty, and potentially great danger.

She writes: 'And then came the thought of the partings and farewells, but His grace is again sufficient, even for this. If we cast our weakness on His might we are able to do what at other times seems an impossibility. And one is comforted by the words of Jesus to Peter: "And everyone that has forsaken homes, or brethren, or sisters, or father, or mother, or wife, or children, or lands for My name's sake, shall receive a hundred-fold, and shall inherit everlasting life."'

So Bessie was a radical. An activist. A young woman with a mission that was the driving force in her life. I wondered what her mission would be, today, at twenty-seven? Would she still have faith? How would she channel her passion to right wrongs? Would she favour direct action? What would be her causes? The universal one of climate change? Women's rights? #MeToo? Gender recognition? The treatment of refugees? Modern slavery?

And what, perhaps most pertinently, would the contemporary Bessie's view be of those who go to another culture, dismiss its belief system, and seek to convert the people to her own? How would a modern-day Bessie look upon her historic self? Would she approve or disapprove? Would she see missionary Bessie as a force for good, or as a person with a misguided 'white saviour' complex?

All these thoughts would remain with me as I followed Bessie's story, but I knew that she was a product of her own time and her own culture, and to take her out of that context and examine her life and judge her actions against modern attitudes wouldn't get me very far.

Bessie had great strength, and great purpose. She was far more radical, far more engaged than the vast majority of her contemporaries, judging from what she wrote. More committed, even, than most of those in her own radical church. I learned of the tradition of strong women that she came from. The Bible Christian church in which Bessie was raised had long had powerful women preachers who were role models for her. Among them was a woman called Mary Toms. She was a rare thing in the 1820s: a female itinerant preacher. So, when she stepped up onto a borrowed chair on the Esplanade in East Cowes on the Isle of Wight to pray and sing hymns, she quickly attracted a crowd. Mary was twenty-seven, the same age as Bessie when she went to China, and a member of this new, non-conformist church. Her gift for preaching earned her the title 'Female Agent,' and a mission to evangelise on the Isle of Wight. Mary wrote:

'On Sunday morning I went to East Cowes... and though [there] was wind and rain I borrowed a chair and sang *Come Ye Sinners Poor And Wretched*, and it was not long before scores assembled, coming from every part of town, some laughing, some talking, but I spoke on and had not proceeded far when the tears began to flow from my eyes and [those of] many others.'

Mary, with the power of her words and belief, had won round an indifferent, perhaps hostile crowd. It was something she would do repeatedly in the coming weeks as she toured the island at a frenetic pace, preaching three or four times each Sunday, at villages two to four miles apart, taking Bible classes in between, and winning many converts along the way.

The Bible Christian message was readily received by farm labourers and the poor, but there was also fierce opposition to this upstart church among the squires and Anglican clergy, and hostility to women such as Mary. Bible Christian services were often held in secret, in cottages, because farm workers feared that if their attendance got back to their employers they would lose their jobs and be evicted from their homes. At a cottage being used for worship in the village of Chale, opponents smeared the gates with tar and excrement and piled tubs of filth against the door. Mary and other women preachers were attacked, and were often in danger of losing their lives from the heavy missiles thrown at them by enraged men.

The reason for all this fear and anger was that the Bible Christians challenged the cosy alliance between the Established Church of England and the landed gentry, both of which fought back hard. Mary Toms was accused of making a riot, and a magistrate, urged on by a clergyman, ordered her arrest. The parson wanted Mary off the island, but wiser heads prevailed, and the charge was dropped.

Beneath the Anglican clergy's fear of Mary Toms lay jealousy. They could only dream of drawing such vast and engaged congregations. Mary received a rapturous welcome when she preached in Wroxall, where Bessie's family originated. One woman, drawn away from the Anglican church by Mary's fame, said after hearing her: 'the pa'son couldn't praich a bit like her.'

Wroxall was one of the first Bible Christian preaching posts on the island, and the Bull family, including Bessie's father Jabez and his brother Augustus, were leading lights of it before the latter's move to Southampton. In the years before they raised the money to build a church in the village, visiting preachers such as Mary used a bakehouse, owned by one of the Bull family, and stayed overnight in his house. One visiting preacher welcomed by the Bulls was the Revd Jas Thorne, who said of the congregation he encountered, 'I perceive the people are very ignorant, but many of them listen with great attention to the word, while their tears bedew their cheeks.'

Bessie's uncle Augustus was a stalwart of the Bible Christians in Wroxall, where he ran the village shop. When the funds were raised to build a church, the foundation stone was laid by his wife. It is still in place, with an inscription recording that it was placed there, on June 14 1886, by Mrs A Bull.

Bessie was the third generation of her family with the Bible Christian fire in her soul. Although she doesn't use the term, I wonder if Bessie saw herself as a Female Agent like Mary Toms, sent out to evangelise not the Isle of Wight but to the other side of the world, and the Chinese province of Yunnan?

I would soon learn that, among the poor of China as in England, the Bible Christian message had a similarly powerful appeal to the downtrodden. But I am jumping ahead. Bessie, when I left her, had completed the river-borne part of her journey. Now she had a long overland trek to make.

4 THE ROOF OF THE WORLD

So that was Bessie, speaking to me for the first time. I would have loved to hear her tell me about the next stage of her journey: the fourteen-day overland trek which would finally bring her to the mission station in Chaotung. But I had to settle for the next-best thing. Her companion, Harry Parsons, kept a diary during that journey, and from it I learned about all that Bessie would have seen.

The party disembarked at the river port of Chongqing, where the Savin family would stay for a while. Bessie, Harry, the Tremberths and their three children were met by John Li, a Chinese evangelist who would escort them to Chaotung, today known as Zhaotong.

Their journey took them 300 miles in a south-westerly direction, to the centre of the region the mission covered. Its territory stretched south from Chaotung to Kunming, the provincial capital, and north to just over the border into Sichuan province, a vast area spanning 400 miles of mountainous country.

When they got to Chaotung they would be met by Sam Pollard, a legendary figure in the Bible Christian mission. Some travellers walk, others go on horseback. Bessie and her companions take a third option: they are carried in sedan chairs. This, says Sam Pollard, is the most comfortable option, but has its drawbacks. 'Given fine weather and strong chair bearers this is all right, but let the roads be slippery and the men weak and bad-tempered, and then the person in the chair has a bad time. Hanging over precipices – for the chair poles are so long that they cannot follow the curves of the cliffs as a horse can – jolting up the slippery steps of the steep hills and still worse down the uneven paths of the narrow roads where the front man's head is only just on a level with the back man's feet, the rider longs for the end of the day's stage.'

The chairs used by Bessie and other women and children featured a seat enclosed in a bamboo frame beneath an oil-cloth roof, suspended on two 12ft long poles. The poles were hefted onto the shoulders of two to four bearers, depending on the weight of the passenger. The men were carried in lighter versions, without the frame.

Harry's bearers dropped him three times. On the first occasion, the back carrier slipped and fell forward with the poles resting on top of him. 'It was an awkward fall, for we were descending a number of steps. The same man caused the second accident by allowing the poles to slip from his shoulders. On the third occasion, a pole slipped when the men were halting, and the chair went to the ground. Falls with no consequence.'

Bandits lurked in this country, on the look-out for travellers they could rob, and so the party was accompanied by a group of eight soldiers on days when the threat was at its highest. Harry was not entirely impressed by them: 'Some of them carry swords which certainly would not pass muster at home, so blunt and rusty are they.' The soldiers also help clear the path, which is often obstructed by fallen rocks. The paths are narrow – barely wide enough for two people to walk abreast – roughly paved and uneven. In rainy weather, they become treacherous.

Their trail took them up the Yangtse valley, rich farming country, and they passed fields of corn, peas and oil-plant, and scores of rice paddies.

On the second day they crossed the Yangtse and followed the valley of a tributary, the Ta Kuan, itself a great, wide river. The path was 'a zigzag one – up and down steps; over and around loose and stationary rocks; at times the chairs overhanging the precipice at the foot of which the river flows. We did 20 li before breakfast.' A li is a third of a mile, but it is also a measure of time. In such mountainous country, the toughness of the terrain has to be taken into account along with distance when estimating a journey's duration.

The inn where they breakfasted was typical: 'The floor is of mud, the small, square tables and forms are rude and uncomfortable; servants bustled around, preparing the meal, the coolies sat near, eating their basins of rice; alongside the empty chairs and boxes; while just below was the river. As we partook of our hurried meal of boiled ham and eggs, men, perspiring and noisy, passed up the narrow path, tracking boats up-stream.'

They don't travel on the sabbath, so spend Sunday at an inn. Word of their arrival spreads among Chinese Christians in the area, and John Li and Will Tremberth preach to a large congregation. 'While we sat at dinner, some of the Chinamen brought presents of a live fowl and a box of sweetmeats. The Chinese crowded in to gaze upon the foreigners.'

Monday's journey began gloriously, the dew sparkling in the sunshine, the birds singing. 'On leaving the village... I saw the clouds of white mist encircling the hilltops, and presently roll away, like a curtain withdrawn, disclosing high, rugged hills, with patches of green and red all aglow with the sunlight. Flowers of many kinds, including the white and blue violet, forget-me-not, and primroses, interspersed with ferns, mosses, and grasses, and a small red fruit, much resembling a wild strawberry, lined the banks by the side of which we rode.'

Their path took them away from the river and over the hills through fields of corn and vegetables; past sugar plantations and by tall, graceful bamboos. 'Blossom covered the fruit trees, clothing them in garments of pink and white.' Next came scores of rice paddies, through which buffalo were drawing ploughs, sinking deep in the water. 'How slowly the animals move. When the beast wishes to rest, it lies down in the water and mud, its body mostly under water.' On the trail they were passed by cows used as beasts of burden. 'With their loads, and adorned with saddles and bells hanging around their necks, the animals looked strange as they were either led or ridden.'

Each day they pass scores of niches in the rock in which idols stand. 'Some are well preserved, others have a dilapidated appearance. With few exceptions, they are filthy. Before most of them incense is offered, and over and around them inscriptions are placed. Many of the figures are grotesque – one had six arms; another a cock's head; a third a bull's head; a fourth has three eyes; numbers of others look most ferocious.'

They climbed a range of hills, with wonderful views from the summit. 'Stretching away for miles could be seen the cultivated hills with deep ravines between.' The next day their path runs through a long, deep gorge. 'Hundreds of feet below the water rushed. For a considerable while we were carried along the brink.' Their path descends by hundreds of steps winding around the hillside and brings them back into the Ta Kuan valley, where they cross from Sichuan into Yunnan.

The night is spent at an inn in the village of T'an T'eo which, in common with the others, was 'dirty, dark and disgusting.' The innkeeper, along with his son – a boy of eleven – is an opium smoker. Late in the evening the father says he wants to give up his idols and kick his opium addiction, and offers his inn as a preaching place. 'In the centre of the village stands a tree with stones surrounding it resembling a mandarin's seal, hat and shoes. These are held most sacred, and form the district idol.' From T'an T'eo they climbed again, until they were hundreds of feet above the river. 'It was a splendid sight. A curious iron suspension bridge spanned the first ravine we reached.' They spent the night at Sheng Ki Ping, perched on the brow of a hill, overlooking the river on one side and the gorge on the other. Far beneath them the water wound around the base of hills which formed the opposite bank, and towered nearly a thousand feet above the river.

'Behind a village, several peaks similarly rise. The hills are majestic. It is an awe-inspiring scene. High up on the side of the hills opposite stand rude inhabited houses. To our unaccustomed eyes it seems a sheer impossibility to reach them.'

The following day they passed numerous stone and clay towers, 'places of refuge when the hill tribes or any enemy sweep down upon the country folk. These erections appeared very primitive and insecure when we thought of the power of our modern guns.'

Another remarkable sight was a place of burial called a coffin cliff. The cliff 'rose many hundreds of feet, sheer from the water's edge, much resembling a wall. Placed on apparently inaccessible ledges of rock, halfway up the face of the cliff, were a number of well-preserved coffins. I counted six, which appeared intact. No one can tell how they were placed in such an extraordinary position. According to local folklore some giant villagers flew there with them 2000-odd years ago; or the coffins themselves flew up and rested there out of reach of some threatened danger. It would be interesting to learn the history of these remarkable sites.'

The next day, April 5, is their final Sunday on the road and the inn at the village of Ki-li-pu is even worse than they were used to. 'The room occupied by Mr Tremberth and myself has, as usual, mud walls and floor. Part of the former had fallen down, hence matting had to be hung up to secure some amount of privacy. The door possesses no latch, and has to be propped by a stick to prevent it swinging open on its creaking hinges. Hanging from the ceiling (through which the sky is plainly visible), is the accumulated dust of months and, probably, years.

'Five sheets of straw matting stretched on dust-covered planks, supported by trestles, form our bedsteads. On these we place our beds and, rolling ourselves in our blankets, dream of cosier corners; yet thankful for even this place of shelter. The room being windowless is lighted by the few gleams which find their way through the apertures in the roof or through the open door. For most purposes, a candle is necessary by day as well as by night... In a room to the left are a number of our coolies either opium smoking, gambling, or sleeping. The inn is cold, cheerless, and void of the bare comfort found in many an English barn.'

Once again, a curious crowd gathers to watch them eat, intrigued by their use of knives and forks, and a table cloth. John Li and Will Tremberth again conduct prayers for the Chinese Christians who seek them out. They sing *Jesus Loves Me* in Chinese. Will is moved to hear this old familiar tune sung under such strange circumstances.

Next day involved a long, punishing climb up to the plain on which Chaotung stood, at 7,000ft above sea level, on the roof of the world. The path led up the face of a cliff, the many steps and sharp turns impossible to navigate in a sedan chair, so all had to climb on foot, children included.

'The upward course seemed endless. One turning after another was taken only to reveal further stretches ahead. The steps were very dirty with mud and water, and in places were nearly obstructed by quantities of earth and stone which had fallen from above. The climb was tiring. Halfway up we rested in a temple.' When they reached what they estimated must be three or four thousand feet above sea level, the landscape changed dramatically. While the valleys were verdant, the hilltops were brown and bare, the ground was parched, as though no rain had fallen for months.

Two days later they were almost at their destination.

'On Thursday April 9 we left our inn early in the morning and took to the road in eager anticipation of the meeting at Chaotung, now only a few li distant. The weather was glorious and our spirits high as we crossed a small hill. The white and blue violets were a welcome sight. On the further side of the hill lay the Chaotung plain.

Six li from Chaotung they saw three figures approaching. This was their welcome party: Sam Pollard, Frank Dymond and Charles Hicks had ridden out to greet them. 'It would be difficult to say who were the more pleased, they or us. Tongues went merrily. Greetings from home were gladly given and as joyously received.'

It had been almost twenty-two weeks since they sailed from Southampton. The following day was Good Friday; they had arrived just in time to celebrate Easter.

5 NEW BEGINNINGS

So now, thanks to the accounts of Harry Parsons and, earlier, Will Tremberth, I feel as if I've been with Bessie every step of the way to her new home in Chaotung. I know what she will have been thinking as the sedan chair was bumped to the ground and she climbed out and looked around: 'At last!'

At last she had reached her destination, and her destiny.

As she approached across the plain she will have seen the massive, encircling stone walls of Chaotung city, with its serrated battlements, and the four city gates. Above the wall she would see row upon row of grey tiled roofs on the closely packed houses, and here and there the gleaming, glazed green tiles of a temple. All around her, encircling the plain, rose the magnificent mountains of Yunnan, range after range rising to 10,000 feet, billowing clouds rolling through the gaps in those mountains, the city itself dwarfed by its setting in this vast amphitheatre.

I can picture Bessie, passing through the city gates into Chaotung and into a very different world from the one she was used to back home in Southampton. Instead of wide roads, smart shops and grand civic buildings, she found herself in a tangle of narrow cobbled streets and mud-brick houses. Buffalo pulled clumsy wooden carts filled with coal or maize, strings of packhorses carried copper ore in great baskets slung over their backs, forcing the mass of people thronging the streets to press themselves against the walls to avoid being trampled.

The appearance of the missionaries among them aroused their curiosity, and some of them came closer to peer at the new arrivals; a small crowd of children started to follow them. In spite of the evil smelling piles of refuse in the side streets, Bessie's spirits will have risen. These were the people she had come to serve. The weather was glorious and a strong breeze from the surrounding mountains blew across the plain and through the city, as she and her companions were led to the mission house by their three new colleagues, Sam Pollard, Frank Dymond and Charles Hicks.

After the dank, gloomy inns on the journey, the mission house was a pleasant, airy building, in the Chinese style but quite comfortable. They gave thanks for their safe arrival and, after a short time for unpacking, began to think about the new lives which were opening before them.

The first challenge to be addressed was the Chinese language: the work they had done during the five months' journey from England had only begun the long process of learning to speak and write Mandarin and, for the next year, Bessie would have language lessons every day with a Chinese teacher. Five months after her arrival Bessie wrote home: 'I am persevering with the language and hope to take my first exam next month.'

This was a further culture shock. Another missionary wrote home to say: 'Fancy sitting at a table for two or three hours a day with a native gentleman, whose breath scents the whole house with garlic, opium smoke, wine, etc., and whose raucous sounds make one feel quite sick... It is not all fun, and then there is the city with its odours and filth.'

Bessie also wrote of her encounter with Chinese religious beliefs: 'We have been having some strange scenes here connected with the ancestral worship of the people. How foolish it looks in our eyes! Yet some of these people have implicit faith in what they do and think it is the noblest act of their lives. It made my heart ache to see them, and I could but turn away and pray that the Light of the World might illuminate their dark minds. I have an unspeakable longing to be able to teach these women of Jesus. I was out with Mrs Dymond last week, visiting them in their homes. The women listened eagerly whilst she preached to them. They are so very ignorant that it is hard for them to really understand and become willing to give up their idols. We rejoice to know that our Women's Work is improving here. Quite a number are unbinding their feet. When old Mrs Chir, who has been a member for a number of years, heard about it, she said she would unbind hers. Poor old soul, she is nearly seventy. She feels she will be doing something for Jesu's sake, and I'm sure He will accept it and bless the effort to her and give her much joy.'

Foot-binding was a particular concern for Bessie. Traditionally, having small feet was considered highly attractive in a woman, and the practice of binding the feet was designed to prevent them growing to their natural size. Girls as young as two had their feet bound. First, a long white cloth would be wound around the foot, bending all but the big toe under the sole. A large stone was placed on top of the foot to crush the arch. The process, which lasted several years, broke the bones, causing excruciating pain, and stopped the foot growing.

Bessie was a great talker, but her progress in the language was necessarily slow; she felt a keen sense of frustration at her inability to chat freely with the Chinese women and girls. Maud Dymond came to her aid in an unexpected way: 'You just need some practice, I'll introduce you to some of the members of the church and you will soon have a circle of friends. But first we must find a Chinese name for you; fortunately your surname can be translated quite easily.'

'Oh no,' said Bessie. "I've had enough of being Miss Bull; all my life I have been teased about bully beef and John Bull. Please give me an ordinary name.'

'We'll call you Miss Wong.' Soon afterwards Maud took Bessie to meet the Chinese ladies in the church. She taught her a short phrase in Mandarin and told her to go over and say it to old Mrs Lee. At this, Mrs Lee burst out laughing and shook her warmly by the hand. The phrase was 'I'm your little sister, don't you know me?'

Mrs Lee had been Miss Wong before her marriage and, from now on, she treated Bessie as a sister. The new relationship did not stop there: Mrs Lee called her 'sister-in-law' and their children called her 'aunt'. There were further ramifications: Mrs Lee had some very close friends, kindred spirits or 'heart-friends' whom she regarded as sisters. If Bessie was her sister, she must also be sister to all these ladies. She was welcome in their homes and in their lives. These unlikely relationships were very real and were to last for forty years.

Missionaries had not always received a welcome in Chaotung. When Sam Pollard and Frank Dymond first came here in 1888, they met with indifference at best, hostility at worst. As Elliott Kendall, a later missionary, would write: 'It was not the city in which, above all others, one would choose to live, because the foreigner was certainly not among friends. The whole population, from the Chinese official in the *yamen* [town hall] to the illiterate coolie who delivered buckets of water, was suspicious of the foreigner. He was unknown and therefore, to be feared. Wild rumours would be whispered from one to another that he could bewitch little children, cause disease by his touch.'

Sam and Frank, who had met at school in the West Country, 'were taking a foolhardy risk,' according to Elliott Kendall, in his book *Beyond the Clouds*. 'They had seemed mad to leave promising careers in England and face the isolation, insecurity and danger of living in Yunnan. Who would choose an uncomfortable house in an overcrowded Chinese city, surrounded by a hostile population, 10,000 miles from home and friends, with the nearest doctor two months' journey away, in preference to a professional career in England?'

They were the sole Christians in the province, living in two cramped rooms in a backstreet house, their attempts to evangelise ignored. 'In an area as big as England they were the only two, unwelcome representatives of the Christian Church, and as they bowed their heads together in their living-room at night, they were the visible Church in Yunnan.'

Yet, 'they had come in response to a call... to undertake a pioneering task which could rely on no local support and which might end in failure and abandonment.' And, in time, it would prove to be 'a venture of faith that was to be nobly rewarded in the following years.' But progress was very slow. Sam Pollard wrote: 'During seventeen years of work, a few churches were formed among the Chinese... Evangelistic, scholastic, and medical work was carried on. A few natives were trained for work among their own people, but things went slowly.'

Bessie happened to arrive just as the breakthrough was about to come, and the accommodation she came to was far superior to that first two-man hovel.

Alongside the new mission house was a chapel and school-room, protected within a gated compound. Bessie was to divide her time in the next few years between Chaotung and another mission in Tung Chuan, later known as Hweitze, a five-day journey away on horseback. She and Harry Parsons had to work hard on their daily language lessons, in preparation for the examinations they were expected to take.

As soon as they had gained any degree of proficiency they started preaching, Harry Parsons helping Frank Dymond at what was called the preaching shop in the centre of the city. They would start by singing a hymn to attract attention, and a crowd would gather round them to listen to what they had to say. Bessie worked under the guidance of Maud Dymond, visiting the women and girls and running Bible classes for them, which soon attracted around fifty members.

Bessie tried hard to concentrate on her demanding work, but her thoughts were often of home and of her fiancé, Alfred Evans.

They had met when Alf came to hear her preach, about four years earlier, at a service in St Mary's Road Bible Christian Chapel in Southampton, where her father Jabez was a lay preacher. Alf didn't come up to speak to her that day, nor for several weeks afterwards, but Bessie became gradually aware of his shy presence. With his high cheek-bones and elongated, shiny face he looked rather like a Dickensian undertaker.

Bessie soon realised that Alf had a will as strong as her own, once he had decided upon a course of action. Later on, when he was studying for the ministry, Alf was well-known for his tenacity in argument. Later still, when preaching, his natural shyness would disappear and he would stride around and thump the table to emphasise his points, occasionally apologising for a particularly loud thump.

Alf was the tenth child of a family of twelve from the village of Holdenhurst, near Bournemouth, and had found his way to Southampton, where he worked in a grocer's shop and lived with his elder brother, Henry. He soon came across the Bible Christian Chapel, where Bessie herself was acquiring a growing reputation as a preacher of great passion. Alf found her determination to go to China infectious. He came to share that ambition. With this goal in common, they got engaged, with the mutual understanding that the marriage would only take place if and when Alf too was sent to China. Alf immediately took the first step and started studying hard. From the outset he distinguished himself in the Local Preacher's Examinations and was then accepted by Shebbear College as a candidate for the ministry.

The village of Shebbear, where the Bible Christian church was founded, lay on the borders of Devon and Cornwall. The college doubled as a boarding and day school for children, and a place where adult candidates for the Bible Christian ministry would study theology, church history and New Testament Greek alongside sixth formers. By the end of 1902, Alf had been appointed as a preacher in St Dennis, Cornwall, but he was not yet a minister.

Meanwhile, Bessie was preparing to leave for China and in November, she and Alf had to say goodbye, without any idea of how long their separation would last, or indeed whether they would ever meet again.

In 1903 Alfred began his probationary period, after which a vote at the Bible Christian annual conference would decide whether he would be accepted into the ministry. Alf's first application, in 1904, produced a dispiriting verdict: 'Having interviewed Brother A. Evans for China, we are of the opinion that he would be capable of general pastoral work in connection with the mission but we do not consider him likely to qualify for medical or educational work in which assistance is specially needed.'

This was not good. It meant that, for now at least, Alf would not be going to China, so he and Bessie would not be marrying.

The news was better for Harry Parsons. He learned that his fiancée, Nancy Bryant, to whom he had been engaged since 1899, was accepted and sent out in November 1904. However, the couple's problems were not over. The Missionary Committee's rules were very strict: there was no question of them being allowed to marry until Nancy had completed two years' work in China. She soon had a further set-back: she caught smallpox during the journey up the Yangtse. She was nursed by other missionaries and soon continued on her way, writing with remarkable stoicism to her brother, Phil: 'Am getting ever so fat, but my face is still a bit rough and spotty and am very nearly bald... [Harry] will think me a sight.'

On arrival in Chaotung Nancy settled in with the Tremberth family and soon recovered her health and looks. She had been lucky to escape with her life. In another letter to Phil, she mentions a family of missionaries who had all caught smallpox ten days after arriving. The father and two young children died, leaving the distraught mother a widow and childless, to recover as best she could. Nancy settled down to work, and to struggle with her Mandarin lessons.

The Missionary Committee discussed Alfred's application for a second time, in November 1904. Again, the news was bad. They refused this request to go to China because they did not have the funds to increase the number of missionaries there.

This second rejection had a devastating effect on Alfred: his hopes for both his marriage and his career were dashed. What was he to do now? In his despair Alf wrote to Bessie, offering to dissolve their engagement. Bessie must have been devastated: she had not seen him for two years, she was far from home, struggling to learn Chinese and to cope with primitive conditions and an alien people.

We don't have Bessie's reply, but she had clearly been discussing all this with at least one of her colleagues. A letter Nancy Bryant wrote to her brother Phil, who knew Alf, shows how concerned Bessie's fellow missionaries were for her. Nancy wrote:

'What is Mr Evans going to do? I hear a whisper that his letters are coming few and far between. We hope he will treat Miss Bull in an honourable fashion. He offered her her freedom, I hear. She has been very poorly these weeks. The weather may be trying her, but I believe it's Mr Evans she is fretting over.

'It is bad enough at home to have the "tip", but out here, well it seems almost unpardonable. Mrs Bull [Bessie's mother] was making sleeping suits for him and doing all in her power to get him ready last year when I was there. If he has decided not to come after all, and I am afraid he has, well then you shake him when you see him and I'll repay you sometime. As yet I have not met Miss Bull, but [I hear] she is a nice girl and ought to be treated properly. She has a very kind heart and I am sure would do her best anywhere.'

Yet, while Bessie's personal life was held in suspension, the great breakthrough that the missionaries had been praying for was about to come to pass, with a sudden overwhelming flood of converts. But that flood would begin with the merest trickle...

6 THE COMING OF THE MIAO

If Bessie had looked out of the mission compound at Chaotung on Tuesday July 12 1904 she would have seen four men walking wearily up the cobbled street towards her, carrying large sacks of oatmeal. One of them approached the gatekeeper and, in halting Chinese, asked to see the foreign teacher, while the others talked nervously in a strange language.

The man they were looking for was Sam Pollard, the senior missionary. Only later did Sam realise the significance of this encounter: 'Little did I dream what it meant for them and for me. Little did any of us dream that this was the revival come at last. God had smitten the rock and the waters were flowing. But we did not know it then.' The men told Sam they were from the Miao tribe, known today as the A-Hmao (pronounced Ahmao) and that they had heard rumours of a new religion which was based on love. They wanted to find out more.

Sam Pollard had recently become interested in the aboriginal groups who occasionally made their way into the city, especially the Miao tribe, which had branches over much of southern China and northern Thailand. The four were from the Hua Miao branch. He usually encountered these shy people as he travelled through the countryside. They lived in small villages of thatched-roof mud-huts, which clung to the steep hillsides on which they tried to eke out a living from the most marginal land. Many lived in feudal conditions, working as tenants or serfs for their overlord who would demand from them labour, rents and taxes, and would often treat them very harshly to keep them obedient. The landlords were usually from the Nosu tribe, who were similar to Tibetans in appearance, and with an independent, reputedly aggressive nature; they normally lived in large family homes, which were built like castles on fortified mountain peaks.

The Miao were despised by both the Chinese and the Nosu for their poverty and ignorance.

Their religion depended heavily on magic and witchcraft, and they worshipped spirits which lived in water, the sky, smoke, trees, rocks and, curiously, doors;

this last was so that the door might prevent evil from coming into the house, but also open the way to good fortune. They believed in ghosts and dreams and greatly feared the wizards, or shamen, who interceded for them with the demons, and preyed on their trust.

Yet a few Miao had heard of another story, one that tied in with their own myths. It was, says W. A. Grist in his biography of Sam Pollard 'a strange, alluring doctrine of a God who was the father of all men, and the fascinating story of the heavenly father's son who was the great elder brother of the Miao.' For the Miao, these 'tidings of a divine ancestry which made the powerful hero-saviour their own kinsman were like a draught of crystal water to their parched tongues.'

The four Miao who came that day had first walked for six days, to the neighbouring province of Guizhou, where another organisation, the China Inland Mission, had been ministering to other groups of their tribe for several years. The bags of oatmeal they carried were their staple food, brought to sustain them on their journey. The missionary at Guizhou welcomed them, but had his hands full with his existing flock and advised them to go to Chaotung, which was only one or two days walk from their home village. So they had walked back. By the time they reached Chaotung they had travelled many miles and were exhausted and covered in dust from the dirt roads.

Neither Sam, the other missionaries nor the Chinese converts at Chaotung knew the Miao language. Fortunately one of the Miao could speak a little Chinese and – through him – Sam was able to invite them into the house.

The Miaos' first question was an unexpected one: 'Please, will you teach us to read Chinese?'

Their own language, which was quite different from Chinese, existed only in an oral form, although they had a tradition that it had once been written down. The story was that an elder of the tribe was once walking along, carrying the books in which their language was written. While crossing a bridge over a stream he tripped and dropped the books into the water, where they were eaten by fish. That was the end of their written language. They had never learned to read, but they knew that the Chinese used writing and felt that a new life would open to them if they could master that skill.

Sam Pollard agreed to help. He prayed that this strange incident might lead to opportunities for more missionary work, but he knew that the Miao only had enough oatmeal for a few days, and could not learn to read Chinese in that time. However, with help from some of the Chinese in the mission compound, he began to teach them. From dawn to dusk the Miao worked hard to memorise as many Chinese characters as they could, only stopping to cook their oatmeal porridge in the courtyard. The missionaries gave them firewood and cooking oil. At night they slept in the mission's school room. After four days the oatmeal had run out, so they left. But, by then, others had arrived.

Sam wrote: 'The following Friday five more tribesmen came, and the day after thirteen more... The thirteen told us they were scouts come to see and, if possible, to open a way for others. They reported that way off in the hills to the north and east there were thousands of their fellow tribesmen anxious to come to Chaotung to see the missionary and to hear about Ie-su [Jesus]. Thousands! Do you blame us if we hesitated a little about believing the story of the thousands. We had toiled for years and had garnered only a few Chinese and Nosu.'

Now the mission was almost overwhelmed. A hundred would be staying with them at any one time. 'They swarmed around us everywhere. Directly the door was opened, in they trooped with their books, begging to be taught. They began at five in the morning, and at 1am the next morning some were still at it.' Will Tremberth, the mission's teacher, and the boys he taught, were roped in. 'Let a schoolboy but show his nose anywhere and down a score of learners pounced on him. When I wanted a bit of quiet, I had to shut the doors and retire to a lonely room at the back, where I was safe from attack. I can assure you it was a glorious, most disconcerting experience.'

They weren't just cramming Chinese, said Sam, 'they were cramming Christianity'. So keen to learn the faith were the Miao that at services they swamped the Chinese congregation. 'Seated in the front, they proved a delightful but embarrassing addition to the congregation. Regular comers had to take back seats, and the preacher in Chinese had several rows of earnest listeners in front of him, who could not understand what he was saying. He had to preach over their heads to the Chinese beyond.'

None of the missionaries knew a word of Miao, and only a few Miao could speak a little Chinese. Using them, Sam wanted to provide services specifically for the tribe. But where to start? Sam wrote:

'We must begin somewhere. The men are all looking up at us and waiting. The Lord help us! Here goes!

'Now, then, Mr Chung, you understand a little Chinese, listen, and when I tell you anything, you turn around and tell it to the others.

'Ready? "We Jesus men worship one God." Tell them that!

'He told them that, prefacing his remarks with an eloquent cough and a clearing of the throat, which almost made one wonder if Mr Chung were not some Bible Christian minister in disguise.

'Sentence two: "This one God is the great Father and Mother of us all. Tell them that."

'He did so, and then we learned the phrase for great father – Pi-nie pi-vie – and so on and so on.

'Our interpreters, for we used several, got quite eloquent, and often moved the audience to shout out with one voice. It was all so strange. Just like a dream. Just like a trip into fairy land. So we have gone on day after day.'

This, after seventeen years of relatively fruitless struggle to convert the Chinese, seemed to Sam to be the breakthrough he had been praying for all along. He was delighted, and so were the Miao as they listened 'for the first time to the story of God and his great love. By and by the men got very excited.

There was a movement all over the chapel. The men with their rough heads and dirt-coloured garments looked at each other and smiled. Here and there they spoke to one another, and all about there was evidence of a new hope taking possession of these poor folk. Here and there they eagerly listened.

'Having explained the gospel as well as I could, I stopped and questioned them. I asked: "Is not that story good?" The answer came in a yell – you can scarcely call it anything else – from all over the chapel: "Zow! Zow!! Zow-Da-Tay!!!" They laughed! They smiled! They shouted! All over the chapel.

'I stopped and said to Miss Squire, who was at the harmonium, "if I only knew a little more of their language I think I could get one or two of them dancing without any trouble." So excited were they.'

Sam wondered what the future would bring: 'The autumn harvests are just being gathered in. The great mass of the Hua Miao are busy in the fields. When the slack season comes, they report that hundreds are coming! Five weeks ago, none of us dreamed of such a move among a people we have never evangelised.'

The news of the foreigners at Chaotung, and their new religion based on love rather than fear, was being passed from one Miao village to another. It offered hope to a downtrodden people and, once the harvests were gathered, the full flood came.

Sam wrote: 'One can never forget those days... The thousands in the hills were free from the heavy pressure of work, and all thoughts turned towards the missionary's home in Chaotung. Almost every Miao village made up a party to go into the city... there came a hundred! Then two hundred! Three hundred! Four hundred! At last, on one special occasion, a thousand of these mountain men came in one day.'

Sam claimed no credit for all this for himself, but others could see that without this remarkable man and his empathy, understanding and abilities as a teacher and preacher, the trickle might never have become a flood. Pollard's biographer W. A. Grist wrote of his power: 'He grapples us to his soul by the intensity of his will and his splendid enthusiasm. Intellectually he was distinguished by mathematical gifts and organising ability. The rich fruit of his humanity was seen in the stories he told. He was chiefly interested in persons and things; abstruse theories and speculations had no attraction for him. He was witty and loved to indulge in fantastic and exaggerated language. He had his mercurial moods and at his best was buoyant and sanguine; but underneath was a stubborn force of character which surprised and sometimes disconcerted his fellow-workers... by thousands he was loved and revered as their spiritual father, the truest image and pledge of the real presence of the Invisible Christ.'

Together with his lifelong friend, Frank Dymond, Sam 'had embraced poverty with the ardour of St Francis.' He was not physically prepossessing: 'a little man about five feet four, with longish pale face, black hair, prominent forehead, and deep-set, large, steady, grey eyes... Of outward appearances this fragile figure made but little reckoning,' yet Sam was a remarkable, inspirational figure. A towering personality who instilled something like awe in Bessie, Harry and the other missionaries who came to learn from him. He was to have the same impact on the Miao. He 'became the apostle and protector of this downtrodden race.'

Nancy Bryant had a very simple explanation of how they had succeeded with the Hua-Miao: 'They are so childlike and think all ministers and teachers are as interested in them and love them as much as we do. Before they became interested in the Gospel no one loved them. The Chinese despise them and the Nosu oppress them. That we love them is something quite new entering their hearts and lives. Life must be such a different thing to them now, with the knowledge of a Father-Mother-God's love, and of a Jesus who died to save, and the prospect of a father's home to which we are all going.'

Initially, Bessie was not directly involved with the Miao, as only men had made the journey to the mission, but once the missionaries began to take their message out across the countryside to the Miao, she spent time living in one of their villages and getting to know their women and children. In a radius of 100 miles around Chaotung there were 500 Miao settlements, and reaching even a proportion of them was a mammoth task.

By Christmas, Bessie had ridden the five-day journey to the other mission base, in Tung Chuan, but she heard how, in spite of several days of snow, many hundreds of Miao walked to Chaotung for that celebration, some sleeping in the mission school, some in the houses and some in the stables. In addition to their bags of oatmeal, they brought small offerings: eggs, chickens, a deerskin.

Much planning had gone into their reception this first Christmas. Sam arranged four days of events, in order to accommodate all who wanted to come. They began the Christmas dinners on December 23, serving 280, with another sitting on Christmas Eve. On Christmas Day, seven services were held, four for the Miao and three for the Chinese. Two of the Miao services were conducted outside, in the large courtyard, with 300 at each. There were 150 more at Tremberth's house.

Pollard's sons, Bertram and Walter, were excited by the dense throngs of people. Sam wrote: 'While I was standing up leading the services B [Bertram] got on his chair and put his arms round my neck, and every now and again would kiss me. W [Walter] worked his way in and out among the crowd enjoying the noise and bustle.'

On Boxing Day the feasting resumed. In the mission compound 400 Miao sat down as paying guests, and hundreds of others came with their own food. In his journal Pollard recorded: 'There were eighty tables of eight persons. We purchased 371 pounds of pork, 6,000 pounds of rice, twenty-eight pounds of salt, sixteen fowls, 220 eggs. We provided also two pounds of honey, capsicum, and pepper.'

Among the visitors this Christmas were a number of Miao wizards, exorcists and witch doctors. Most Miao and Chinese believed in devils, and employed wizards to protect them from evil and mischievous spirits.

Sam insisted that all converts must renounce witchcraft. But, writes Grist, 'it was very difficult for the Miao to suffer sickness and fear the approach of death, and yet refrain from employing the professional exorcists.'

Sam and his colleagues spent the holiday teaching the Miao the Christmas story; then, on Boxing Day, he was approached by one of the Miao wizards, who was blind in one eye. He asked Sam to rid him of the demons which he believed possessed him. At the service that evening Pollard called the wizard to the front. 'I told the people what we were going to do. Then I thought there may be others in the same case, and asked for any other wizards. Another stood up. Then another and another... At last we had nine... I told the people that we were more powerful than all the devils, that the devil is very afraid of Jesus... then I questioned each. Each said he wanted to trust Jesus. I prayed first alone, then all nine repeated after me, prayed and prayed for deliverance... The whole audience prayed and at last unitedly clapped their hands. The whole scene was exciting and wonderful!'

As it was for Sam, the coming of the Miao was the answer to Bessie's prayers. It confirmed her faith, expressed in the piece she wrote just before leaving for China, that 'the voice of the Master has come, saying, "The harvest truly is great, come ye, and work in my vineyard." This, to Bessie, was that harvest.

7 STONE GATEWAY

Bessie was still alone. However fulfilling her work as a missionary might be, there was still an aching void in her life. Alf's application had still not been accepted, so she had no idea when – or even if – they might be reunited and eventually marry.

Bessie was angry with herself for thinking of her own personal happiness when there was so much work to be done among people whose circumstances were far worse than her own. She never would have raised Alf's situation with Mission House back in London, but other missionaries did so on her behalf. After their annual meeting in Chaotung in January 1905 they wrote: 'We beg to remind the committee of the engagement existing between Miss Bull and Mr Evans and hope that Mr Evans' case will have their earnest consideration and suggest that in future when engaged persons offer for China their cases be deliberated upon and decided together.'

The position of single women such as Bessie and Nancy Bryant was a puzzling one to the Chinese and Miao. Nancy wrote to her brother Phil: 'The natives who are not used to us, think we are not unmarried at all – that we girls are simply second wives or something worse. It is most unpleasant to be a single girl here. I wish our committee only knew this. But it is not a nice thing to talk about to them and they can't or won't see our difficulties here.'

Nancy's fiancé, Harry Parsons, also had his grumbles. He had originally been allocated to Tung Chuan for most of 1905, apart from three months with Pollard with the Miao. However, as it turned out, he spent much of the year working among the Miao, while Nancy was in Chaotung, five days journey away on treacherous roads, with stays in verminous inns, making it almost impossible for them to see each other.

In spite of their personal trials, Bessie, Nancy and Harry would have immediately conceded that their problems were as nothing compared to those of the people they had come to minister to. One greatly pressing concern was the backlash against the Miao from their landlords, the Nosu, and the Han

Chinese. Hostility to the Miao had a long history, and stemmed from the fact that the Chinese were not the native inhabitants of these lands. As Sam Pollard explained to his readers back home:

'The Chinese are strangers in a land which has only been theirs for a few centuries. Here is the land of the aborigines of China, of the great Miao and Nosu nations, who at one time reached right down to the sea coast and looked across at Japan... As the Anglo Saxons drove back the Britons and Welsh to the hills of Cornwall and Wales, so the Chinese rolled back the Miao and Nosu to the west and south-west. The Miao and Nosu are thus the Cornish and Welsh of China.'

The Nosu were the dominant of the two native races, and expected subservience from the Miao. The movement of thousands of Miao in the hills did not go unnoticed. Sam wrote:

'Everybody was asking: "What means this unrest among the Miao? Why are these long lines of aborigines going every day to the foreigners' homes?"

'Before long it was whispered that the Miao meditated rebellion and wholesale massacre. It was said that the foreigners were supplying each band of Miao with bags of potent poison, which the Miao were casting into the wells, so that the Nosu and Chinese might be killed off, leaving the land for the Christians... a great fear filled the hearts of many.

'The quest after truth became distorted into a murderous conspiracy. Rebellion! Poison! Anarchy! Arson! Massacre!... Before the Miao had been coming many months a most dangerous situation was created, which might at any time have ended in a great massacre. As it was, a number of people lost their lives.

'Nearly every day came stories of Miao being driven away from the markets, of men and even women being beaten, of others being captured and cruelly tortured, of murderous attacks and chained prisoners. In fact, we were face to face with the most difficult and dangerous situation we had ever met. What could we do? At all costs we must prevent an outbreak. We must keep these poor Miao, on whom the promise of dawn had risen, from being massacred. On the other hand we must not let the Chinese and Nosu adopt an attitude of hostility leading on to fierce persecution. We knew what would be the outcome of that action on their part. Others would come from the Chinese headquarters to stamp out the persecution. That would mean soldiers and pillage and robbery and a peace leaving in its train hatred to Christians and missionaries. How could we save the situation and turn treacherous opponents into friends?'

Sam decided he had to confront the accusers: 'Into the danger zone! Pursue the rumours! Bring the dreaded foreigner right to the doors of the people who feared him, and let them see how weak and helpless and just like themselves this foreigner is.'

He was fortunate that he was a good friend of the Prefect of Chaotung, Mr Chang, 'who was a perfect gentleman of the old school in China, clinging to the ancient traditions, and yet wise enough to treat kindly the incoming of new ideas and thoughts.' Through him, Sam got a letter of introduction to the Chinese mandarins and Nosu landlords in the area around Weining, to the south of Chaotung, where the unrest was most severe.

Sam, accompanied by two Chinese Christians, also carried a proclamation from the Emperor. It included an imperial edict, commanding mandarins and landlords to protect Christians from all ethnic groups. Two official messengers were appointed to accompany Sam's party through the disturbed districts. One Saturday afternoon they reached a place the missionaries called Sheep Market, right in the danger zone. 'We attended the market which was held on the hillside, and to hundreds of people we told our story and read the official proclamation.'

It had the desired effect. From Sheep Market 'we struck out for the castles or baronial residences of several feudal lords... Again and again on this journey the people turned right around, and there was peace where before there were fear and unrest. It is all very well to hate an absent, unknown foreigner but there is no special fun in such an attitude when that foreigner stands before them dressed as one of themselves, small enough to be knocked down by any strong man among them... On Sunday, about a hundred Miao came to visit us, and it was a great joy to comfort and help them.'

One of those feudal landlords proved to be a great benefactor.

'We came to the home of one of the biggest landowners in the district, a Nosu chief and a rare educated man. His name is An-yung-cher and his position among the chiefs is a very strong and important one. By many he is respected and feared, and again by many he is hated and feared. On his land are sixty villages of Miao, and we were most anxious to win his friendship, as he could make or mar much of our work.'

They were invited to his castle at Ta-Kwan-chai, which means the Fortress of the Great Ruler. 'Our stay here was a most fruitful one. Until midnight we chatted with An-yung-cher, explaining our position, preached the gospel and pleading for religious liberty for the Miao. Next day when we left, the great chief assured us that all the tenants in the sixty Miao villages would be allowed to do as they pleased in regard to Christianity.'

An-yung-cher's friendship did not end with this tolerant attitude: 'In our difficulty he proved to be the very friend we needed.' The chief was concerned that if his Miao tenants spent too much time in the city of Chaotung they would 'lose their simplicity, and not be so easily ruled by the lords in the castles.' To make such journeys unnecessary, An-yung-cher offered Sam a piece of land on his estates for a missionary settlement. 'This offer was a quick answer to our prayers, and a great load was taken from our hearts when we heard of it.' The land was a 10-acre plot at Shimenkan, 75 li or 25 miles east of Chaotung. The missionaries named it Stone Gateway, after the narrow, rocky path up a ravine that led to it.

'I had been to that place once before, but did not dream that in that lonely situation, right among the hills, a mission settlement would be built... The Miao

Christians were delighted with the situation. They knew more about it than I did. They knew that the hills at Stone Gateway are full of beautiful smokeless coal, well named by the Chinese Black Gold... we found a good water supply, splendid clay for brick making and plenty of stone... The Lord had given land to His people.'

Money was the only thing missing. None had been allocated by Mission House in London for work among the Miao, so the Miao raised it themselves. In a year, these dirt-poor people managed to raise 'a million of money', equivalent to £100. Sam immediately set to work.

The first project was to build a chapel. The walls were made of wattle and daub (essentially mud and sticks), and easily built, but for a watertight roof they needed clay tiles. Those they had to make. So, they built a kiln, and bought a buffalo to knead the clay beneath its big feet and make it ready for shaping and firing. After many months and much trial and error the first 10,000 tiles were ready. 'That happy day came too late to stop much misery from the rain, which refused to be kept out of the chapel because of such a trifling obstacle as a roof thatched with dried grass.

'When the building was completed, the Miao rejoiced with a great joy, for now at last they owned a "God's Home" of their own!' It was not, however, anything like the chapels the Bible Christians built back in England. 'Poor, damp, ugly little chapel! How insignificant compared with the chapels in the home land. At most it can only have cost £25. Were they wrong in their rejoicing over such a place? They were not the only ones who rejoiced, for over and over again God's presence has dwelt in that little chapel, bringing peace and light to the distracted dark heart.'

On Sundays, up to 1,500 worshippers came, and a series of services had to be held. During the week, the chapel doubled as a school. Next came accommodation. 'We built nine rooms in sets of three, where people coming to worship could stay the night, and where the Chinese preachers and teachers and the schoolboys could live. Gradually there arose a settlement. The whitewashed buildings could be seen for many miles and formed quite a feature in the landscape.'

One building was 'an Englishman's home' for the use of the missionary. 'At first my Chinese assistants and I lived in a corner of one of the huts in the hamlet of Stone Gateway. Then we moved down to the chapel. All the while I longed for the little home where it would be possible for wife and children to join me. It was not satisfactory, they living in the city, and I living among the hills so far from home. The building which the converts erected out of their own money for the missionary's use cost about £5... the house was only a small one and very economically built.' It had three rooms and the lack of glass in the windows meant they had to keep a fire burning to deter the wolves, leopards and tigers that roamed the area from leaping in through them.

The back wall was also cut into the hillside, so what became known as 'the £5 House' suffered from damp. With so many Miao converting to Christianity, ministering to them had become a full-time job for Sam, and he was persuaded to leave the mission among the Han Chinese to others and move to Stone Gateway to work full time with the Miao. In August 1905 the house was considered habitable and Emmie Pollard, two of their boys and Lettie Squire, missionary and teacher, moved in for a while.

They also set up a dispensary: 'All day long people were coming for help. We rendered assistance wherever we could, giving first-aid to as many as possible. Cases which needed a doctor we sent in to the city, where Dr Lewis Savin and Dr Lilian Grandin were always ready to attend to everybody.' A constant stream of sick people came to them, sometimes a hundred in a day. With so much contact with the Miao at Stone Gateway, and by travelling constantly between their villages, a great bond was established.

Once Sam, who was a fast learner, had mastered Miao, he moved on to another great challenge: creating a written version of their language. In doing so he fulfilled a prophesy, told by the Miao alongside the story of how their books were lost, that they would one day get their written language back. This was perhaps as big a draw for the Miao as hearing about Jesus.

As soon as the Miao had a written language, the Bible could be translated into it. Sam's approach was simple, but ingenious. He invented a script based on Pitman shorthand. In that system, consonants are represented as lines and vowels as dots, placed alongside the consonants. However, there was a complication: the use of different tones in spoken Miao. The tone in which a syllable was pronounced gave it one of a number of meanings. Sam likened this to the relationship between the words of a song and the tune.

Sam wrote: 'The Miao language is monosyllabic, and in nearly all cases the vowels end the words. By adapting the system used in shorthand, of putting the vowel marks in different positions by the side of the consonant signs, we found that we could solve our problem. The signs for the consonants are larger than the vowel signs, and the position of the latter by the side of the former gives the tone or musical note required. It was a great joy to us when we had solved our problem, and could give the people a simple phonetic system.'

What he created became known as Pollard Script or Pollard Miao. He took the basic idea from a written language created by James Evans, a Methodist minister working among the First Nation peoples of North America, and known as the Cree Syllabics. Sam credited his Chinese pastor, Stephen Li, for giving him much assistance.

Once Sam had the written elements of the language, a typeface could be created using it. Printing blocks were cut, and primers containing the Ten Commandments, the Lord's Prayer, and an account of the life of Christ were printed. Mark's Gospel was to follow.

Sam wrote: 'It is hoped also to print an edition of hymns in Miao. One great thing Brother Stephen Li has done this year is the adaptation of hymns to Miao chants. In many scores of Miao villages, women and children are every day singing in their own chants, the story of Jesus, the story of creation, the story of Noah. Also such hymns as *There is a Fountain, The Great Physician, Jesus Who Lived Above the Sky* and many more.

'This chanting has been of the greatest assistance in our work, and these singing women are one of our principal hopes.'

8 THE FEAST OF FLOWERS

The day Nancy Bryant first went to Stone Gateway coincided with a time of great celebration. It was the day of the fifth moon, marked by a festival called the Feast of Flowers.

When she reached the flight of stone steps leading up to the village she found the way lined by Miao women, all wearing their best flowery dresses. 'On each side of the steps was the huge cliff covered with foliage. I have never seen so pretty a sight.'

In her letters home, Nancy gives a very human account of the Miao, particularly the women, who she encountered during the festival. She writes in far greater detail than Sam Pollard or Harry Parsons of how the Miao live. The male missionaries are more interested in their spiritual life, Nancy is more holistic. She describes their staple food of ground maize, steamed with vegetables, capsicum and salt, eaten either with chopsticks or a large wooden spoon; and their houses, just four walls with neither window nor chimney, and a mud floor. Sometimes a house was divided with railings into three compartments: one for cows, sheep and pigs; a central area used for cooking and eating; and a sleeping section where the family lay down on the bare mud. 'It is a pitiable sight to see anyone who is sick lying on the floor on a very thin straw mat with no pillow and only a thin woollen cape for covering.'

The Miao, Nancy learns, are almost entirely self-sufficient: they build their own houses, grow almost all their own food, and make their clothes from hemp which they grow and weave into cloth. Onto the cloth they trace a traditional pattern in beeswax, mainly of flowers, plus stars and other emblems, then dye it blue. When dry, the material is boiled, melting the wax and leaving a white-on-blue pattern that gives the Hua Miao their other name: Flowery Miao. The women make the cloth into kilts bordered with red, and other bright colours. Other branches of the Miao bear names that refer to the preferred colours of the women's dresses. There are the Red, Green, White, Black and Striped Miao tribes.

The women's hairstyles are also distinctive: 'Little girls do their hair into plaits at the back and have short hair in front. Young [unmarried] women place the plaits around their heads or do them up into coils at the back, while the mother does her hair in a horn style on the top of her head.'

Harry Parsons was also impressed by the Miao women who came to the Feast of Flowers: 'A noticeable feature of the crowd was the number of women present. The simpering, false modesty of Chinese ladies was absent. Miao women command and maintain equal rank with their men. Indeed, as I watched their independent bearing, and remembered that numbers of them had walked that day, a distance of 50 to 80 li [16 to 26 miles] side by side with their husbands and brothers, and seemed not at all fatigued, I could not help remarking that some of the men would fare badly in a tussle with the ladies.

'Children had not been forgotten; they were present in scores, laughing and playing and having a merry time. The younger bairns had been brought strapped to their parents' backs. It just resembled the jolliest of Sunday school treats.'

The Miao poured in from all directions, flowing in their many hundreds across the hillsides and valleys in their brightly coloured clothes on this warm, sunny spring day. So many were streaming in that the missionaries realised their buildings could not accommodate them, so an open-air rally was quickly substituted. A platform was erected around which gathered 1,500 or more Miao men, women and children. For Harry Parsons 'It was an imposing sight. The costumes of the people showed to best advantage – a contrast to the sober dress of a Chinese crowd. For two hours, the brethren preached and prayed; the people sang and recited.'

The Miao loved hymns. A favourite was *Jesus Loves Me, This I Know* which was sung not just at services but scores of other times during the day. Between services, with their long, rousing sermons, there were games and other entertainments. The missionaries had a device called a galvanic battery which could administer a very mild electric shock. With no knowledge of electricity, the Miao were amazed and delighted with this remarkable toy: 'How folk laughed when the current passed through their hands and arms, and as again when one after another attempted to take cash from a bowl of magnetised water. It was fun both for them and us.'

In the evening there was a magic lantern show, in which images were projected onto a large screen. The first screening was for women and children, the second for men. Again, such technology 'delighted and astonished' the Miao. The shows featured Bible stories: 'How appreciative [they were] of the truth of the Biblical scenes portrayed. The infant Jesus, and the Saviour blessing the children, greatly appealed to them. How thrilled they were at the sight of the crucified Saviour and also of the Saviour risen. We were led to think as we watched the eager attentive throng, that human nature is the same the wide world over. Divine love brings all the sons of men in one grateful company to the feet of Jesus.'

After the magic lantern shows, further services for men and women were held. The crowds were by now so whipped up that when they were asked 'Whom do you want, Satan or Jesus?' the resounding cry came back, shouted out by 600 people: "We want Jesus." To the question: "Whom will you serve?" came "Jesus, only. We do love him. We will be his good disciples.'"

Did the Miao know what they are pledging themselves to? 'The people, as yet, understand but the barest elements of Christian truth.' However, Sam Pollard wrote: 'To have waited on and watched that crowd of simple, ignorant Miao, was to be assured that the love of God was based not on perfect knowledge of him. "We love Him" not because we have a perfect knowledge of Him, or that we are able to perfectly serve Him as we would, but "because he first loved us." Through their love, the Miao are learning God's, and are slowly but surely being led to the light and beauty of Christian lives.'

Between the two services, a dozen wizards, men and women, asked for deliverance from devils. This had become a pattern when the missionaries preached and, they believed, the transformation in those who publicly denounced 'the devil, and all his works and accept Jesus as their Saviour from sin, is conclusive proof that their faith and petitions are not in vain.'

It is nearly 11pm when the crowds disperse, the women to the Miao village to shelter with friends, the men sleeping on the floors of the six mission buildings, and under the skies when they become full. Harry Parsons and Sam Pollard retire, 'tired out in body but happy in spirit, feeling that something had been attempted, something done to hasten the coming of the Saviour's Kingdom of purity and peace.'

The words 'purity and peace' are key to what the missionaries feel they have achieved at the Feast of Flowers which, to them, had become the epitome of evil. They hope they have successfully Christianised a celebration that had descended into a decidedly heathen affair.

In the past: 'Thousands of people, mostly young men and maidens, would gather together and, to the playing of pipes and the singing of love-songs, they would let loose their passions.' The outcome was 'to leave scarcely a single virgin amongst the many hundreds of girls in their teens belonging to these tribes. If the girls become mothers then they are considered wives, and go to the home of their husbands. This is the only form of marriage the Miao possess, and this method of courting, in their eyes, has nothing wrong with it – it is an old established custom.'

So, the Feast of Flowers had to be appropriated. Sam Parsons wrote: 'We realised at once that we must keep our people away from such scenes. It was easy to say "Thou shalt not," but we thought something more was needed. It was decided to capture that day for Christ and keep it in memory of the greatest Hero of all. We should have a great festival of our own [on the same day], where the young people could enjoy themselves in the presence of the great King, and so find out that Jesus is the source of all true joy and happiness.'

Their success was just the first battle in a war. Such old customs could not be stamped out easily. 'It is difficult to make the young folk believe that that which their parents, grandparents, great-grandparents have done, is wrong for them to do... we shall vigorously bestir ourselves to root out the evil – though it will not be completed in this generation; however there is hope for the next.'

Elliott Kendall, a later missionary, explained the tactic further: 'A pagan festival must either be absorbed and redeemed by the Church, or it will infiltrate with heathen ideas into the faith. Pollard acted quickly and effectively. Before the first year was out, he had taken hold of their age-old festival and organised something new and better... In place of the drunkenness were feasts organised by the Church and to replace the nights of immorality there were crowded services in which they listened and sang together late into the night. It was a remarkable change. Whatever the new religion meant to them it was certainly a power which was turning their tribal life upside down.'

9 THE MIAO SONGS OF LOVE AND MARRIAGE

The Feast of Flowers had not always been a mass orgy. Keith Parsons, son of Harry and himself a missionary, would later learn that the Miao's descent into 'drunkenness and unbridled sexual licence' at such festivals was a relatively recent thing. He writes:

'When they were still a free people, before being conquered by the Chinese, they no doubt had proper tribal taboos which regulated relations between the sexes. Their young adolescents probably underwent tuition and initiation as is common practice in other tribal groups all over the world, and this was carried out in special initiation houses by tribal elders. Traces of the old customs survived, but much of the tribal structure had been destroyed by conquest and the ancient taboos had degenerated.'

The missionaries did not know at the time that the tribe had once had a great many traditions and rules surrounding love and marriage.

There was a whole framework, expressed in traditional songs and stories, governing every aspect of courtship and union. These covered how courtship should be conducted; how a man should respect the wishes of a woman who was reluctant to enter into a relationship; which families might intermarry and which could not. There were songs which revealed the lengths to which parents went to identify a suitable partner for their child; and others that covered the use of a middle-man to carry out negotiations between the two families; and the payment of dowries.

It was not until 1946, over forty years after the first Christianised Feast of Flowers, that the songs and stories that had been passed down orally for centuries were recorded on paper, using the Miao script invented by Sam Pollard. As well as traditions regarding love and marriage, they cover everything from the Miao's creation myths, the history of the tribes, and the details of their animist beliefs and ancestor worship.

The songs of love and marriage are beautiful, and I find myself engrossed in reading them. *Song of a Youth and a Maiden* is about a young woman who is not prepared to respond to a youth's amorous advances. It reads:

The youth sings.
The young man is on the high hill,
The young woman there below.
The young man with sighing and yearning called,
Called to the young woman below.

Then the young woman below called back,
Called to the young man on the high hill,
And the young man was overcome with restless longing.

The maiden sings in response to the youth.
Young man, oh young man!
When you see a flower do not pluck it,
When you see a maiden do not deceive her!
Just let the flower drop in the place where it stood.
So I will go round and about and return to my home,
And you shall go round and about and return to your place.

Youth, oh youth!
Do not be like dropping yellow leaves fallen in my way,
Do not be like drooping flowers fallen in my path!

For I, the maiden, the young woman, am like the rising sun,
While you, the youth, the young man, are like the full moon.
O youth, so it is!

In the song, the maiden is asking the youth not to obscure her destined path through the wood, a metaphor for life, and in the final lines makes reference to the Miao idea of the sun being a maiden and the moon a youth, each with their appointed course of travel.

There were strict rules about which families could intermarry, partly to avoid incestuous relationships, and families that broke them could be excluded from their clan. *A Woman's Song* has a potential partner asking:

From what landlord's estates do you come,
And of what clan are you a son?
Come let us two, maid and youth, check our names.
If careful checking shows us unrelated,
Let us two, maid and youth, go on together.
But if we are related,
Let us two, maid and youth, not hesitate to go our separate ways.

A third, *Song of a Woman and a Man*, is about that perennially anxiety-arousing ritual: meeting the parents. It runs:

The woman sings.
If you are a bachelor I am willing to go with you,
But I fear your mother and the man, your father, will not approve of the bride!
That your mother and the man, your father, will bring out
The most complicated costumes to test me.

The man sings.
My mother is good and my father is good,
They are not people like that.
I am willing to marry you,
But I fear your mother and the man, your father, will not approve of the bridegroom!
That your mother and the man, your father, will bring
The untrained ox out of doors,
And the untrained ox will drag me across three hills and three valleys.

There are also six songs about the stages involved in arranging a marriage. Often, before the middle-man was called in, male members of the two families concerned might meet for a preliminary discussion, during which much wine would be drunk. Each set of relatives would extol the virtues of their family member as part of the haggling over the marriage settlement.

In *Song About Entertaining the Middleman and the Headman* a bride's household sets out to make as good an impression as possible on two marriage negotiators, one of whom also happens to be the headman of the village. The bride's father is thinking of the additional livestock a good marriage settlement would bring to his farm, and the bride's aunt demonstrates the young woman's skills as a seamstress by displaying the fine garments she has made. The song ends with these beautiful lines:

For there will come a day when the daughter, the adult young woman, like,
Like a shadow passing over the crops,
The swaying crops, will go to her marriage.
There will come a day when the daughter, the adult young woman, like,
Like a shadow passing over the harvest,
The swaying harvest will go to her marriage.

Sometimes disputes arose when one side accused the other of not honouring the deal that had been struck. *Song of Collecting Livestock From The Bridegroom's Family* tells of a bride's family who consider they have fulfilled their part of the bargain, turning up with the bridesmaids, as promised, and in their finery, but the groom's family do not deliver the quality of livestock that has been agreed:

Our appearance was worthy
Worthy from the outset of the marriage,
But we collected a marriage cow only the size of a deer!

Our appearance was worthy,
Worthy from the outset of the marriage,
But we collected a marriage sheep only the size of a small rabbit!

There are other songs about how parents identify suitable partners for their offspring. In one, untitled, the father of a boy spots the fine yarn woven by a young woman and, deciding she would make an ideal bride for his son, sets about breeding livestock as a suitable wedding gift:

With her smooth hands the girl had joined the hemp strands,
And now the weather came out fine and good,
Just right for the girl to carry her skeins to the river.
Very soon the girl's skeins, the girl's yarn was hanging,
Hanging to dry in the garden plot.

Now the man, the father had heard,
Heard about that daughter, the adult young woman,
And the man, the father, mated his ewes for breeding,
And mated a pair of spotted pigs.
So the man, the father, made arrangements,
Mating all the flocks and herds.

However, when the youth's father approaches the girl's parents, they reject him.

They grieved that their daughter, the adult young woman
Might rise and leave the shelter of the door.
They grieved that their daughter, the adult young woman
Might rise and quit the shelter of the house.

Sometimes, children rejected the partner their parents had negotiated for them. *The Song Of The Runaway Girl* is about a daughter who wants a suitor who is a talented musician, skilled at playing the pipes. When her father fails to find anyone suitable, the daughter runs away with a man referred to in this song as 'the strange suitor'. Her father sends his son to track his sister down and bring her back:

When someone becomes a bride she may come home,
But when Yeu-rang's run-away daughter became,

45

Became a bride she could not come.
So Yeu-rang sent,
Sent Yeu-rang's eldest son.

His eldest son followed,
Followed the magpie bird,
The magpie bird flew up in the sky,
While Yeu-rang's eldest son travelled on the ground,
And passed through ninety-nine valleys.

He passed through forests, through the edible bamboo,
He passed through forests, through the bamboo hanging low,
He passed by forests, by the tall bamboo,
He passed by forests, by the bamboo bending down.

The strange suitor had brought,
Had brought Yeu-rang's run-away daughter and arrived,
Arrived at the great mountain range of Niu-lu,
And stayed on the great mountain range at Drao-cie.

So the magpie bird brought,
Brought Yeu-rang's eldest son and arrived,
Arrived at the strange suitor and Yeu-rang's run-away daughter's place.

Then Yeu-rang's run-away daughter declared,
Declared that the strange suitor behaved,
Behaved like a bird of passage,
And Yeu-rang's run-away daughter could not remain.
Therefore Yeu-rang's run-away daughter would accompany,
Accompany Yeu-rang's eldest son and come back.

Thus Yeu-rang's run-away daughter and the strange suitor
Returned then, came back...

So having crossed ninety-nine mountains,
Yeu-rang's eldest son brought
Brought Yeu-rang's run-away daughter,
Along with the strange suitor, and they came and reached,
Reached Yeu-rang's home.

The father now accepts his daughter's chosen husband and welcomes him into the family:

Yeu-rang took the strange suitor's pipes,

46

And set them down against the partition wall.

Then Yeu-rang provided arable land
For the strange suitor to farm,
And Yeu-rang provided a site,
Where the strange suitor might build,
Build a house with timber frame and tiled roof to settle as a family and live.

At the time of that first Christianised Feast of Flowers the missionaries had no idea that such traditions had ever existed, but they associated the Miao's singing, and dancing, with immorality, and suppressed it.

Elliott Kendall questioned that policy. In his book *Beyond the Clouds* he writes: 'In the rapid and sudden changes which were made, some harmless features of their tribal life were cast out with the more undesirable elements. In making a clean sweep with the past, they swept out some things which could well have remained. Unfortunately, their immorality was closely associated with dancing and music; in abolishing the places and opportunities for immorality they also killed the traditional music and dances. Perhaps their enthusiasm for reform carried them to excess; it may have been impossible for them to disassociate the harmless from the abominable. At any rate, the tribal pipes and dancing, of evil association, were lost in the revolution that took place.'

10 SHIPWRECKED

At last, Alf was on his way. Bessie's reply to his letter offering to end the engagement has not survived, but it had the effect of encouraging him to apply again to the China mission and, perhaps aided by the plea from the other missionaries in Yunnan, permission was finally granted at the annual conference, in July 1905.

It was agreed that Alf and a medical missionary, Dr Lilian Grandin, should travel to China in January 1906, together with a married couple, the Revd Charles Hicks and his wife Maria with their small son Charlie, who were returning from furlough. Alfred was still a probationer at this stage but, the Bible Christians' annual conference was told, he had 'proved himself an able and faithful minister at home and obeys a deep and abiding conviction in giving himself to China.'

Alf left for Shanghai from Southampton on January 11 1906 and was given a great send-off by many relatives, including most of Bessie's family, who gathered at the docks. Alf was presented with a camera by the congregation of St Mary's Road Chapel. Packed in his trunk were the sleep suits Bessie's mother had been making for him.

However, Alf's journey was even more perilous than Bessie's had been, and could so easily have ended in tragedy. All went well until they reached Yichang on the Yangtse and transferred from a small river steamer to an even smaller houseboat to negotiate the rapids in the narrow gorges. Alf had little to say about the drama of their perilous journey, merely commenting 'I shall not be at all sorry to part with the excitement of travelling... were I possessed of a poetic nature I might attempt to describe some of the scenery we passed. But these things are by the way.'

Fortunately, they weren't by the way to Lilian Grandin. In her diary, Lilian records that, after about ten days, the *laopan* (captain) insisted on stopping early so he and the crew could have 'an evening's amusement' at the town of Kwei-fu. The next morning, the missionaries awoke early to find the crew much the worse for wear. Lillian wrote: 'A day to be long remembered by this little party! We woke anxious, for an early start had been made, and the river was rough with a strong up-river wind blowing. We were rolling from side to side, and travelled at a great rate! Though no fault could be laid directly to anyone's account, it seems to us that there was recklessness – due to the dissipation of the previous night.

'About 11am, as we were sitting at our Chinese lesson, suddenly we crashed onto a sunken rock, and were pitched about from side to side.' The boat was steered immediately for the riverbank where it was beached safely. 'Had the bottom of the boat not been so new, we would probably have gone down in mid-stream.'

The two pilots, responsible for navigating a safe course upriver, ran off, fearing they would be blamed for the shipwreck and beaten or even hurled into the river. Some of the trackers went too, as it seemed to them their services would not be required until the boat was repaired. It was only when they were reassured that Charles Hicks would not have them punished that they returned, and the missionaries' many boxes could be offloaded from the swamped hold and set to dry on the riverbank. They would not know whether their things had been ruined until they arrived at Chaotung and they could be unpacked and inspected.

'Our cabin furnishings were flung out of the windows, and we carried them up gradually to the shelter of the rock, where Mrs Yang (the captain's wife) sat taking care of a little girl and of Charlie [the Hicks' little boy]. The latter was very quiet and sober for a long time... The most trying thing was the strong, cold wind, which drove the sand into our eyes and nose and mouth.'

A shelter was created by piling up the boxes around a rock, creating a space in which the travellers could sleep if the boat could not be repaired. 'At first, we thought that the boat was done for, and that Mr Hicks would have to go back to Kwei-fu for another.' In fact, when a carpenter had arrived from a village 15 li away he told them he could repair the damage.

'We were able to get back to the boat about 5pm and have the use of the two bedrooms, while the saloon was left for the trackers to sleep in. Mrs H and I put up our beds in what was my bedroom; from the other room, Mr H and Mr E were to keep watch on the goods piled on the bank above – it was a bitterly cold night. Fan-san [their guard] stayed on the bank and told Mr Hicks that he would fire his pistol if any robbers came. But happily for the safety of the boxes, rain came down, and Chinese do not go about in rain if they can help it.

'The boat settled down, and about 12pm bailing out of water had to be renewed, when she righted herself again. Our chief feeling was one of gratitude that our lives have been spared, and that we had so much left to us – many have been wrecked and lost all. And so, in a wrecked boat, on an unfriendly shore, we were conscious of the all-surrounding, all-loving care of our Heavenly Father, and we rested in that thought.'

Next morning repairs were made. 'The carpenter, who is a good workman, but an opium smoker, arrived about noon; in the meantime, an emissary was sent down by the village elder, to whom Mr Hicks had sent his card, to mount guard over our wrecked property on the beach. The men tilted the boat over on her side, and we had to sit at an angle of thirty degrees with the horizon to eat our midday meal. But it was better than being out on the bank, for the wind had risen again.

'There is snow on the heights far away and we are glad of the heat of an open charcoal stove. The sound of the carpenter's plane and hammer is a cheerful one to our ears; there are three holes, all well forward, while there may be strain elsewhere. No putty is to be had here; we should have to get it further on at some place which is either 15 or 75 li away! This putty is made of beef suet and flour, mixed together into a paste, and is used to caulk the seams of the boat.'

That night, Alf Evans and Charles Hicks took it in turns to stand guard over their possessions while the *laopan* slept on. Next morning, the boxes were put back on board. 'After a great deal of talking, the carpenter agreed to come with us to finish his job of repairing the boat; he did not want to, but Mr H refused to let him have the money until assured that the boat would not leak – so he had to come. The *laopan* had a straight talk from Mr H, and looked very green over it. How thankful I am that the head of the party knows his own mind, and is able to make these people obey him; we should be at their mercy otherwise, that would not be worth much.'

At last, at 2pm, they were able to continue their journey. Each day, the distance separating Bessie and Alf was just a little less.

11 TOGETHER AT LAST?

It had been three-and-a-half years since Bessie and Alf had seen each other. They hadn't heard each other's voices, nor seen any photographs. At times Bessie had lain in bed trying to picture Alf's face, and failing. She feared she would forget what he looked like. How would he have changed? He had always looked older than his years with his long, pale face, high forehead and serious expression.

When they were finally reunited they had just three short weeks together, staying with the Pollards, before being separated again. Alf was sent to Tung Chuan, Bessie to Chaotung. Could they really wait the two years that the missionary society insisted upon before being allowed to marry? Harry Parsons and Nancy Bryant couldn't.

Harry became dangerously ill with typhoid in February 1906 and Nancy hastened to nurse him. When he was beginning to feel better, they decided that they could wait no longer. So, in defiance of the rules, they travelled to Kunming, to be married in the presence of the British consul, who acted as registrar. They received the following chastisement from the Missionary Committee in London: 'We are surprised to hear from Br Parsons of his marriage in May last, so long before the time stipulated by the decision of the conference. We consider that such a distinct departure from our decisions should not be taken without the sanction of the Chairman of the Mission, who should be prepared to justify the sanction given by a full statement of his reasons for so doing.'

However, they were separately sent the committee's best wishes. Nancy wrote to her brother Phil: 'We are amused to receive from one committee-sitting congratulations and [also] condemnation over our marriage. We are getting both resolutions framed and hung up in our study (when we have one) as a gentle reminder of the grand possibilities in logic for our committee. It has made some big blunders over our work here this year. The sooner its worthy members learn to leave the legislating of the work in China to persons who know the work and its needs, the better it will be for both parties.'

This was a time of upheaval for the Bible Christian Church. It amalgamated with two other branches of Methodism in 1907, to become the United Methodist Church.

Alf set to work to learn the language. Study was divided into six parts, with all missionaries expected to complete the first three or four parts. The fifth and sixth concerned mainly classical Chinese and Confucian philosophy. Bessie had completed the four essential parts, and was able to speak and preach fluently, but Alf went on to complete all six and, in later life, enjoyed discussing Confucian philosophy with local Mandarins.

It was quite an achievement, given that one of the reasons for the Missionary Committee's reluctance to appoint him had been their fear that his lack of higher education would make it very difficult for him to learn the language adequately.

Then Alf became ill, struck down with typhoid fever. Harry and Nancy Parsons went to help Bessie nurse him, under Dr Savin's supervision. Although he was out of danger by mid-December, Alf was still feeling weak four months later, when Nancy commented in a letter that a sovereign remedy would be a trip to the regional capital to get married.

Bessie spoke regularly in the preaching shop, and sometimes in the surrounding villages, which she would visit on horseback, accompanied by a Chinese Bible woman. Earlier attempts by the missionaries to dissuade people from binding the feet of young girls had been greatly advanced by the formation of an Anti-Footbinding Society among the Chinese, who were working to end the practice. Bessie also dispensed medicines and learned how to set broken bones.

The other missionaries were only too aware of the difficulties that Alf and Bessie were experiencing in having to wait for permission to marry. A number had faced the same problem. It was hard for a single missionary to be stationed alone in a town so far from any colleagues. Alf used to fit in visits to Bessie with his work, sometimes travelling for a week each way on horseback. His route often passed a very fine rose bush and, when it was in flower, he would pick a bloom to take to her.

Having lobbied for Alf to be sent to China, the other missionaries stepped in again on the couple's behalf, asking that they be allowed to marry when Alf had only been in China for fourteen months. Their District Meeting, held in Chaotung in January 1907, sent the request to the Missionary Society in London, but it was refused: 'We cannot recommend the marriage of Brother Evans and Miss Bull earlier than our regulations permit because we are not furnished with any reasons why such a departure from our rules is necessary.'

It was a cruel blow.

12 THE TAMING OF MRS LIU

Now that Bessie's spoken Mandarin was so much better, she was able to talk freely with the women and girls and, being a great chatterer, enjoyed her work among them much more.

She visited them in their homes, inviting them to attend church services and the women's reading classes which were run by the female missionaries. Nancy Parsons tells the story of a nice man called Mr Liu, very gentle-natured, who made and sold beautiful paper flowers, and who had been coming to the services for some time. 'His wife persecuted him terribly. One Sunday she even came to chapel and rowed with him as only a woman knows how. A few weeks ago he brought his idols and said he would have them no longer. He also told us that his wife had got so unbearable he would have to leave her. Well, we all prayed much for them.'

The missionaries daren't try to visit Mrs Liu, convinced she would slam the door in their faces, but one day she came to the house of another woman, Mrs Lee, where the missionaries were holding a get-together, and there Bessie and Nancy were able to make friends with her. One afternoon an invitation came from Mrs Liu for Bessie, Nancy and Lettie Squire to go to her home for tea. When Mr Liu heard of the invitation, 'he was so excited, he didn't know what to say or do. "It is all God's doings" he remarked "we must trust God and not man."' This was a breakthrough for the missionaries that spread far beyond Mrs Liu: 'Everybody in that crowded street will consider her a Christian now.'

Mr Liu escorted Bessie, Nancy and Lettie to his house. Nancy wrote: 'He was so overjoyed that he took us a queer path – over wide ditches – along narrow banks between deep water. It was a mercy we didn't fall in. And didn't we go at a rate. I had to run to keep up. It was a long walk but we reached the home at last. I wish I could describe it. We had to go through a shop and then along a very narrow dark passage with homes on either side. Then through a courtyard full of homes into another courtyard. One of the homes here belongs to the

Liu family. 'The house possesses two rooms only. The room downstairs is scarcely any larger than our fireplace at home... We went outside and sat in the courtyard and a goodly number of women and children gathered to look at us and to talk about our clothes. I wore my plaid blouse and dearie me wasn't it admired. Mrs Liu meanwhile was busy preparing the meal and soon we were invited indoors. I wondered how they would manage, for there was positively no room downstairs.

'When we got in, we were invited to ascend a ladder which brought us into a small dark loft, where I could scarcely stand upright. It was the bedroom, but a small square table served our purpose exceedingly well. Mrs Liu and her sister remained downstairs for some time, cooking the various niceties and then handing them up to Mr Liu, who took them and placed them on the table for us and some other guests.

'We couldn't see much [of] what we were eating, but I, (for one) could feel when I put a large piece of capsicum in my mouth. The cooking finished, Mrs Liu and her sister joined us and didn't they load our basins. I ate and ate, but couldn't eat more than half of what they gave me. They treated us so royally and no mistake, you can imagine what a strain it was. We wished to move carefully to feel our way gently.'

Over this feast they learn that Mrs Liu was so hostile to them because of her treatment by another missionary denomination. 'It was a misunderstanding which made her so bitter. She thought all foreigners were as bad as the Roman Catholics, and so she wanted to have nothing to do with us.'

The meal finished, the three missionary women went into the yard, where the residents of the many houses that surround it asked them to sing hymns chosen by Mrs Liu: *There Is A Fountain; Hark, The Herald Angels Sing;* and *Heaven Is My Home.* After each was sung, Bessie and Lettie explained what the hymns were about.

'The people were all so pleased with the singing. They wanted to know when we intended to come in again, so we promised to go again soon and to take the little harmonium with us. We came away with happy hearts, and with a feeling that we must tell somebody the good news [about] this mighty triumph of the Cross.'

For Nancy this success is a great milestone: 'It was worth coming to China for. At home, your friends cannot realise half [of] what yesterday's victory means. It is not merely one woman who has been won, but all her people who have hitherto been so bitter, and then all those persons in those courtyards, who gave us such a warm reception, and listened so well. "Praise God from whom all blessings flow." We shall find the work most interesting.

'What strikes me is that the people receive us so kindly. They laugh at their own stupidity in worshipping idols, and yet they are afraid to dispense with these false gods. The poor people are living in mortal dread of evil spirits. If a person is bitten by a dog, the relatives take Chinese ink, and write the character for tiger over the wound and so deceive the devils.'

13 BEAT! KILL!

Sam Pollard was a marked man. His success in Christianising the Miao had made him a target for Nosu and Chinese who resented his hold over the class they considered their serfs. They chose the night of April 8, 1907 to kill him.

Sam had travelled to the village of Ha-lee-mee, two days' journey from Chaotung, where the few Miao Christians lived in fear of Chinese and Nosu violence. He hoped to be able to calm the situation. Sam and three Miao companions arrived at 5pm and were warmly welcomed by the Christians. He conducted a service for them, then retired to a Miao home to rest.

Between nine and ten he heard rifle fire. His host told him that a man was sick in one of the villages and the people were trying to frighten away the evil spirits. Sam would soon learn that his host had deceived him. The firing was a signal, calling together the militia, which had been ordered to arrest him. Unsuspecting, Sam went to sleep. Here is his account of what happened next:

'At midnight the continuous barking of dogs woke us, and soon afterwards there appeared a lot of lights around the small house, practically a hut, in which I was staying. The bamboo door was pushed open and I saw a crowd of armed men with torches. They were shouting for me.

'I asked a Miao what it meant. He quietly answered: "Capture; murder".

'I hurriedly slipped on my gown and, as there was no possible way of escape, I went out to them and was immediately surrounded by about sixty armed men.' The three Miao were beaten by the mob but one, a boy, managed to escape. Sam and the other two were led away. 'We came to a bank with a stream below, and they again began to beat one of my men and knocked him down the bank. In the confusion I thought I might escape; so I jumped the bank and ran down the stream. The crowd rushed after me and forgot my Miao, who went the other way and got clean off. I did not give them a very long run, for they headed me off with cries of "Beat! Kill!" (Ta, ta! shah, shah!) They got me fairly in the bed of the stream and then began to beat me with great force and anger. I expected every blow to be my last: they used iron weapons as well as clubs to beat me... Just as I expected eternity to dawn a man with a sheepskin jacket stooped down, put his arms around me, and ordered the beating to cease.' Sam later gave Nancy Parsons a fuller picture, saying that this was a mysterious figure, a Chinese man dressed in a white gown, who bent over him and said: 'Don't be afraid, I'll take care of you,' at which point the mob dispersed. But Sam was not released.

'Three men took me, and after 50 or 100 yards we came to a walnut tree, and here the three leaders were waiting for the band. The armed men lined up. Ropes were sent for, but this order was countermanded, and then my trial began... The one great charge against me was that I deceived the people.

'I had tried my legs before, now I tried my tongue and pleaded for all I was worth. At last the leaders seemed to hesitate, and then they gave their verdict. I was to leave their district and never return. If I came again they would kill me without hesitation; and if any action were taken against them for this night's work, then they would kill all the Miao in the village.'

Sam was carried back to the village, where he lay in a hut, semi-conscious, in great pain, and close to death. The Miao sent a messenger, who ran all the way to Chaotung, and Dr Savin. The doctor went to see the chief magistrate and got a military escort to go with him to the village and bring Sam back, a journey that in itself was enough to kill him.

Lewis Savin, in his report to the British consul, wrote: 'I found Mr Pollard unable to move even slightly without great pain. On making a superficial examination I found that his body was a mass of bruises, the only part that had escaped injury being the head. On more closely examining him I found that he had received a wound in one lung and that air had escaped into the surrounding tissues: one or more ribs were injured, or broken. The wound of the lung was just below the heart. For some days Mr Pollard was in danger, as some pneumonia followed the lung injury.

'Mr Pollard had narrowly escaped with his life. If the blow that injured the lung had been delivered an inch higher he would have been killed on the spot... At the time of writing, three weeks after the assault, Mr Pollard is able to sit up in bed, but cannot turn on his right side. He still has considerable pain at the site of the injured lung. It will be some time yet before he will be able to leave his room, or will have recovered from the shock to his nervous system.'

Sam's wife Emmie was on furlough in England when the attack happened. As soon as he was able, Sam wrote to her: 'Thank God I am a little better. The doctors are gradually patching me up. The only place which gives anxiety is the torn lung. This, however, seems better, or is no worse. Dr Savin is hopeful and so am I. We have much to thank God for. It is a marvel I am alive at all.

'Another marvel is that while they set to work to kill me as men would kill a deadly snake, not a single blow touched my head. The right hand is also as good as new. Legs, arms, left shoulder, ribs, chest, stomach, left thigh, they got at; but my head quite escaped. Thank God with me. The people are all so kind. My poor Miao have been distressed beyond measure... I want to say so much, but I have not the strength. I think all is going on well, and God never makes mistakes. How much I miss you at this time! Good-bye, my queen. Love to the boys.' While he was in the early stages of his recuperation, Sam received a letter from his mother, which was dated a fortnight before the attack. She wrote: 'My dear son, I have been led to pray for you. "Touch not mine anointed and do my prophets no harm".' Sam was struck that his mother's prayers had been offered up two weeks before the attack on him. It made him wonder, was the mysterious man in white actually Jesus, answering his mother's prayers?

Three years passed before Sam discovered that this man was a Chinese named Yang-shih-ho, who lived near Ha-lee-mee and had always shown kindness towards the Miao. That night he had done what he could to dissuade the men from beating Pollard; but when he saw that they intended to murder him, he threw himself on the prostrate missionary and so risked his own life. When Sam learned this he at once determined to revisit the area north-west of Chaotung where the attack had happened, hoping to meet his rescuer and thank him.

At Ha-lee-mee he stood under the walnut tree where his trial had taken place, and tore off a piece of its bark to send to his boys. 'I saw the place where I stood and pleaded for my life with the crowd of armed men: then we came along the road where I was carried wounded and tired. I walked down the side of the stream and saw where they beat me, just across the water. The jump I made that night was a big one; but I did not run far. Then we came up to the village, and from the house where I stayed that night the daughter came and called me in.

'The place was dirty and looked wretched. The old man who played traitor was there and looked as vicious as ever. But here I am after four years, still alive, thank God!' Sam saw the ruins of the village chapel which the rebels had destroyed ten months before, and determined to efface, as far as he could, the memories of that period of terror from the minds of the Christian villagers. He found a builder who would supervise the congregation as they repaired the chapel. Before he left he vaccinated fifty children.

Such acts won more converts, and in March 1911, Sam wrote to Emmie with good news: "The Miao traitor and nearly all the aborigines of Ha-lee-mee, where they beat me, are now learning our books and profess Christianity. They seem very much in earnest.'

That September, on his way to meet Emmie as she returned from furlough, he returned to the village to find 'one of the nicest chapels in Yunnan.' On the Sunday 250 came to worship in the still-unfinished building, and Sam baptised twenty-three new members. In the congregation were the son and daughter of the man who, four years before, had betrayed him to his enemies.

14 PEARL DISCOVERED

And then came Pearl. There had been the vaguest of stories told about her in my family, tales I had heard from my father, Douglas, about his aunt and the baby she found abandoned. One version was that she was found floating in the Pearl river, set adrift in a basket, hence the name Bessie gave her, which sounded very biblical.

Now I had another, fuller account, from John, her adopted brother. I haven't got to his part in the story yet, but for now let me tell you what Bessie told him about finding Pearl.

Bessie was travelling through Yunnan, carried in a sedan chair. The men were stepping slowly along a rough track, when suddenly Bessie shouted 'Stop!' and jumped down. She stood, listening, then stepped off the track and walked slowly through the long grass of the rubbish tip. 'And there she was – a tiny baby, lying in the grass, crying mournfully.

'Someone had thrown her into the field, not long after birth... discarded her like an empty bottle. She was a tiny thing, a baby girl, lying naked on her back, squawking pitifully. Her scalp was bleeding in several spots. Birds had found her helpless, and had been picking at her soft head. Mother Evans pulled her from the grass, swaddled her, took her home, and adopted her, naming her Pearl. She was fifteen years older than me and lived with us in Kunming, the only sibling I ever had.' John's stories would help enormously in bringing Pearl to life. But I am getting ahead of myself. John will come later.

For now, I want to think about how Bessie felt when she found this helpless, abandoned baby. So much must have been going through her mind. In the course of everyday life, Bessie saw some terrible sights; sights which had a profound effect on her. The abandonment of unwanted infants, especially baby girls, came as a tremendous shock: the tower in Chaotung into which mothers threw unwanted babies, where they were left to starve to death; other infants strangled and thrown over the city wall.

Such abandonment was part of everyday life for Bessie and her companions. They all had horror stories to tell.

A missionary called Will Hudspeth was in a rural inn with companions, just spreading their blankets to sleep when the innkeeper's wife came in and asked if they had any medicine for sore eyes. 'She explained that she needed the medicine for her little girl, six years of age. After a few minutes the child was brought to us, and a sorrier sight we have never seen. The child was almost naked, had not been washed for months, and the hair was hopelessly matted. We drew near that we might see her eyes, but the poor wee lassie was quite blind. Reluctantly we told the mother that nothing could be done, and then I begged her to look after the child and make her happy. "We women haven't time to look after blind children. I'll wait until the river rises and then I'll throw the child in; then, perchance, the water-dragon will give me a boy who can see," was the reply.'

Harry Parsons had his own horrifying experience at Chaotung: 'Last week outside the East Gate I saw a couple of dogs devouring the body of a three-year-old child. The head and body had disappeared, only two legs and an arm remained. T'was a gruesome sight. What an outcry would be raised in England if such a thing were to occur.'

He tells another terrible story in a letter to his sister and brother-in-law: 'Less than a month since I saw a fifteen-year-old girl lying by the roadside, dying. A few rags and a dirty straw sheet were her only covering... No woman was near to moisten the parched lips or drive away the flies. Helpless and almost forsaken the sufferer had to wait for release. Three or four men stood near indifferently watching the scene. It transpired that she had been mistaken for dead; and only when being taken to her grave was it discovered she still lived. Returning a short while afterward, the girl had disappeared, probably taken and buried whether her body had ceased to breathe or not.'

There was another reason Bessie's maternal instincts were heightened. When she found Pearl, Bessie had just finished caring for a baby girl whose mother had died shortly after giving birth. In the previous October, she had gone to stay in Kunming to help Mrs Graham, wife of one of the missionaries of the China Inland Mission, who was nearing the end of her pregnancy. Shortly after giving birth she caught a virulent strain of measles and died a week later.

Bessie agreed to look after the baby until the distraught father could make other arrangements for her. She seems to have enjoyed caring for the little girl and continued to do so for at least six months in Chaotung. In April 1907 Nancy Parsons wrote that 'Mr Graham's baby in Miss Bull's charge is growing a bonny girl.'

Eventually the baby went back to her father, leaving Bessie feeling rather bereft. Only a few months earlier, she had heard the sad news of the death of her little brother Leslie, at the age of four, his death following that of her nine-year-old sister, Gladys.

So all of this was still fresh in Bessie's mind when she discovered Pearl. Somehow, she found out who the parents were and took the baby back to their house, begging them to keep her. The child's father was away and it may be that the mother could not afford to feed her. Bessie made several visits to the mother over the course of a weekend and eventually it was agreed that Bessie would eventually adopt the little girl and raise her, but that the mother would continue to look after her for a while, with the help of money which Bessie would give her.

Alf was a week's journey away, so there was no way of first asking what he thought about adopting this baby.

She was given the name of Baozhen, which means Precious Gem. In English, she was always known as Pearl. So Bessie had a daughter, but would not be allowed to marry for almost another year. That may have been one of the reasons she left Pearl with her mother, paying for her care, rather than taking her right away.

The other missionaries were again lobbying for Bessie and Alf to be allowed to marry, and engineered a *fait accompli*. At the Tung Chuan mission, where Alf was based, there was a staffing crisis. There was no female missionary to work with the women and girls. The local committee appointed both Alf and Bessie to Tung Chuan, thus implicitly allowing them to marry. Alf immediately wrote to the British consul in Kunming, and they married on January 11 1908. Bessie was thirty-one, Alf twenty-eight. Alf took a cutting of the rose bush which he had so often passed on his lonely journeys to visit Bessie; he planted it in the garden of their first home together, where it flourished, while the original bush went into a decline and died.

15 BESSIE, ALF AND EDWIN DINGLE

If you were to open a book called *Across China On Foot*, written by a young Englishman called Edwin Dingle, you would see this dedication: 'During my travels in interior China I once lay at the point of death. For their unremitting kindness during a long illness, I now affectionately inscribe this volume to my friends, Mr and Mrs A. Evans, of Tung Chuan, Yunnan, south-west China, to whose devoted nursing and untiring care I owe my life.'

That's not the half of it. Alf and Bessie spent months caring for and later travelling with Dingle as he suffered first from a broken arm, then a bout of malaria, and finally dysentery.

There is something of Evelyn Waugh's hapless hero William Boot in Edwin Dingle. Boot is the nature-notes writer who ends up in darkest Africa in *Scoop!* Dingle was a twenty-eight-year-old English foreign correspondent, based in Singapore, whose thirst for adventure and a good story drove him to attempt to walk across China. Something, as he says in the introduction to his book, no white man had ever done: 'So far as I know, I am the only traveller, apart from members of the missionary community, who has ever resided far away in the interior of the Celestial Empire for so long a time.' He only mentions in passing that he has a 'retinue' to support him, so his is not exactly a solo mission.

At the time they encountered Edwin Dingle, Alfred and Bessie had just set up their first home together, in Tung Chuan, in 1908. In December, Bessie collected Pearl from her birth mother in Chaotung and brought her home with them. It must have been very unsettling for a baby of about eighteen months to be uprooted and given to adoptive parents, let alone of a different race and culture.

Alf and Bessie's work at this time involved much travelling around remote settlements in the mountains with a small group. Sometimes they travelled together, sometimes Alf went without Bessie. These were dangerous journeys across rough country – and often in atrocious weather – to remote villages. At one destination, Alf discovered the village he was to visit had just been entirely washed away in a flood. He fought his way home through torrential rain. Reaching a dangerously swollen and fast-flowing river, he wrote: 'My horse, fortunately, is well-accustomed to water and carries me safely over these dangerous parts. The same evening [as] we crossed, two poor fellows, not of our party, were carried away by the rush of waters and one was drowned.'

On another occasion, Alf and Bessie were travelling together in a small group to the Miao village of Loh-in-Shan. Along the way, no-one would offer them shelter for the night until Alf told one villager that they were going to stay with him whether he liked it or not, and would pay for any inconvenience caused. So Bessie was allowed to spend the night on the mud floor, with a bamboo partition separating her from the sheep and goats, while the Miao accompanying them slept on a platform above her, and Alf and the other missionaries spent the night outside in the yard, with two of the horses. He remarks stoically: 'The weather being fine, I and those with me... had the best of the bargain.'

They were about to set off on another of these journeys when a badly injured Edwin Dingle turned up at their door. He writes of how he came to be in such a state:

'At Chaotung I had bought a pony in case of emergency – one of those sturdy little brutes that never grow tired, cost little to keep, and are unexcelled for the amount of work they can get through every day in the week. Its colour was black, a smooth, glossy black – the proverbial dark horse... The first I saw of it was when it was standing full on its hind legs pinning a man between the railings and a wall in a corner of the mission premises. It looked well. Truly, it was a beast!

'On the second day out, whilst walking merrily along in the early morning, the little brute lifted its heels, lodged them most precisely on to my right forearm with considerable force – more forceful than affectionate – sending the stick which I carried thirty feet from me up the cliffs. The limb ached, and I felt sick. My boy – he had been a doctor's boy on one of the gunboats at Chung-king – thought it was bruised. I acquiesced, and sank fainting to a stone. On the strength of my boy's diagnosis we rubbed it, and found that it hurt still more. Then, diving into a cottage, I brought out a piece of wood, three inches wide and twenty inches long, placed my arm on it, bade my boy take off the puttee from one of my legs, used it as a bandage, and trudged on again.

'Not realising that my arm was broken, in the evening I determined to chastise the animal in a manner becoming to my disgust. Mounting at the foot of a long hill, I laid on the stick as hard as I could, and found that my pony had a remarkable turn of speed. At the brow of the hill was a twenty-yard dip, at the base of which was a pond.

'Down, down, down we went, and, despite my full strength (with the left arm) at its mouth, the pony plunged in with a dull splash, only to find that his feet gave way under him in a clay bottom. He could not free himself to swim. Farther and farther we sank together, every second deeper into the mire, when just at the moment I felt the mud clinging about my waist, and had visions of a horrible death away from all who knew me, I plunged madly to reach the side.

'With one arm useless, it is still to me the one great wonder of my life how I escaped. Nothing short of miraculous; one of the times when one feels a special protection of Providence surrounding him. Pulling the beast's head, after I had given myself a momentary shake, I succeeded in making him give a mighty lurch – then another – then another, and in a few seconds, after terrible struggling, he reached the bank. We made a sorry spectacle as we walked shamefacedly back to the inn, under the gaze of half a dozen grinning rustics, where my man was preparing the evening meal.'

That evening he had a poultice of warmed bread wrapped around his injured arm. 'Whilst it was hot it was comfortable; when it was cold, I unrolled the bandage, threw the poultice to the floor, and in two minutes saw glistening in the moonlight the eyes of the rats which ate it.'

He tried to sleep, but couldn't. Finally, the pain made him pass out. 'Shuddering in every limb with pain and chilly fear, I at length awoke from a long swoon. Something had happened, but what?... a dream had dazzled me and scared my senses. And then I knew that it was malaria coming on again, and that I was once more her luckless victim.' It had him 'whimpering like a child.'

Despite his afflictions, Dingle fights his way on, through storms and gales, wracked with malaria, in constant pain from his arm, only realising it is broken after four days of agony. Alf and Bessie are his saviours.

'At Tung Chuan the Revd A. Evans and his extremely hospitable wife set my arm and did everything they could – as much as a brother and sister could have done – to help me, and to make my short stay with them a most happy remembrance. It was, however, destined that I should be their guest for many months.'

Dingle wanted to press on to Kunming, so Alfred and Bessie, who were setting out to meet the Revd Clement Mylne, a newly arrived missionary, agreed to go with him part of the way. They could see he was too weak and helpless to travel alone. Dingle describes their journey: 'It was a fine spring morning, balmy and bonny. It was decided that I should ride a pony, and this I did, abandoning my purpose of crossing China on foot with some regret. I was not yet fit, had my broken arm in splints, but rejoiced that at Yunnan-fu I should be able to consult a European medical man.'

Two days out, a messenger caught up with Alf, to tell him that he no longer needed to meet Mylne, and so his journey could be abandoned. However, fearing Dingle would not survive if they let him struggle on alone, they decided they should still accompany him.

Unfortunately, two more days into the journey, Dingle suffered a further attack of malaria, which made him delirious, and unable to go on. 'It was not until I had been there six days that I was again able to be moved. During this time, Mr and Mrs Evans nursed me day and night, relieving each other for rest, in a terrible Chinese inn – not a single moment did they leave me. The third day they feared I was dying, and a message to that effect was sent to the capital, informing the consul. Meanwhile malaria played fast and loose, and promised a pitiable early dissolution. My kind, devoted friends were fearful lest the innkeeper would have turned me out into the roadway to die – the foreigner's spirit would haunt the place for ever and a day were I allowed to die inside.

'But I recovered.'

Eventually, Alf and Bessie were able to take Dingle on to Kunming, where he had arranged to stay with a friend. Shortly after they leave him, Dingle contracts dysentery, and it is several weeks before he recovers. Once he can travel again he goes back to Alf and Bessie's home, staying with them for 'several happy months.' Dingle acknowledges all the Evanses did for him when he writes: 'Had it not been for their brotherly and sisterly zeal in nursing me, which never flagged throughout my illness, future travellers might have been able to point to a little grave-mound on the hill-tops, and have given a chance thought to an adventurer whom the fates had handled roughly. But there was more in this than I could see; my destiny was then slowly shaping. Throughout the rains, and well on into the winter, I stayed with Mr and Mrs Evans, and then continued my walking tour.'

During his convalescence he studied Chinese, learned about its people and travelled extensively, on occasion with Sam Pollard, who he describes as 'one of the finest Chinese linguists in China at that time.'

What Dingle doesn't mention in his book – but alludes to obliquely when he writes 'my destiny was then slowly shaping' – is that, during his stay, he met and later married Dr Lilian Grandin, who had come to Yunnan on the same boat as Alf. She resigned from her work and returned to England, but the marriage broke down. During the First World War she was in her native Jersey, but would return to China in 1920 and resume her work as a medical missionary. Sadly, she died four years later, in Chaotung, of typhus.

16 REVOLUTION

Meanwhile, the ripples of revolt were spreading across China, even reaching Yunnan in the far south-west. The Qing dynasty had been founded by the Manchus way back in 1644, but by 1908 there were increasingly severe rebellions against imperial rule and, in 1911, the Qing dynasty collapsed, the government was overthrown, and China was plunged into lawlessness and chaos. Many provinces declared themselves republics.

The years building up to revolution had seen a resurgence of fear and suspicion of foreigners, who were blamed for many of China's troubles. There was plenty of reason for China to resent foreign interference. Western powers including Great Britain, Russia, Germany, France and the United States had long sought to carve China up among themselves in the interests of trade and the exploitation of its resources. The most notorious assault on the well-being of China and its people was Britain's flooding of China with opium, imported from India, enslaving much of the population to the drug.

A key target of fear and resentment in Yunnan province was the railway being built, by a French company, from Haiphong, on the coast of French Indo-China (now Vietnam) to Kunming. Many Chinese feared it would be used to bring in foreign armies. The arrival of surveyors, who came in advance of the construction workers, sparked an uprising in which the rebels captured three cities before they were defeated.

Because of the mountainous terrain, the route chosen for the railway proved hugely challenging. The line wound in and out of the valleys, climbing nearly 6,000 feet in 100 miles, requiring 107 bridges and 155 tunnels. The climate was very hot and humid, over 40c in summer, when tropical infections and plague were likely. The railway also crossed a valley which had a well-earned reputation for being the source of the Black Death. Navvies were brought in to start work, but the accommodation provided was very primitive and they began to fall ill with the fever. With no adequate medical care the outbreak was soon out of control, and the death toll rose to 15,000. The railway was completed by 1910, but when the surviving navvies made their way home, they begged from house to house and told their story, which grew ever more extreme. Some of them accused the westerners of demanding that babies be sacrificed to the 'iron road' to make it work. Alf later recalled this time in a talk he gave about his life:

'My wife and I were living in Tung Chuan. Because we had been there a number of years, nearly every house was open to us... My wife would be welcomed by the mothers, with their children... But when that rumour spread and they saw us walking down the street, they would bang shut the big doors and lock them on the inside so that you could not possibly get in. Fear had overcome all the previous friendship that they had had for us. How did they know that we were not there simply for the purpose of getting their babies, to offer in sacrifice?... And there were Chinese peddlers who were stealing babies to take to Kunming to sell... so the rumour gained ground as it went around.'

For many, the missionaries were the embodiment of those resented foreign powers. Some women missionaries and their children were advised to leave outlying areas and move into the city of Chaotung, under the protection of the mandarin, because the Miao villages were targets for the rebels. Miao houses were looted and burned down, and several people were killed.

Then the rebels marched on Chaotung itself. Harry Parsons describes how they were defeated by government soldiers who shot many people and took many prisoners, some of whom were later decapitated: 'Thirty or forty heads were hung up over the four city gates – a gruesome spectacle. But the most revolting scene of all was that of the soldiers cutting out the hearts, livers and tongues of some of the beheaded rebels and eating them. The savage lurks but a little way below the skin.'

However, Alf and Bessie were able to ride the storm, and suspicion of them died down. By now, Bessie had been in China for nearly eight years and was beginning to feel the effects of the harsh conditions and constant overwork. She spent three days each week in the dispensary, setting limbs and dressing some terrible wounds, although she seems to have had no medical qualifications beyond perhaps a basic nursing course. The patients would begin to arrive at about 6am and continue until 6pm. Many of them were in a very bad state. They had tried traditional medicine first and only sought help from the missionaries when all else had failed.

She would visit sick people throughout the city, as well as running evening services for women, playing the organ in church and leading the singing. She also tried to supervise the girls' school at Tung Chuan, but was unable to spend as much time on this part of the work as she would have liked.

By the summer of 1911, it was clear that Bessie urgently needed to go home for a rest. In September she was given a royal send-off by the people of Tung Chuan: in the morning her Chinese friends began to gather, some having come long distances. The *Missionary Echo* reported: 'As the missionary in her sedan chair wended her way through the streets, accompanied by more than 100 people, many women came out of their houses to offer good wishes, such as 'May you have peace all the way'... Not a few persisted in giving her a profound bow.'

Alf escorted her to Hong Kong via the new railway from Kunming to Hanoi, followed by a sea journey. They travelled with Sam Pollard who was going to meet his wife Emmie and small son, who were returning from England.

Bessie arrived home in Southampton on December 20 1911, nine years after she had set out for China, although furlough was normally taken every seven years. She felt in need of complete rest, but immediately received some very sad news: Alfred's mother was dying. She hurried to her bedside, just in time to say goodbye, on Christmas Eve.

After leaving Bessie in Hong Kong, Alf, Sam and family set off back to Yunnan by train, only to be told on arrival at Kunming that the British consul had ordered all British nationals to leave the area for their own safety.

The revolution had broken out in southern China and many soldiers had deserted the imperial army to join the uprising. Local government control of law and order had broken down and anarchy reigned. On October 30 Yunnan had been declared a republic under the leadership of General Ts'ai, who was proclaimed president. He set up his headquarters in the large government college which dominated Kunming from a nearby hill.

The British consul ordered Alf and a group of other foreign missionaries to get back on the train and go to the border with French Indo-China, where they waited to see what would happen next. When anti-foreigner riots broke out nearby at Meng-tzu, they boarded the train again with a guard of 500 soldiers and ran the gauntlet, arriving safely in Haiphong, the port of French Indo-China.

By mid-December, all the other missionaries had joined them in Haiphong, with the exception of two of the single men, Clement Mylne and Will Hudspeth, who stayed in Kunming.

While civil war raged in the neighbouring province of Szechuan, in Yunnan there was little loyalty to the Manchu Empire, so the fighting was mainly among Republican factions. The majority of revolutionaries followed Ts'ai, who was from Hunan, but a minority wanted to be led by a Yunnanese.

The other problem was that there was no money to pay the army, so the troops rioted and looted to keep themselves from starving. Alf wrote to Bessie that there were some examples of anti-foreigner feeling, with mobs crying 'Kill the foreigner and destroy the church.'

The struggle between imperialists and republicans entered its final stage. General Yuan Shikai, the leader of the imperial army, switched sides, declaring his support for the republic. He later became leader of the nationalist party, the Kuomintang, and was declared president.

The missionaries were encouraged to hear that Yuan had sent his sons to Methodist missionary schools. General Ts'ai managed to get control of the situation in Yunnan fairly quickly, and so Alf returned to Kunming to join

Clement Mylne and Will Hudspeth. There he found that some French priests had been allowed to return to their missions in other cities, so they persuaded the British consul to allow them to return to Tung Chuan. Chaotung was still considered too dangerous. According to Mylne: 'We cleared out of Kunming before the consul could have time to repent. It snowed a blizzard the day we left, but it would have taken something considerably worse to have stopped us.'

He also noted a strange result of the revolution: the Manchu emperors had insisted men wear their hair in a single plait; the republicans now banned that style and ordered men in Kunming to shave their heads. The order was enforced by the police, who would stop anyone with long hair and cut it off on the spot, leaving piles of hair on the street.

In May 1912 it was safe for all the missionaries to go back to their stations, so Alf continued to work on alone in Tung Chuan, with the additional task of being secretary to the district, a time-consuming administrative role.

Progress among the Han Chinese continued to be difficult and took up much of his time, but among the aboriginal tribes there was real enthusiasm for Christianity, especially from another tribe known as the Gopu, who had sought out the missionaries in their thousands. They had already built five chapels in their hillside villages and the evangelising work was being carried out largely by six Miao preachers, under Alf's supervision.

The missionaries were working to establish schools in six centres, from which the surrounding villages could be visited. Alf ended his report to the annual conference with an urgent request for the appointment of another missionary to take a more active charge of the mission to the Gopu than was possible for him.

By 1913 Alf's furlough was due, so in spring he set off for England. Pearl was left in China with the Li family. They were prominent members of the Methodist Church in Yunnan: John Li became the first Chinese to be ordained, and his brother Stephen was also an evangelist. John had escorted Bessie's party from Chongqing to Chaotung when she came out to China in 1903. The Li's sister, Li Shuang-mei, initially trained as a nurse and later helped in the girl's school. She will appear again later in this story.

So where had Pearl been since Bessie returned to England? Had Alf taken care of her for those two years? We can't know, but it seems more likely that she had been with the Li family since 1911, rather than from when Alf took his furlough. If that's the case, Pearl would have spent over three years with the Lis, from the age of four to seven. How much of a father had Alf been to her during these formative years? Who did Pearl see as her main family in that time? So many questions, so few answers. It would be a few years yet before Pearl came truly to life for me.

17 CIVIL WAR IN CHINA, WORLD WAR IN EUROPE

Three times within a few days Sam and Emmie Pollard were forced to flee for their lives, escaping in the night clutching their three sons and walking for hours to remote villages where they might be safe.

The imperialists might have been defeated in Yunnan, but the republicans were now at war with each other, and Sam and the other missionaries were caught in the fallout. Large armies of badly paid soldiers were living off the land, requisitioning goods and destroying what infrastructure there was. Armed bandits organised protection rackets and some landlords built stockades and forts so that they could terrorise their own tenants and fight their neighbours to gain more land.

Sam Pollard heard that the Miao mission at Stone Gateway was to be attacked. An escape route was planned to a village six hours walk away, and in the surrounding hills lookouts were stationed. They were to sound the alarm by blowing cornets and the school whistle. One night in June 1914 the alarm was given.

Sam later wrote: 'The cornet alarm was a false one, but we did not know that it was so... As fast as I could I went up to our house shouting to Mr Hudspeth as I passed his study. Ernest [the youngest of his three sons] was in bed asleep. It was the work of a few moments to snatch him up, and in two minutes we were all off. Fleeing from the supposed attack of men who, had they really come, would have made short work of us all. It was half-past eight when we started, about an hour after dark. We kept on till two o'clock in the morning, when we reached a small Miao village right up among the hills. We judged that we should be safe there for a day, and that by that time assistance would reach us from the officials in the city.'

After a day or two among the hills they returned to find that all the Miao had gone back to their homes. But, two hours after their return, Will Hudspeth brought news that a rising was to take place all over the district within a few hours, and they were forced to set off again, this time in another direction.

'By four o'clock,' writes Sam, 'we came to a river ferry on the way to Mi-ri-keo where we encountered a storm of rain which soaked us to the skin. We just got across before the waters rose and made the passage impossible. We were like drowned rats; but we were glad to think that the rain would put off any attack upon Shimenkan [Stone Gateway]. Two days later we reached Mi-ri-keo.'

Yet they were not safe here. Thirty-six hours after their arrival they were told that a thousand Boxers were due to attack Mi-ri-keo. It was the Boxers who had forced the missionaries to flee from Yunnan in 1900. They were told to go to another city, Ko Kuei.

'Again we travelled all night; just before dawn we all lay down by the roadside and tried to sleep a little... An hour after dawn we reached Ko Kuei where the mandarin made us welcome... The Boxers in the district made their expected attack, but the soldiers and militia defeated them with great slaughter. The leader, a so-called emperor, was executed on the spot, and the enchantresses who were supposed to be able to stop the bullets with their magic fans had a terrible awakening that day...

'There were attempted risings in four or five different places. Two proved abortive, another was put down with considerable loss of life, and at a fourth centre many who took part in the rising were killed. Yesterday the officials here executed two of the leaders. One was a girl of eighteen who was evidently a tool. She claimed occult powers; but these could not save her. She was dragged through the streets and shot as she lay in a swoon on the execution ground. Mr Dymond and I begged that her life should be spared, but orders had come from headquarters and they were carried out.'

While civil war was tearing China apart, the First World War was doing the same to Europe.

Sam heard the news of the war's outbreak as he made his way back from Ko Kuei to Chaotung. He wrote in his journal: 'It is ten years since the Miao first came to us at Chaotung and here we are away from our stations. What an end to the ten years!' What should have been a truly auspicious anniversary was clouded by the terrible news from home. Sam writes to his friends in England:

'I dread the days that are coming... Like you I feel that England is after all the best Christian country in the world, and has a lot of good men and women in it. But I remember also that Judea just before it was destroyed produced some of the finest men and women the world has ever seen... Yet the place was wiped out and by a people who were at times as ruthless as the Germans. I pray God to be merciful and in some way to bring peace soon that mothers' sons may no longer be cruelly murdered or maimed for life... May God give you all light and comfort in your days of intense darkness!'

Sam was appalled that Christian statesmen could not prevent such a tragic conflict. He heard the Miao praying 'that the war might stop and the peoples of Europe should practise the law of Christ' and felt humiliated. He remarked later: 'The people still come round us in large numbers, but they are puzzled at the idea of Christians killing and hating each other in Europe.' In August 1917 China, which was initially neutral, became a player in the conflict when it declared war on Germany. A hundred thousand joined Chinese battalions that travelled to France where, although not directly involved in the fighting, they played key supporting roles. Many of them were tradesmen such as masons, carpenters and blacksmiths who proved to be very useful in repairing tanks and other skilled work. The coolies, or unskilled labourers, built roads in northern France or loaded and unloaded ships.

Many of the officers in the Chinese battalions were missionaries and Will Hudspeth was among them. He believed it was necessary, if he was to truly fulfil his mission to the Chinese, to be alongside those men, so he joined up. He wrote: 'I felt a thrill of joy to think that these coolies... came from chapels founded by missionaries... Many of us feel that we are doing a much-needed missionary work in France, and that is why we stick it. We don't like being in the army – it is irksome to have to obey orders – but we do intend to present the very best of the British nation to the Chinese.'

After the war Will went to Cambridge to study Chinese, before returning to China.

18 TYPHOID, AND THE DEATH OF SAM POLLARD

Alf and Bessie had struggled to get back to China after their furlough in England. Their booking, in August 1914, was on a German ship, and was cancelled when war broke out. They finally found a Japanese ship which could take them to Hong Kong. They left in November, travelling with Kate, Lewis Savin's wife, and her three children, Kitty, Agnes and David.

They arrived in Kunming in early January 1915, and were destined for Chaotung, to take some of the load from Frank Dymond. He wanted to concentrate on the training institution which provided boys with a good general education combined with religious instruction. Most of the students were baptised in the course of their time there and some went on to teach in the villages, and preach in their spare time.

Alf and Bessie threw themselves into their work in Chaotung. Alf supervised the building of a new chapel. He was a practical man, and found he really enjoyed building projects. Bessie supervised the girls' school while Lettie Squire was on furlough, but also spent quite a lot of time helping Kate Savin, who was pregnant again and whose husband had several severe attacks of a painful illness, possibly due to appendicitis or gall stones. This hindered Lewis's work at the hospital, so Bessie helped here, too, nursing typhoid patients.

In the summer of 1915 she and Alf went to Stone Gateway for a short rest. Sam Pollard had been hard at work translating the New Testament into Miao, finishing a few months earlier. As he did so he was weighed down by increasing weakness, and found himself struggling against exhaustion. He had achieved so much. There were now 10,000 Miao Christians, and they could read the Bible in their own written language; a language Pollard had created for them.

It was probably one of the Miao women who came to cook for the boys at the school who brought typhoid to Stone Gateway that summer.

Sam Pollard had foreseen the dangers associated with a great concentration of pupils at the mission, and had done all he could to guard the health of the

300 scholars. No boy was allowed to go home in term time without special leave, in case he brought the infection back with him. Sam had tried, unsuccessfully, to get proper medical staff for the school. Dr Savin sent a nurse, but she proved to be unfit for the post. So, when the outbreak came, there was no dedicated medical practitioner on hand.

The Miao cooks, the probable source of the infection, were only there because Sam had been told to cut costs. He had had to dismiss the Chinese servants who cooked at the school hostels and find cheaper staff among the Miao. Emmie Pollard wrote: 'Sam wrote pleading that a foreign missionary should be withdrawn rather than that the native organisation should be disturbed,' but his fears were dismissed.

That decision was to prove fatal.

In his vulnerable state, Sam might have been the first to succumb to the disease. In the event it was Will Hudspeth. Will had been inoculated so, believing himself to be safe, immediately took charge nursing the sick boys. When Will fell ill, Bessie stepped in, but Sam insisted on taking charge of the boys' care.

Sam's scribbled notes to Frank Dymond chart Will's decline over the next ten days: 'Uncle Will is in the thick of it and feels very tired. I think, however, he is going on all right and in due time will get well again. He feels it very much and thinks he is having an awful time...

'Mr Hudspeth is still unwell with [a temperature of] 101f this morning, after a bad day and night. If he is not better by tomorrow none of us will be able to come in as I must stay and nurse him... If he does not get better soon I will ask Dr Savin to come and look at him...

'Mr Hudspeth is still ill, highest temperature to-day 104.5, lowest 104. He is, however, fairly easy and bright and has slept a little. He ought soon to be getting the change, ninth or tenth day, to-day. I hope he will be well soon... This sick-nursing makes me very tired.'

Will's temperature dropped but, just as it did, Sam himself became ill.

His wife, Emmie, turned the schoolroom down-stairs into a bedroom for their son, Ernest, and placed a Miao girl in charge of him, while she moved into her husband's sick room to nurse him twenty-four hours a day. The following day he fainted twice and was very languid. He told her: 'If it is typhoid I am afraid I shall not pull through, but I hope, please God, I shall get well for your sake.' He slept heavily, as if unconscious. Lewis Savin paid a visit from Chaotung, though at that time Emmie was hopeful Sam would survive.

A week dragged by, Sam lying mainly silent. At one point he spoke of a cheque he needed to sign, but Emmie refused to let him attempt any business. On the Sunday he said to her: 'It is not time for service yet.' On Tuesday he said nothing, but twice looked into his wife's face and smiled.

'Months afterwards it dawned upon me,' Emmie later wrote, 'that they were smiles of farewell.' As Sam was dying, his old friend Frank Dymond came in. Sam said to him: 'Well, old man!' and smiled.

Then a great silence fell. Sam's eyes took on an intense, fixed gaze. On Wednesday he went into a coma, never moving, his eyes wide open but unseeing. At 4pm on Thursday afternoon, September 15, Sam's face became ashen, and he stopped breathing.

Will Hudspeth wrote: 'As he lived, so he died. It was this unselfishness, this love of others, that cost him his life... Mr Pollard nursed me; but after fourteen days he became ill, and alas! was unable to endure the strain. It came as a great shock to me, for he was in one room and I in the next. Though I knew he was ill I had no idea of what was coming. He passed into eternal rest just as I was beginning to recover.'

Sam was just fifty-one, and had been in China for twenty-seven years.

His funeral was a scene of much sorrow, especially among the Miao tribesmen. W. A. Grist has this account: 'They said: "He is ours, let us bury him; we will arrange for coffin, bearers, grave, and tombstone; for we loved him more than our fathers, and he was ever kind to us."

'They chose his grave on a far-seen hill-slope. Away up through the maize fields, wailing a dirge, they carried all that was mortal of him, followed by 1200 mourners, 400 of whom were scholars from the school he had founded and maintained. His lifelong friend, Frank Dymond, conducted the interment and has described the scene: "Singing and prayer were followed by short testimonies... That night men stayed upon yon hillside watching near the open grave, and so for a few successive nights, lest the tomb should be rifled. Among the sapling oaks, surrounded by Miao graves, he lies. Mr Evans erected a cross and beneath its shadow the body of Sam Pollard rests."'

Alf also built an imposing tomb for Sam, and later helped Emmie Pollard organise her journey back to England. Even before Sam's death she had been under doctor's orders to go home as soon as she could. Before long, Lewis Savin would also die. The huge pressures of their work; the increasing danger of meeting a violent death at the hands of a mob; and typhoid were taking their toll on the missionaries. And things would only get worse. Much later, Bessie would also succumb to this illness.

19 CHINA BETRAYED

While the world of the missionaries was undergoing its own personal turmoil, China, already torn by civil war, suffered another body blow.

Japan had seized the opportunity provided by the outbreak of war to capture the German stronghold of Qingdao in Shandong province – on the coast midway between Beijing and Shanghai. It pursued its advantage by going on to make a series of demands for China to concede extensive territorial rights, economic privileges and military concessions. With his armies too preoccupied by the civil war to mount a counter-offensive against the Japanese, President Yuan Shih-kai was forced, in May 1915, to concede to their demands.

Yuan's dictatorial rule was making him increasingly unpopular across China. Harry Parsons wrote, later that year: 'All [elected] local authorities have been dismissed and a return to government by official only taken place. The baneful influence of Yuan Shih-kai is even being felt in this remote corner of the kingdom. One cannot help feeling that the country is sadly drifting onto the rocks ... unless the present regime is radically altered.'

Yuan, clearly widely out of touch with the feelings of his subjects, decided to inaugurate a new imperial era, declaring himself emperor in December 1915. That sparked a revolt in Yunnan. On December 29 *The Times's* correspondent in Peking wrote:

'REVOLT OF CHINESE PROVINCE,
PROTEST AGAINST MONARCHY

'The province of Yunnan yesterday declared its independence. The efforts of the revolutionaries to secure the co-operation of other provinces have so far failed... The military governor of Yunnan yesterday issued a proclamation declaring the independence of the province and saying that Yuan Shih-kai had broken his presidential oaths and had failed to comply with exhortations to

75

restore the republic. Numerous reinforcements of northern troops are being transported southwards.'

Yuan was forced to renounce the throne he had only just won. He died in disgrace in June 1916, leaving China without a strong leader, and the country descended into a period of control by warlords, who fought for control of cities and provinces.

Despite living in such uncertain times, the missionaries continued their work. Bessie took over the medical work in Stone Gateway, treating several cases of typhoid, plus many burns. However, her health deteriorated: early in 1916 she was said to be suffering severe haemorrhages which left her seriously debilitated. Six months later Nancy Parsons wrote that Bessie could not be left alone and 'has been ill a good deal this year. Can just manage to walk a little now.'

We can't know what this illness was. It might have been the result of a miscarriage, which would have had a devastating effect on her spirits. She would have realised that her last chances of having children of her own were fading fast. Or, perhaps it was caused by hormonal problems related to an early menopause. Whatever it was, maybe because gynaecological matters were never discussed openly in those days, no references to it have survived.

Because of Bessie's illness, the missionaries decided that both the Evanses and Will Hudspeth should live at Stone Gateway, and amalgamate the Miao work with that among the Nosu, with Will and Alf arranging their travel around the villages to ensure that Bessie was never left alone.

Whatever the cause of her illness, her health seemed to improve gradually with time. She managed to help Alfred run a Women's Bible School for ten days in August 1916, which attracted about 100 Nosu women. The differences between the lives of the Nosu and Miao women were striking: the Nosu were much more prosperous. The women came dressed in their finery and accompanied by their children and servants. They were taught St John's Gospel in the mornings; in the afternoons they learnt hymns and had practical lessons on health and hygiene. The favourite hymn that year was *What Can Wash Away My Sins*. Bessie gave short talks on childhood illnesses and how to treat them. She found that many of the babies had never had a bath before and found the new experience very enjoyable.

She wrote: 'One afternoon... I impressed upon them their great responsibility in training their children for God. I felt this to be especially necessary because among Nosu women each child has its nurse, and she has more to do with the child than its mother. One has only to listen to these nurses to know what a baneful influence they exert upon the child.'

The Parsons were stationed at Tung Chuan, but when Nancy became pregnant again they returned to Chaotung in September, where she gave birth to twin boys, Philip Kenneth and Richard Keith. Both would one day become missionaries, and feature later in this story.

At the January 1917 meeting of the District Committee it was agreed that Alf and Bessie would go back to Tung Chuan, as they had been hoping since their return to China in 1915. A key part of their work would be building and staffing a school for girls, but they struggled to raise the funds needed for the project.

When Bessie found that there was a demand for English lessons for the children of some of the wealthier Chinese, she started regular classes under the trees in her garden, and was able to put her earnings towards the wages of the workmen building the school.

And here, at last, comes a mention of Pearl. She took part in the classes for girls. This is the first time she is mentioned, other than as a baby, in the records which have survived, but it is a fleeting mention. Pearl will remain beyond my grasp for a little while longer.

The year 1918 began with some very sad news. Dr Lewis Savin caught typhus from a wounded soldier he operated on. Weakened by his previous illness, he could not withstand the infection and soon became very sick. His wife Kate nursed him, but he died, and was buried in Chaotung. Kate and the four children were effectively stranded in China, unable to travel home because of the war, so she was engaged as a missionary in her own right and had to balance her work with the care of the children. She moved to Stone Gateway with them, where she did her best to help Nancy Parsons, but was hampered because she could not speak Miao.

Quite apart from such tragic events, there were numerous daily threats that the missionaries had to be aware of. They had to have their wits about them at all times. While they were widely accepted among the general population, some would seek to exploit them for their own purposes, or use them as scapegoats.

Nancy Parsons related a sinister event early in 1918: a coal miner had asked Harry to come and help his crippled wife, who had toothache. Harry was on his way to market and promised to bring his forceps to take out the tooth. Nancy cleaned and boiled up the implement and left it ready for him to take.

Soon after Harry set out, he realised that he had forgotten to pick up the forceps so, as he passed the cave where the man was employed digging coal, he called out that he could not remove the tooth now, but would come back later and do it. Almost immediately the crippled woman died. Her husband had given her poison because she could no longer work, expecting that she would die just after the tooth was extracted and her death could be blamed on the missionary, who would be forced to pay for her coffin and funeral and might even be expelled from the country. Nancy was convinced that the hand of providence had saved them by ensuring that Harry forgot the forceps.

Another brutal blow to China's esteem came with the unfavourable settlement the nation received following negotiations at the end of the First World War, in November 1918. Although China had declared war on Germany and Austria-Hungary in 1917 and was thus on the winning side at the peace conference, the end of the war did not bring an end to its troubles.

The Russian Revolution of 1917 had shown Chinese intellectuals and workers that socialism could be effective in making significant changes in a country of comparable backwardness, and this marked the effective beginning of a Chinese Socialist movement.

While the civil war was continuing, it became known that the Treaty of Versailles had ceded Germany's former rights in Shangdong province to Japan, which had seized the area, instead of returning the region to China. The civil war had left China weakened and without credibility in the region, while Japan, which had joined the Allies in 1915, was an important supplier of munitions to Europe and in a much better position to extract concessions.

The terms of the Treaty of Versailles provoked a protest march by students in Beijing in May 1919, which led to national demonstrations, strikes and a boycott of Japanese goods. These became known as the May Fourth Movement. Merchants organised a run on the banks, and the combination of intellectuals, workers and merchants was too much for the government, which gave in and refused to sign the treaty. After the Communist takeover, May 4 became a national holiday, in recognition of the fact that this event had paved the way for the founding of the Chinese Communist Party.

20 THE YEAR OF FAMINE

In 1919 there was another horror for the people of Yunnan to face: famine. A cold, rainy growing season caused the failure of the maize crop, the Miao's staple food. There was starvation at Stone Gateway. The mission did all it could, feeding 10,000 Miao, but many thousands more had to resort to digging up bracken, the roots of which could be boiled and made into an edible paste. Children were sold into slavery for a handful of maize. Gangs of half-starved robbers, often defeated soldiers, roamed the land.

On February 7 1919, Nancy Parsons wrote to her brother Phil Bryant from Stone Gateway: 'I wish you were here to help in the famine relief work. It is terrible. We have sent two boys off today with a little meal, made from popped maize, to about six families who are dying from starvation. I do hope we'll be able to keep them alive, but they are too weak to dig bracken, too weak to look pleased when the boy gave them a little meal to mix with water and drink.

'James [a helper] went around to the different places where the folk are washing bracken, and he just stood and cried to see the suffering of some of the folks. We are trying to give all the children one or two meals per week... Some [Miao parents] are selling their girls as slaves to the Chinese for about a peck of maize. We are talking of redeeming them, but don't know what we could do with them.'

Later she writes that they have managed to help two children: 'We have found homes for two of the slave girls, so the next thing is to buy them out. They go to live in Miao homes as mother's helpers until they're old enough to marry. We shall have to supply them with food until the next harvest comes on.'

Some parents were so desperate that they prayed their children might die: 'One father took his children among some Chinese covered with smallpox, and then into the thick of the influenza, hoping they might get ill and die, but afterwards he thought: perhaps God would not be pleased with him. He told James if we couldn't give them a bit of food, just a message of love and hope would keep them alive. To be here in a famine year has always been a dread to me. But it is a good thing that the famine has always been confined to the high lying lands. In the lower places, even the Miao have almost sufficient to last. About thirty years ago, the famine was so universal that many of them died with silver in their hands on their way to buy food.'

Harry Parsons wrote: 'We are having the most strenuous time of our lives. The famine relief business has kept our hands very full. At times we have had nearly 400 people on the compound. Some Sundays we have had over 500 children and mothers to a meal. Week by week we have had to superintend the dispensing of maize from a score of centres. As far as relief moneys have permitted, we have been succouring nearly 10,000 of our people. We have opened relief work, employing the people in drain laying, house building, swimming bath building, and road making.

'We are building 10 li (3 miles) of new road between Stone Gateway and Chaotung. The new road obviated crossing a gully which in the rainy season is very dangerous. Almost every year men and women are swept away in trying to cross the torrent. A year ago a Miao girl of sixteen or eighteen was drowned in the gully when returning from service at Stone Gateway. By blasting through some rocks, we have succeeded in making a road which runs up one side of the gully only. Formerly the water had to be crossed four times.'

The missionaries struggled to cope in the face of such suffering. The annual report for 1919 says: 'This calamity has been a crushing burden to Mr Parsons, and both he and the native preacher wept, as they tried to relate to the district meeting the frightful scenes they had witnessed. Local mandarins sent large quantities of food for the famishing multitudes, and Mr Parsons used to the utmost the means placed at his disposal, but all the supplies fell immeasurably short of the need.'

Many families fled the district, often to perish on the road. Mission work ceased, the schools closed, and teachers were switched to relief work. And while they did all they could to feed the starving, the missionaries were under constant threat themselves from marauding bands of robbers.

Alf writes about the danger he faced as he travelled his vast district, which was as big as England: 'From the commencement of the year, the whole district has been infested with bands of robbers. Towards the end of the summer, the district was reported free, but only after the most severe measures have been taken, whereby some of the bands were completely annihilated.

'On behalf of the village headman and the local officials, it must be acknowledged that it is a very difficult thing to keep their parts of the country free of these marauders, for in all of the bands are some local men, and the slightest movement on the part of the official to capture them is known to the robbers, and swift vengeance is taken upon him. Consequently, he often shares in the plunder that is taken by the men.'

Alf had been robbed at gunpoint by twenty ex-soldiers. The one unarmed policeman who accompanied his group proved no deterrent. Alf lost the £120 he carried, (worth over £5,000 today), two pairs of boots, his watch, a knife, some clothes and even the saddle on his horse, but none of the group was hurt. It could have been much worse: 'A seller of pigs was caught by them at the same time, and because he shouted over his silver he was badly beaten.'

Against all this, Alf was to face a new challenge. He was appointed to re-establish and lead a mission in Kunming, the provincial capital, where the Bible Christians had had a base until the Boxers drove them out in 1900. This would become an administrative centre, from which money and supplies could be sent out to Tung Chuan and Chaotung, and the Evanses moved here late in 1919. To cap it all, Bessie caught typhoid almost immediately, but fortunately made a good recovery.

Alf rented a house with storage space which could be used as a chapel for about 100 people, in addition to living quarters. It also had a courtyard lined with rooms which doubled as consulting rooms for patients coming to the dispensary, and guest accommodation. Later, a Sunday school was established.

The first service in the new church was held on January 4 1920, with a congregation of seventy turning out, despite it being a bitterly cold day. Bessie led the singing and played a tiny organ.

Across the street from the church, a row of fine houses had just been built. These, it turned out, were for the concubines of wealthy men. Such women were sometimes found in order to provide a son, if the first wife had been unable to. The first wife might well submit to this arrangement and move to another part of the house. Bessie and Alf were invited to the first birthday of a baby boy who was born in this way.

It was only after they had offered congratulations that they learnt the mother was the second in the household and number one wife was upstairs in her room. The young mother took Bessie to the first wife, introduced her, and left. The room was large and comfortably furnished, and it seemed to Bessie as she spoke to the first wife that while she was sad about the arrangement, she accepted it without bitterness. Such relationships were open, and generally understood.

Bessie was able to increase the income of the new mission by giving English lessons to local women, including some teachers from the government-run school. She and Alf were also responsible for work among the villages of the Gopu tribe in the surrounding countryside but, because of the number of robber bands which roamed the area, they had not been allowed to visit them for nearly three years. These gangs were growing ever larger, joined by many peasants driven to desperation by hunger, and the high rents charged by absentee landlords.

During a peaceful period, Alf and Bessie were granted permission to visit some Gopu villages, and made a detour to attend the annual meeting at Chaotung.

And, I learn, they took Pearl with them. I clutch at this further mention of her and try to use this scrap of information to build my picture of how Pearl's life was developing.

They rode their ponies from one Gopu village to another for thirteen days, trekking high into the mountains. The congregations were overjoyed to see them. As they approached a village, children waving flags would come out to greet them. There was excitement and laughter when they reached the church. On most days they were travelling from one place to another and might not arrive until early evening. A feast would be laid on in their honour, but would not be ready until six or half-past, so it would be very late before they could even begin the meeting. One night it was midnight before they got to bed.

Next morning, Pearl and Bessie would dispense medicine outside for an hour or two, before heading to the next village. It gave Pearl an idea of what she wanted to do with her life: nursing.

If my portrait of Pearl were a jig-saw puzzle, I would so far have just two or three pieces in place. She has stayed with the Li family, probably from the ages of four to seven, attended Bessie's English classes, gone with her adoptive parents on missionary journeys, and helped Bessie with her work. I'm about to place another, very significant, piece.

21 PEARL IN ENGLAND

When she was 15, Pearl sailed to England with Bessie and Alf as they went on furlough.

From now, the baby found abandoned on a rubbish dump was to have a very different life: she would become an English boarding-school girl. Her adoptive parents would return to China a year later, but Pearl would not go back to her home country for nine years. When she did, it would be as a senior nurse.

What happened in the years in between: the years Pearl grew from childhood to adulthood? The official trail is a thin one. She sailed to England on May 25 1922 on a Japanese ship, the Atsuta Maru, via Singapore, Aiden and Port Said. The ship's passenger manifest mis-spelt her name as Perl and gave her date of birth as 'about 1906'.

She returned on January 21 1931, when her age is put at twenty-four, on the Samaria from Southampton. Alf and Bessie would return to China without Pearl in the autumn of 1923. She would not see her foster parents until their next furlough, in 1927-28. By then she was training to be a nurse, at the Royal South Hants and Southampton Hospital, and would later work there until her return to China.

I do have one photo of Pearl, with Bessie and Alf, taken at this time, and you can see it overleaf. It shows Pearl, in a simple, loose-fitting dark dress, a hint of white lace showing at the neck, standing between her foster parents, who are seated. Alf, in his dog collar, has a sheaf of papers in his hand, as if looking up from a sermon he has been composing. Bessie is the only one smiling. Pearl's hair is cut short, parted on the left and swept across her forehead in an almost boyish style. In her right hand she holds a full-flowered rose. She does not wear the spectacles she has in later pictures. She looks confident, yet out of place.

Alf, Pearl and Bessie in England

The set in which the photographer has placed them is very English: a faux panelled wall behind them, a painted sash window from which a drape is drawn back in a tie. If this was the first picture you saw of the three of them, you might wonder why this young Chinese girl had been photographed with these westerners. How did they fit? Could she be a trusted servant?

Pearl was enrolled at Edgehill College, a girls' boarding school run by the Bible Christians in the Devon seaside town of Bideford. Harry and Nancy Parsons' daughter Elsie went there the year before Pearl, but she was just eleven. So the decision to give Pearl an English education seems to have been a late one. Many missionaries sent their children to Edgehill, usually for two or three years, but Pearl stayed for five.

According to the school's records, her previous education is shown as 'desultory teaching in China,' so her first year at Edgehill was spent trying to catch up on some of the general education she lacked. The next two years were in preparation for the School Certificate, and she passed the Second Class certificate in 1925 and the First Class in 1926. She stayed on a further year as a 'pupil teacher': she would have taught some of the younger pupils in return for widening her own education, without further expense to her parents. By the time she left, in 1927, she was twenty.

Edgehill had been set up in 1884, as a companion school to Shebbear College, to educate the daughters of Methodist clergy. The school motto was 'Beyond the best there is a better', which one teacher said sounded exhausting. When Pearl arrived there were around 210 pupils, 152 of them boarders like her. The school was housed in a substantial three-storey country house, with a number of other premises spread over its twenty-five acres.

The prospectus praises the 'beautiful and spacious' dining hall, 'large and pleasant' sitting room, a library with several hundred volumes, and bedrooms that were 'pretty little boudoirs. The diet is liberal and varied. An abundant supply of pure milk is obtained from the college dairy farm.' There were hockey pitches, a croquet lawn, tennis courts and gardens.

An advertisement read: 'The study of the Holy Scriptures and the Moral and Religious Instruction of the Students are objects of especial care and solicitude, on principles decidedly Christian, but unsectarian.'

Two years into Pearl's schooling, Dr Brook, the bursar, summed up Edgehill's charms. The building, he said 'is a record in stone of high devotion, of no little sacrifice for noble ideals. The scenery is unforgettably magnificent. The view from the terrace [is] of rolling hills and wooded valley, with pleasant homesteads embowered in luxuriant greenery, equal to some of the most famous beauty spots in the British Isles... One can hear on wild nights the mad music of the waves against the pebble beach of Westward Ho!... Coming from Bideford town and ascending the Northdown Road one is conscious of a distinct and delightful change. Something particularly vivifying is in the air.' At the school: 'There breathes in it the spirit of eternal youth. It is spring time all year round at Edgehill, with the joy and laughter, the brightness and beauty of that season.'

In 1920, a couple of years before Pearl arrived, a major fire had broken out in the night, causing extensive damage to the main school building. The local paper called it 'the most disastrous fire in the district within living memory' leaving the school 'totally destroyed'. It wasn't until 1928 that the school was fully rebuilt, which meant that while Pearl was there things were rather ad hoc, with lessons conducted in a range of buildings around the town. Art classes were in the art school on the quay, gym sessions at the boys' grammar school, music lessons at White's Music Shop in the High Street. A number of borders had lodgings in Bideford while their 'pretty little boudoirs' were out of action.

What, I wonder, did Pearl make of all this? She was thousands of miles from home and from everything that she had known up to now, transplanted from deepest China to a west-country seaside town, being turned into a middle-class English girl. For forty weeks a year she was in this alien environment, spending the twelve holiday weeks with Bessie's family.

No letters from Pearl describing her school days have survived, but in a book, *When You Were There,* a number of her contemporaries paint a vivid picture of what it was like.

'Our lives were regulated by the bell which was rung in the hall... a warning [was rung] at 7am and at 7.30 Miss Kyle, (we called her Jane) came round to see if we were all properly dressed and, if not, it cost us a 3d fine. It was also 3d if we spilled anything on the table cloth.'

'Miss Kyle was a very strict disciplinarian who insisted on every inch of your jotter being filled before you could have a new one. A friend of mine had to report to her every morning for a week to make sure that the kiss curl on her forehead was greased back. Her father was dead. Her mother had four children, three of them at Edgehill – and Miss Kyle said "If your mother can't control you, I will." All because of a curl!'

Boarders ate in the dining room, napkins on lap, a member of staff at the head of each table, the headmistress at the top table. 'None sat down until she was in her place.' The dinner menu rotated between such English staples as cottage pie, stew, roast meat, hotpot, and rissoles, followed by rice pudding, prunes and custard, and spotted dick.

'We were allowed a parcel from home for either a birthday or a "giving-round day" at which one girl shared the contents of her tuck box with the other pupils on her table. 'We were allowed to ask permission to go shopping in the town on a Saturday morning, for this we had to write a note and state the purchases we wished to make. Saturday was tuck shop night and we were allowed to spend up to 1s [5p]. On Sundays we attended the High Street Methodist Church, both morning and evening.'

There were regular outings, ordinarily walks to the seaside village of Westward Ho! or Abbotsham cliffs, occasionally day trips by coach to Exmoor, Dartmoor, Ilfracombe and other seaside towns.

One highlight of the year was the celebration of the headmistress, Miss Johnson's, birthday. 'Borders may have celebrated their birthday with no more than a parcel from home, but they all shared in the celebration of the headmistress's birthday, with a free afternoon and evening. After dinner, up hills, vaulting gates, crawling through prickly hedges, went a jolly crowd of cross-country runners, finally arriving at Westward Ho! They trooped back to Edgehill, weary but happy, just in time to change for tea.

'Girls and staff took it in turn to provide the entertainment in the evening.' That year it was the mistresses' turn. They put on a comic play, *Eliza Comes to Stay*, accompanied by a small orchestra. 'All that was needed to make us believe we were actually at the theatre was a box of chocolates.' In the interval, one of the teachers recited a poem in praise of the head, and after the curtain came down 'there was dancing in the gym and then off to bed we went.'

In 1924 a new head arrived. Miss E. Cuthbertson Hill had a more modern idea of how girls should be raised, and a broader vision of what their aspirations might be. Under her leadership, 'the demure schoolgirl, hair tied back with its huge bow of navy-blue ribbon, was giving place to the New Woman.'

In 1926 the speaker at prize day urged the girls to 'play for all you are worth at hockey, win back the laurels at Wimbledon, take your degree... but not if by doing so you lose a woman's chief charm – the capacity for sympathy and love.' However, the girls were still expected to become ladies 'and a vase was still being awarded to the table who had needed the least correction about their posture when sitting at meals.'

Bessie and Alf stayed with Bessie's family in Southampton during the two periods of furlough while Pearl was in England, and will have seen her in her school holidays and in her breaks from nursing. While they were away, Pearl kept in close touch with Bessie's family. She spent her school holidays with

George and Clarrie Bull, her uncle and aunt, and later visited them when she was nursing. My father, Douglas, and his sister Gwen came to know her well during this time.

There is a record of how Bessie's family found her during their furloughs. Among those they stayed with were Bessie's sister Ida and her husband Jack, an engineer on a passenger liner that sailed from Southampton to South Africa, and who was only home intermittently. Their daughter, Joan, says such visits could be rather a mixed blessing.

'Alf,' she says, 'was a great favourite with us children; he was also from the mission field but not making so much noise about it as his dynamo of a wife who rushed around, plucking souls from the burning whether they wished it or not. Singing! Painting! Sewing! Much was forgiven her though, as she had gone on long journeys on horseback where no Englishwoman had been before and could tell hair-raising stories – of waking up in a filthy Chinese inn and, [in the dim light] seeing rows of old Chinese crones bending over her and smoothing her pink face and golden hair and muttering "So white! So fair!" She was quite fearless. A rather lengthy grace was said by Alfred [before meals] and Bess was narrowly prevented from repeating it in Chinese...

'Delusions of grandeur were upon her throughout that furlough. I am glad to say that next time she was home [in 1927-8] painting in oils had superseded this and she went out for hours far afield with easel and paints and brushes; that was far easier to live with... She was a wonderful aunt and did not utterly fail with me – I never set the table for a true dinner party without blessing her and still subscribe to at least fifty per cent of her robust Methodist faith'.

Pearl will undoubtedly have become assimilated during her nine formative years in England. When she returned to her homeland her written Chinese was poor, and she must have felt and seemed more English than Chinese, something that would cause her great difficulties in the coming years.

22 JOHN IS ADOPTED

With Pearl gone, a new Chinese child entered Bessie and Alf's life: a boy they named John.

John's earliest memory of his foster mother was when, aged three or four, he awoke from a nap, nestled in her lap, and heard organ music. It was a magical sound. They were in church, in Chaotung, and Bessie was playing during a service. John felt as if he was waking inside a dream: in heaven, safe and secure in her arms.

I am looking at a picture of John now. It shows him as a small boy, holding Alf's hand outside the gateway to the house they had by then moved to in Kunming. Bessie would have been about forty-seven and Alfred forty-four at the time. Alf looks very middle-aged to be fostering a small child. I have another photograph, taken in the same place, but with Pearl, before she went to England. Having the two pictures, showing the same scene but with a different child, suggests to me that, whether they were conscious of it or not, John was Pearl's replacement. With Pearl far away in England, I think they felt the loss and wanted another child in their lives. And along came John.

So now I had another young life to follow, another flickering image of a person to be fleshed out and woven into the story I was pursing. But how to find John in 2001, eighty years on? Was he even alive? And if he was, where would he be?

By a miracle, I found him. I learned that he was living in America, where he had emigrated after the Second World War. And, by another piece of great fortune, John was able to give me the clearest picture yet of Bessie, Alf and Pearl. John had written a memoir, and he shared it with me.

It gives a wonderfully vivid and human picture of his adopted family. A far clearer portrait than I had been able to establish so far.

I learn that John was born in Chaotung. John's son told me: 'My father was too young to understand or remember the circumstances of his adoption, and

Alf and Bessie never broached the subject with him. Eventually he learned that some troubles within his extended family grew to engulf his parents, who became unable to care for him sufficiently. I have been unable to find out in detail how the Evanses became involved, but they stepped in to care for John and ultimately to adopt him, at the age of about three.'

John writes: 'Bessie spent a great deal of time with me when I was young. When I got sick she brought me food, drinks, cold compresses for my feverish head, and sat patiently beside my bed, darning my socks while waiting for my condition to improve. When I slept, she was there beside me. Like a guardian angel she always took care of me.

'My foster mother gave me the joy of language, reading to me almost every evening... as a child it was Hans Cristian Andersen's fairy tales, and later, it was Alexandre Dumas' Three Musketeers, and Charles Dickens' A Christmas Carol.

'Afterwards, we'd discuss the novels, the different characters, the plots, and the messages. I was educated continuously from the minute the Evanses came into my life. My parents encouraged me to talk, and so I did.'

John found Alf a more reserved, remote, less sympathetic figure – perhaps typical of men of the times – but kind. He was less socially accomplished than Bessie, and could be stern, and formal, but with family and close friends he relaxed and opened up.

'The English Methodist Mission ran the elementary school in Chaotung. One time my grades plunged: I was flunking. Father Evans was not happy. Several times he called me to his study to review my report card. This made me very nervous. I was scared of him. It wasn't fear of being beaten or abused. It was fear of losing his respect.

'Father Evans tried to tutor me, but it was hard for me to concentrate. It's hard to focus when you're afraid. My mind drifted off into space sometimes. He got frustrated, but never yelled. He just looked angry. I discovered that sometimes you can't learn from the best teachers: your parents.'

John felt Bessie was closer to him than she was to Alf. 'I had more consistent interaction with my mother than she did with her own husband. He was a brilliant man but always very busy. Their marriage was one of the times – they had mutual respect and affection, but were very reserved. Who knows what happened behind closed doors. But on the surface, it was very cool. It was very British – a culture more reserved than America. They were man and woman, together in marriage, perhaps distant in intimacy and romance, perhaps not.'

Yet Alf was something of a romantic figure to John, a man who 'travelled alone, mostly on horseback, wearing a broad-brimmed hat. Looking back he reminds me of a cross between Harrison Ford and John Wayne.'

John saw how ready Bessie was to help those in need.

'I can't remember a time my mother wasn't helping someone. Our home was a safe haven, a beacon of light to many over the years. One time, a woman of the Yu minority knocked on the door. She was pregnant, but had a belt tied tightly around her waist; so tightly you couldn't tell she was expecting. In her tribe it was a disgrace to be pregnant without a husband, and she had run away. Mother Evans helped her into a bedroom to sit down, loosened her clothes, removed her shoes, fed her. Mother knew nothing about the woman's background, but she took her in anyway. 'Within a few days the Yu woman gave birth, by herself, in the middle of the night and was rushed to hospital. She almost died. She stayed with us for several months after the birth. She did some housework to earn her keep.

'Another time, my mother helped a young girl named Xiao Hua, which means Little Flower. Xiao Hua was a slave girl sent by the well-to-do Li family to work for their daughter, who had married an Air Force pilot in Nanking... But their marriage broke up after a dispute with the father-in-law over land. The family splintered, and the little slave girl had no place to go. She ended up at our door.

'In the brief time she was with us, my foster mother gave Xiao Hua perhaps the only love she'd ever known. But sadly it was not enough. In those days, a common way to commit suicide was to drink raw opium. Xiao Hua had tried this once before, but someone saved her, just in time. The next time she got her way out. It was so tragic. Here's a girl killed by circumstance. Had she been loved, by anyone, she'd have found a reason to live. My foster mother gave her that for a brief time. But the rest of her life did not.'

John's childhood with Alf and Bessie was clearly a happy one. He remembers holidays they took him on. Once they travelled twelve miles into the country, carried in sedan chairs, to the foot of the mountains, and Da Long Dong or the Big Dragon Cave. Alongside the cave was a temple where a Taoist priest lived, and above it was an apartment, where the Evanses stayed.

A spring rose in the cave; the cool, clear, perfectly pure water forced up in a fountain and flowing through the temple. The temple was centuries, perhaps millennia old, and drew many to it, including Buddhist monks. It was a profoundly spiritual place, but John found it fascinating for another reason. In the nooks and crevices beneath the dark water there were frogs.

'Our cook waited until night to catch them, using a flashlight. It was a ritual, and the capture was a practiced art. When the light hit them, the frogs froze. The cook barbequed them. They were delicious – a genuine delicacy. It was a magical memory for me, exploring the caves, drinking the fresh water, chewing the frogs' legs.

'We stayed at the Big Dragon Cave for several weeks. Father Evans spent his time studying Chinese books with the aid of a dictionary. He read me many of them, including books on Confucian philosophy and by the Taoist philosopher Lao Tzu. He was deeply interested in Chinese culture and shared with me his western perspective of my country's ancient roots.'

This is John remembering the happy times, and perhaps as a child he was shielded from some of the horrors that would blight his adopted family's life. However, within a few years the idyll would be shattered as the conflicts that were rocking China poisoned life in Yunnan province.

23 UNDER SIEGE

Chaotung was under siege. For two weeks a rebel army had been trying to fight its way into the walled city and defeat the troops of the ruling warlord, Long Yun. Alf, Bessie and John stayed within the mission compound, which was outside the city walls, where the attacking army left them alone. Finally, the attackers appeared to give up. Rapidly, the army left, but their leader came to the mission to speak to Alf. What happened next was among the most terrifying episodes in John's young life. He remembered it like this:

'Their leader asked father to take a letter to Long's army commander inside the city. Ostensibly, the letter was to discuss terms for peace. Mother prepared a large white flag with a red cross in the middle, showing that her husband was travelling on a peaceful mission. She was terrified and fussed over father tremendously before he left. Father was accompanied by a servant holding the flag. The two men walked slowly out of our compound, across the fields and into the walled city. The walk took forty-five minutes and thousands were watching with heightened anticipation.'

Alf didn't know it, but that letter was not a peace proposal at all, but full of insults and abuse. Delivering it almost cost him his life. Long's commander read the letter as Alf was taking the long walk back to the mission compound, and safety. Suddenly a shot rang out. Alf heard the bullet whistle past, missing his head by inches, and punching a hole through the white flag.

John was only four or five at the time, but even if his understanding in the moment was incomplete, he would have had plenty of occasions to ask questions about what he had seen, and fill in the blanks. Now that I had found John I felt so much closer to Bessie, Alf and Pearl. Here was someone who was part of their family, who grew up with them, and had first-hand knowledge of all that happened in their lives over the next twenty years.

These were increasingly troubled times for China, and for the missionaries. They had been making progress on various fronts in the Yunnan missions, but all was now in doubt. Alf had made great strides in Kunming, where he had been posted before Chaotung. He had supervised the construction of a new church, which opened in 1925. It was the only Methodist church in the city, and held 700 to 800 people. It was on one of the main streets in the business district. The £30,000 it cost had been raised by the Methodist Missionary Society in England. Alf had also supervised the building of a new mission-house in the city, so that they no longer had to rely on rented buildings to live and work in.

In Stone Gateway, Harry and Nancy Parsons had used their own savings to buy a plot of land near the mission, which had rich deposits of open-cast coal, and a fresh-water spring, from which they could provide both village and hospital with new supplies of fuel and clean drinking water. They also set up an experimental farm on the site, so that trials of seed corn, potatoes and maize could be undertaken to find which varieties best suited local conditions, in the hope of preventing another famine, and raising the income of the people.

However, despite their best efforts, famine worsened and large numbers were dying daily. At night, wolves and jackals prowled outside the Parsons' garden, digging down to devour the corpses of those too poor to be buried in a coffin. Harry wrote: 'Yesterday I was asked to take a girl and rear her; babies are being thrown away and wives and children are sold.'

It all became too much. When Harry and Nancy left for furlough early in 1926 because his health was deteriorating they expected to come back in a year. They never did. Harry suffered a serious breakdown soon after arriving in England, and Nancy became diabetic. Harry recovered sufficiently to work on the Methodists' English circuit, and they settled in Ventnor on the Isle of Wight.

There were constant reports of Miao villages across Yunnan province being attacked. Preachers were captured and homes looted. However, Will Hudspeth – now fully recovered from the typhoid that had almost killed him – reported that, on one occasion, 'when the brigands discovered that the captured men were preachers of the Gospel they were immediately released and the looted goods returned to Christian villages. In this the Miao trace the hand of God, and who will say they are wrong? This exceptional treatment of our Christians on the part of brigands is remarkable and is, I believe, very rare.'

Yunnan had been invaded by an army from the neighbouring province of Sichuan. The incident with Alf and the white flag was not the only time Chaotung came under assault. The mission school just outside the city was attacked, in fighting that went on for several days. With the city gates closed, many women and children took refuge in the mission hospital. Eventually the soldiers in the city drove away the attacking troops and took many of them prisoner. They showed no mercy. Will Hudspeth wrote: 'Some were bayoneted to death, others were decapitated, and in not a few cases were cut up like pigs and their hearts eaten, as it is believed that the eating of the heart conveys considerable bravery to the eater.' Anti-foreigner feeling was growing once again, and the missionaries were caught up in it. Resentment was stoked by an incident in Shanghai in May 1925 when British troops killed a number of unarmed students who were protesting at the death of a striking Chinese worker in a Japanese factory.

In 1926 civil war broke out, initially between a short-lived coalition of the right-wing Kuomintang and the Communists under Chiang Kai-shek in the south, against the regional war lords in the north. The war lords rapidly swept over Shanghai and Nanking, but soon Chiang had broken with the Communists and many of their troops were massacred in Shanghai.

By April 1927 Chiang had taken over all the provinces south of the Yangtze river except Yunnan, and in London the Foreign Secretary, Sir Austin Chamberlain, told the House of Commons that the consular officers in Yunnan had been warned to prepare to evacuate.

The end came suddenly and unexpectedly for Bessie, Alf and the other missionaries.

April 6 was a beautiful day, and Alf went to the cemetery in Chaotung with a group of schoolboys to plant trees and hold the annual memorial service for the dead.

That evening a telegram came from the British consul, telling them to leave immediately. They were completely unprepared. They could pack very little luggage, just clothing and a few of their most precious things. As they took one last melancholy look around their home, they feared that everything they had built up over the years would be looted as soon as they were gone.

By May 2 all the missionaries had arrived safely in Kunming, and set off for the journey home via Haiphong in French Indochina. It would be a year before Alf and Bessie could return.

John was by far the most valuable thing they left behind. He was placed in the care of a woman called Li Shuang-mei, who was John's aunt and the Chinese companion of Lettie Squire who ran the Methodist school at Chaotung.

This was a bitterly unhappy time for John. He felt abandoned. In contrast to his earliest years with Alf and Bessie, he remembers this as a time of misery. One episode in particular stands out for him.

Shuang was also looking after two other boys. One was Wang Cheng Eng, who was related to John. 'One day Shuang Li took us to visit the house of Wang Cheng's family.

There we met a boy of our own age. It was a pleasant visit and we returned home. About a week later Wang and I went off on our own to visit our new friend. When we came back Auntie Li was waiting for us. She found out where we had gone without her permission.'

Her response to this minor infringement was extreme. 'Her reaction was swift and brutal. She took me into the garden, broke a bamboo cane from a bush, pulled down my pants and beat me as hard as she could. My screaming brought out the students and teachers from the elementary school next door... The beating continued for twenty minutes or more... I really hated her for causing me such pain... She broke the bamboo stick on my back and bottom.'

John would never forget this humiliation.

24 LETTIE AND SHUANG AND THE CIVIL WAR

It was the middle of the night when Lettie Squire heard men's voices in the house, and learned that a rebel army had once again taken the city. The year was 1929, and the missionaries had only recently returned, having had to flee two years before. Lettie was the only missionary within Chaotung's city wall when the soldiers came. She and her Chinese companion Li Shuang-mei were running a girls' school there. Other missionaries were occupying the mission compound outside the city wall, not far from the East Gate.

There had been very heavy gunfire and shelling for hours, making sleep impossible. At around 2am the men broke in. There were three of them, soldiers loyal to the ruling warlord, Long Yuin, who were defending Chaotung. They told the women that troops under the command of a rebel general, Chang-ru-ih Chang, had got into the city. The men had deserted their posts, and wanted to hide their guns in the house, but Lettie refused, and they left.

That wasn't the end of their troubles. Lettie wrote: 'After a short interval, to our surprise and dismay, we heard thundering blows struck on our doors. The outer and courtyard doors were burst open, one after the other, and then they were outside the door of the house. Someone shouted peremptorily "Open the door," and at the same time shots were fired. Shuang called out and immediately six soldiers with rifles and bayonets burst open the door to the sitting room where we were sleeping, and came pouring in.' These men were among the first of the attacking troops to get into the city. Chang's forces would rout Long's and hold Chaotung for a while.

'They demanded silver, and the goods of some wealthy Nosu with whom we had nothing to do. At the same time they began picking up things that were in the room. I was not fully dressed and was on the sofa-bed. Shuang was up, and they surrounded her, threatening her with their rifles. This was all before dawn. The men were in a very dangerous mood.

'So Shuang had to point out a few boxes to them – things we had stored for people. They smashed these open, taking all they could carry with them. They also opened my bookcase, cupboards and drawers. I didn't know what they had taken, until Shuang began shouting for them to give my glasses back. They had taken both pairs. Shuang followed them out to the street, begging them to return the glasses, and at last got them back. But they have taken my gold watch, my new fountain pen, a little clock I bought in Bideford, and a gold broach.

'All that morning we had company after company of armed soldiers coming through the burst-open doors. After the first horrible and unexpected attack, Shuang and I went out to meet each party that came. I said to them: "I am English, I have been looted once. How many more times are you going to loot me?"'

'Distressing as were these experiences we are grateful for the gracious Providence which prevented any bodily injury, excepting the inevitable nervous shock befalling anyone on our mission premises.' Chaotung would be under siege three times during 1929, but this was the most terrifying episode.

Curiously, the families of these two rival generals, Long Yuin and Chang-ru-ih Chang, both had connections with the Chaotung mission. Chang's daughter and a sister-in-law had both attended Miss Squire's school, and the Longs had been linked with the mission's work for years.

The attackers had been bombarding the city for nine or ten days. Heavy shells rained down in a near-constant barrage, crashing through houses and destroying them. Long's forces sought to drive the rebels off by throwing bales of straw soaked in kerosene down from the city walls onto the houses beneath, in which the attackers were sheltering.

The schoolgirls were terrified, and beds were made up on the ground floor, which offered greater shelter from the bombardment. On the Sunday a plane flew overhead, dropping leaflets in which General Long urged the citizens to hold the city until relief troops arrived.

Alf and Bessie were back from their furlough, and in the mission compound outside the city wall with John, who was living with them once more. Alf's desperation at not being able to protect Lettie and the others in the school was extreme. He had little idea how they were faring under the bombardment. Once he managed to persuade the defenders on the wall to pass a letter on to her, and once she managed to get a message out, but he knew that at any point a direct hit on the school could kill them all.

Again, it fell to Alf to try to broker peace, as he had attempted with near fatal consequences two years before. On the Monday he sought to secure an armistice, and got the agreement of Long's attacking forces, but Chang's defenders refused to negotiate. On Tuesday the bombardment increased in intensity, with shells that dropped short landing in the mission garden, and the city fell.

General Chang held Chaotung for a fortnight before the approach of Long's reinforcements led him to withdraw. 'Since then,' Alf wrote, 'we have had the Yunnan troops in charge, but nasty rumours are floating around all the time, and the people have spent, and are still spending, their days in greatest dread. Some of the Yunnan troops are now returned and a barricade is being put up outside our East Gate, so it looks as if the rebel troops are coming back again. It is reported that it will be a stiff fight for the province of Yunnan between Long Yuin, our present governor, and his rivals Hu and Chang, generals under the previous Governor T'ang.'

The trouble didn't end there. As Alf had feared, another battle ensued. Three rebel generals lined their troops up on three sides of the city, besieging it for a week. Again the school was in the centre of the fighting, and there were great fears for Lettie, Shuang and the schoolgirls.

Alf, Bessie and John were also in the firing line. Alf reported: 'the attackers were on both sides of us, and had reinforcements just behind the house. We succeeded in keeping them off the premises, but we could not keep the bullets off the house, for the defenders directed a lot of their fire at the soldiers around it. Very few of the rooms were habitable; we had to seek shelter in the passages and the back rooms. We had about a hundred folk who had come in for shelter, many of them had had their houses destroyed. For several days we were short of water and had to depend upon what we could get from holes dug in the ground. However, we have come through safely, and were glad when the generals decided to move off.'

Hu and Chang's troops moved on to attempt to take Kunming. A state of panic gripped that city. Frank Dymond wrote: 'Trenches were dug in several quarters, and we were requested to allow the solders to make rifle-holes in our garden walls. Just when things looked at their darkest, on the afternoon of July 11, a terrific explosion took place, caused by the ignition of 300 boxes of gunpowder brought into the city by the army.

'Over 13,000 people were affected by the explosion, and 2,700 people are being fed and housed, being entirely destitute. Three hundred and eight-five people were killed, and several thousands were injured. Over 2,500 Chinese houses were destroyed and many partially so. The Bible Society houses were destroyed, and the British Consulate was damaged badly. It was an awful time for those living in the vicinity; the darkness, the smoke and dust, the falling houses and the screams of distress causing great panic.'

However, Kunming managed to resist the assault, and the rebels moved off to attack the western city of Talifu.

Stone Gateway had also suffered terribly in 1929. Six thousand rebels stopped there on their way to attack Chaotung. Will Hudspeth wrote: 'Not only were they a nuisance during the actual troubles, but since then the unsuccessful rebellion has led to a greater degree of brigandage than has ever been known before.

'Defeated troops invariably become bandits, and the whole countryside has been terrorised by large bands of these robbers, who stop at nothing in their outrageous conduct. Some of our districts have suffered especially, and in three villages our Miao have been looted of all their possessions and particularly of their cattle, the wealth of a Miao peasant. Two chapels have also been robbed and left in a shameful condition, with all windows broken, and from one centre our preacher was tied up and led away, to be kept a prisoner, with constant threats of torture, fearful for his life, until he paid the ransom demanded.'

In his review of the year, Alf brought all that Chaotung had suffered together: 'The year that has just closed has been a peculiarly trying one to all the people of this city and neighbourhood. From the end of March until the middle of August, the people have been harassed by the arrival, short stay, and departure of various bodies of troops, for and against the government; and during the remaining months the people outside the city have been distressed by assaults from brigands. The work of the church, equally with all other work, has suffered from these conditions, and much that would have been attempted, of necessity, has had to be postponed or abandoned.'

It had all seemed so much more hopeful at the start of the year. Lettie Squire wrote: 'After the evacuation of 1927, with the uncertainty about our future work, it was a great joy to reach Chaotung once again at the beginning of 1929... it was with especial gratitude I realised how, amid great difficulties, the work of the girls' school had been kept going.' There were 100 pupils, twenty-five of them boarders. 'Though the city at times had been full of troops, and in spite of keen anti-Christian feeling, the teachers, under the guidance of Miss Li Shuang-mei, remained loyal.'

Shuang-mei and Lettie Squire were both formidable, strong-willed characters. Shuang was from a traditional Chinese home, but learned of Christianity at the age of six, rejected the animist beliefs of her parents, and insisted on being baptised. She also refused to have her feet bound and, in her teens, rejected the suitor her parents arranged for her. She became the first Chinese nurse to work with the Methodist Mission, later teaching at and helping Miss Squire run the girls' school. Shuang-mei was devoted to Lettie Squire. When, in 1916, Lettie had been taken seriously ill while on furlough and might not return, Shuang – having never left China – travelled alone to England to nurse her.

Nancy Parsons wrote to her brother, Phil Bryant, at that time: 'The girl Li Shuang-mei who lived with Miss Squire has started off on her own to go to England. I can't think what will become of her. Am quite worried about her. She knows so little English. I wouldn't like to take the journey alone. But no one could persuade her to remain at home as soon as she heard Miss Squire would scarcely return. We are thinking of giving her a letter for you saying what boat and when she expects to land. If you will kindly meet her and send or take her to Lettie Squire, we will pay all expenses... She deserves to be treated well. Her idea is to become a servant, but she would do better as a children's nurse. Her position here has always been that of well-to-do farmer's daughter with servants to do all the work.'

All the troubles they had endured during the year left Frank Dymond questioning whether he and the other missionaries could actually do any good in China. Frank was a veteran, a missionary in China since 1886 and the great friend of Sam Pollard: 'The year has been such a strange one with its surging tides of opinion and varying moods. At times the air has been full of anti-Christian animus, to which missionaries are particularly sensitive, then a lull comes and one has been grateful, [only] once again to be disturbed as a new political situation suddenly threatens civil war...

'Is there really any need for us to be here? I heard someone say that Kunming is regarded as one of the wickedest places in China. It reeks with vice in many quarters. Ask a doctor what he meets with or ask the people, and you hear of 80 per cent being opium addicts, gambling everywhere, a terrible sordidness among men, and as to noble manhood, pure and sweet and good, it is rare. Unwanted infants are placed in boxes, a bell rung, and the poor wee mite is received into a sort of home where 70 per cent are never reared. Three girls were recently sold for eleven shillings the lot.'

25 A FAMILY AT LAST

In 1931 Pearl slipped back into Bessie and Alf's lives in China. They were stationed now in Kunming and Pearl got a job at the Hui Tian Hospital, run by the Church Missionary Society. She had clearly progressed in her career in England and now, aged twenty-four, she was managing nurse, an administrative role overseeing the nursing staff.

In 1935, Alf and Bessie would go on furlough again, and both Pearl and John would move to other cities in China. However, in the interim, they were a family of four for the first time. Or, at least, they were when Alf and Bessie were not travelling around the province on mission business.

I try to imagine what it is like for Pearl, after nine years in England where she went first to a girls' boarding school, then trained and worked in an English hospital. How Chinese could she feel after such a long stretch away? In the last four years, living in the same town as many of Bessie's family, she will have got to know them well. How much did she feel a part of that family? And now, back in China, did she feel English or Chinese?

The four years they spent as a family were not without their problems. In 1932 Alf became seriously ill, with what seems to have been a nervous breakdown, and Bessie's mother died. A notice in the *Missionary Echo* reads: 'Another sorrow has fallen upon Mrs Evans in the news that her mother had passed away. The shadow deepened as letters reported her mother's long illness and sure decline. A very deep affinity must have existed between mother and daughter who so much resemble each other. The richer the treasure the keener the sense of loss.'

The following year, 1933, she and Alf celebrated their silver wedding anniversary. They should have gone on furlough in June of that year, but Alf requested a delay of twelve months partly because 'it would help us in connection with the schooling of John.' John, it is becoming clear from his own account, was something of a challenge for Alf.

John tells us: 'When I was eight the Evanses decided to move to Kunming and enrol me in an Episcopalian-sponsored elementary school called Eng Guang Xiao Xue (Merciful Light Elementary). It wasn't easy. Elementary school kids can be very cruel. Some students teased me, called me names like 'false foreigner', because they knew I was adopted by missionaries.'

In the wider world, China was suffering another great threat in those years. In 1931 the Japanese had invaded Manchuria, in the north east of the country, creating the puppet state of Manchukuo and placing the last Emperor of China, Henry Pu Yi, as ruler of this false republic. From there they extended their influence, and would ultimately attempt to subjugate the whole of China.

For John, Manchuria was a long way away, and such events meant less than his own personal troubles. He writes: 'Eventually I made friends at the Eng Guang school, despite my rocky start. In fact, from that difficult baptism came deep rewards. There were five boys with whom I spent most of my time.

'At that age we were always hungry, and didn't seem to get food at school. After school we'd scrounge some money and get something to eat on the streets. The streets were filled with cooking stands. The vendors would fire up rice noodles. We'd sit there and pay a few pennies for a full bowl. It was a good deal... tasty, homespun Chinese cooking. One thing I liked was smelly tofu, fermented and grilled over charcoal. They smother it with bean paste and spicy peppers and roast it until the outside is tough and black. It's very chewable.'

When John talks about Alf, he is full of praise, but the list of his achievements gives some idea of the pressures his step-father was under: the pressures that seem to have led to his breakdown.

'Evans taught himself architecture and the related engineering and mathematics. He built the church compound where we lived: a stately main house and several outbuildings – perfect mini bible-study sanctuaries. He also built our home – a two-floor structure with two studies: one for mother, one for himself. Behind the study were a dining room, a kitchen, a pantry and a hallway. On the right was a drawing room. His study was in the front. Outside the dining and drawing rooms was a porch, facing south, so it attracted lots of sunshine all day long and became a great place to relax. Beyond the porch was a large garden. It was a beautiful place.'

There was happiness and fulfilment for Alf and Bessie too. 'Because of the temperate climate in Kunming, my foster parents had more success gardening than maybe anyone in England. They were prolific in their plantings. Our house featured a large garden and many varieties of flowering trees and bushes. I still remember the wonderful fragrance of the pure-white camellia.'

It's clear that Alf set high standards for his adopted son; standards which John struggled sometimes to live up to, and which would later cause conflict. But this appears to have been something of a golden time.

'Evans was a very wise and talented man who read a lot of books, including Chinese literature. He travelled extensively and spoke Yunnan Mandarin. He was a Western Renaissance man, living in China. Education was vitally important to him. One time I was sick and he didn't want me to fall behind in my studies. So he came to my bedside every few hours to take my temperature and see if my fever was abating. When it dipped he would sit on the edge of my bed and help me with my schoolwork. It showed how much he valued education, and revealed his love for me.

'It wasn't just showing concern – he thought about me too, and helped me his entire life. He and mother always wanted the best for me, and they showed me in many, many ways. In this way they were great parents.'

Faith was central to family life. 'We prayed every morning in the drawing room, right after breakfast, kneeling down to give thanks to Jesus and bless the new day... Father would usually lead. We made our daily requests, and always included a prayer for someone who was sick or needy.

'Many times there were four of us, but we also had guests. Travelling missionaries stayed with us frequently, and they in turn blessed the day. The practice of giving blessings before meals was branded into me.'

John was about to be sent away to middle school in Chaotung, but would return to the house in Kunming in the holidays. There were family vacations, taken in Su Jia Cun, a small town two hours boat-trip away across the great Dian lake to the south of the city. The Evanses rented part of a schoolhouse, and stayed for two summer months.

'Our rooms were on the top floor, and the sun flowed through the windows each day... I remember one morning watching Father Evans draw. He used a Chinese brush and sketched the lake as he saw it from the balcony of the schoolhouse. Mother also painted a number of beautiful landscapes that are still etched on my mind.'

26 MILDRED, LESLIE AND PEARL

Have you ever had someone tell you about a person that, actually, you know much better than they do? I get that sensation when I read a letter written by a young missionary, Leslie Pacey, who stayed with the Evanses on his arrival in China.

By now, thanks to John, I have quite a strong sense of what Bessie and Alf were like, but Leslie adds rich detail. But, because I know a good deal about them already, I know what he gets wrong about them, as well as what he gets right. Leslie also helps me begin to get to know Pearl. Leslie is significant because the woman he is to marry has a very close friendship, and quite possibly an intimate relationship, with Pearl. But that story comes later.

Leslie, you can tell from the way he writes, is young, and pretty green. But he gives a very vivid picture of life at the mission in Kunming, and of how the Evanses enjoyed their family time. Here's what he wrote to his parents about Pearl, Bessie and Alf. It is 10pm and Pearl has just knocked on his door, delivering two letters from home:

'It is a very nice place to stay. The Evans are great folk, very nice people, and after thirty years in Yunnan, they can tell me a good deal that I'm glad to know. Mr Evans is fifty-six. Did I tell you about Pearl and John, their adopted children? I think their own must have died. Mrs Evans found Pearl when she was only a day old; she was nearly dead, having been left naked out in the open somewhere. The Evans have looked after her ever since. She, like John, calls them Mummy and Daddy. They both speak English and are just like an ordinary son and daughter.

'Pearl is only just back after nine years in England, where she went to school, trained as a nurse at the Southampton and Southsea Hospitals. She is now a sister at the Church Missionary Society Hospital here. The Evanses adopted John, who is now ten or twelve, when he was three. They came across him somehow, and as it was famine year, no Chinese family could take him in. He is at the higher primary school here... Mrs Evans is a great gardener. Just now her garden is full of colour – carnations, larkspur, roses, sweet peas, geraniums, pansies etc all in full bloom. I have a vase of carnations and two of sweet peas in my bedroom, and there are lots more in the rooms downstairs. It is a real old-fashioned English garden, from which you may pluck whole armfuls of flowers without making the loss noticeable...

'Last Monday we had a boat trip to Hsi Hsan (Western Hills). I shall have a photo of the boat to send you next week. We were rowed by two women and a man. Just outside Kunming is a big lake. We crossed over at the end where it is only a mile or so across. Further down it is nine miles wide, and altogether some forty miles in length. One of the servants came with us and there was a little fire on the boat so we had porridge and eggs for breakfast. On the other side I saw the loveliest little white foal. We walked up the hill through groves of bamboo and other trees. It was a glorious day.

'The blue waters of the lake and the little sailing boats could be seen below us through the trees. I was just thinking of Shanklin when Mrs Evans turned to me to ask if I knew Shanklin Chine: her home is at Southampton.

'The Evans are excellent Chinese speakers and, with their jokes and conversation, they are known to quite a number of people. We called at a temple on the hill where the priests knew them. I was very glad of the tea they provided. There was a young Indian priest there. He is on some sort of pilgrimage and has walked from temple to temple all the way from Bengal across Burma into China. I think he was glad to see us for he could speak English, but not Chinese, and so Mrs Evans was able to interpret for him. The only language he had in common with the Chinese priests was the language in which their Buddhist scriptures are written.

'We got back to the boat about 2.30pm and immediately sat down at a little table under the cover to a Chinese meal which the boy had ready for us. The sun is very hot and it is necessary to keep one's head well covered. I am wearing the sun helmet that I bought at Port Said. We were able to sail back. I sat in the prow, and listening to the water lapping on the front of the boat, I shut my eyes and thought of Purfleet. We got back into the canal just when many of the boat dwellers were at their evening meal, squatting on their boats with basin and chopsticks in hand. Talk about *Three Men In A Boat!* I saw some with men, women and children, not to mention a pig and a few chickens, and there they live all their lives.

'Early Tuesday morning I saw the other folk off on the bus... John was at school all day, so Pearl and I were on our own for lunch and tea. She took me to the post office in the afternoon, dressed in a smart English summer frock. I couldn't help wondering what she might have been like if someone else had picked her up.

'Every Wednesday afternoon the Evanses hold an At Home. Ten or twenty people turned up this week. The tennis court, croquet lawn and garden come in very useful for this event. By this means the Evanses are making friends with some of the better class of Chinese, who often suspect their motives. It is a good way of breaking down the barriers and showing them that we only want to be their friends. One girl, who has done brilliantly in some government exams, is the image of a girl I know in Nottingham. She, and one or two others, seem as though they may be on the verge of making the decision for Christ.

'On Thursday Mrs Liu, the mayor's wife, brought along her husband. That may prove to be a valuable contact. Peggy, the girl just mentioned, first introduced Mrs Liu. The girls like to take on an English name when they become friends...

'The Lord bless you and keep you
All my love
Les.'

Leslie Pacey was about to meet someone who would become the most significant person in his life. She was a missionary nurse, Mildred Button, based in Chaotung. Mildred would become hugely important not just to Les, but also to Pearl, and Pearl to her. Mildred had been ill, and was to be escorted to Kunming for treatment. Leslie was asked to meet her when she reached Tung Chuan, where he was based, and guide her the rest of the way. On his return journey he would escort Lettie Squire and Li Shuang-mei, who were returning to Chaotung.

Les's journey with Mildred took six days, travelling with a group of porters and two soldier guards. Mildred was on her horse, Rusty, Les walking alongside her most of the way. It was a fine, sunny day when they set out, and Leslie took off first his jacket, then his sweater, and – having forgotten his own – borrowed a porter's hat because the sun was beating down.

That evening, after dinner at their inn, they wrote letters. Mildred wrote to her friend, Cathie, wife of Kenneth May, a Chaotung missionary. She told her how Leslie Pacey was being embarrassingly attentive in all sorts of ways, such as holding her horse's bridle every time she needed to mount or dismount. In her student days, Mildred had often referred to young men who showed an interest in her as nuisances. She was so set on her vocation as a missionary nurse that she did not want the distraction of boyfriends. Writing to Cathie now, she put Leslie in the same category: he was becoming a nuisance.

Les described the sleeping arrangements at the inn: 'All coolies in one private room, and we shared what was left. Miss B had a bit partitioned off and I filled in the doorway with an oil sheet. Rusty occupied the open end of her section and I had my bed in the public room. I fed, washed and shaved in the semi-privacy of her bedroom.' He sketched a rough plan and attached it to his letter. Ominously, in the corner close to his bed, Leslie has written 'Pigs'. Next night, he notes that at this inn the walls are so thin that he and Mildred can hold a conversation from their beds.

Reaching the Evanses' large, comfortable house with its secluded garden felt like coming home, after six nights of squalor. The house was crowded, with Lettie Squire and Li Shuang-mei and other visitors. Les confided in his diary: 'it seems odd to be separated from Miss B. after six days together on the road – good to be with people and yet don't like to share her with so many.' On the Sunday after their arrival Roger Arnold of the YMCA popped in before breakfast to ask if Les would help him with that morning's church service in English. Les writes: 'Had to accept, as only reason I could think for not doing so was that my mind was wondering what to do about Miss Button, and I couldn't tell him that.'

Finally, late that afternoon: 'I found myself alone with her in the drawing room – again talked of the weather (!) until I managed to splutter: "Do you think we could have a talk together before I go back?" She made some irrelevant reply about me going on Tuesday and wanting to talk with Uncle Alf first. I (rightly) thought this was intended to put me off, but managed another effort: "About us two, I mean," just before Auntie Bess came in with some flowers. We busied ourselves with these in silence until she said, "Shall we walk in the garden?"

'I waited a long time while she fetched her blazer – Auntie Bess nabbed her on route. Then we walked up and down the tennis lawn. I said that I wondered if we could develop our friendship, and then we talked so quietly and simply as we walked, and I found she loved me too.

'It was marvellous. We had only met ten days before, but were both willing to take the risk of the unknown future. That she should love me was more than I had dared contemplate. That talk together was so quiet and beautiful. I don't think I actually proposed – we just evolved. After a time, I asked if I might use her Christian name, but she called me "darling" before she called me "Les". Then I put my arms round her, and we walked like that. The black cat kept running in front of us. It was dark now and soon a voice coo-eed across the lawn, it was Auntie Bess come to warn us of the approach of dinner. She guessed what had happened and was a good sport.

'Going upstairs to wash our hands, we had our first kiss on the landing – the seal of our engagement! Dinner was exciting – we two sitting opposite and only Auntie Bess knew what an historic night it was.'

A day or two later, Leslie wrote to his parents saying he now had 'a young lady', and sent an enigmatic telegram to a close friend worded simply: 'FOUND A BUTTON'.

Mildred's diary entry for that day read simply: 'How many hours between?!'

Four days later, Les set off back to Tung Chuan with Lettie and Shuang. On the same day Mildred visited a doctor, to try to discover the reason for the episodes of dizziness and sickness she had experienced at Chaotung. She feared she had heart problems. Her diary entry reads just 'all OK', but she immediately wrote to Les, saying she had been advised to spend six months somewhere on the coast to recover from the effects of Chaotung's high altitude.

They wrote to each other every day while they were apart. Mildred rested, made a dress for herself, and took trips on the lake with Alf and Bessie, on one occasion visiting Hua-T'ing-Si, the Buddhist temple on the far side of the lake that Les had visited with them six months earlier. While Mildred recuperated in Kunming, a friendship developed between her and Pearl. On December 27, Mildred noted in her diary that she and Pearl 'Gave a party for the foreigners – tea on the veranda.'

On New Year's Day, Alf, Bessie and John left for Chaotung. John was now twelve and was to attend the Methodist Middle School in the city, there being no church middle school in Kunming. He would stay with Mildred's friends, Cathie and Ken May, in the mission compound. Cathie was the daughter of Frank Dymond, who had come to China with Sam Pollard in 1886.

Alf and Bessie went on to attend the church's synod meeting, and were away for several weeks. While they were away, Mildred and Pearl had the mission house to themselves. The only entry in Mildred's diary for the rest of January is: 'Pan-yan and Chutney keep house for a month'. Pearl's Chinese nickname was Pan-yan and, as at the time Pan-yan was a popular brand of pickle among the missionaries, she called Mildred Chutney.

Mildred and Les's son, Arnold Pacey, believes that Pearl suffered greatly from being brought up between two cultures, and felt neither Chinese nor British. She was probably often lonely, he believes, and adds: 'When Mildred stayed on in Kunming after Les returned to his post at Tung Chuan, she and Pearl became very close.'

So, the woman who had committed herself to a man she had known for just ten days had now forged a second profoundly close relationship.

27 A SKELETON, CLEAN, WHITE AND SHINING IN THE SUN

War suddenly became starkly, brutally real for John in Chaotung. He writes: 'One day while we were eating lunch a servant bounded in to report he had seen a strange sight – a skeleton not far from our house, near the graveyards outside the city. We'd never heard of anything like this, so we went out to take a look.

'We walked for a few minutes into the graveyard and there it was: a skeleton, clean, white and shining in the sun. The bones looked moist, not dry. It was pretty fresh and had a rope still knotted around its neck. Wild dogs feasting in the night had removed all the flesh from the bones.

'After staring at the remains for a few minutes, we went back. It was a quiet walk – that sort of sight can silence you somewhat.'

The horrific scene at the graveyard was a small part of the long-running civil war in China: the fight between the nationalists, or Kuomintang, led by Chiang Kai Shek; and the Communists, led by Mao Tse-Tung, later known as Mao Ze Dong. At this time, 1935, Kuomintang troops had moved into Yunnan from the neighbouring province of Sichuan, intending to halt the Communists, who were headed there. Mao's troops were on what became known as The Long March, a retreat that took them right across China but which led, ultimately, to victory. John saw the pursuing Kuomintang troops enter Chaotung: 'They just marched into town and moved into people's houses. Some peasants objected, but not too strongly, and some were chased out of their homes by bayonet.'

So that was why there were murderous soldiers in town. When John went back to school that afternoon, he told his classmate Zhong Yu Song what he had seen, and Zhong told him a story he could barely believe. Zhong's house, near the city's East Gate and alongside the school, had soldiers billeted in it. The previous evening, Zhong had heard an argument break out.

The soldiers were drinking, and gambling at cards. One of them, a big, tall man according to Zhong, kept winning. After several hours a drunken argument broke out between the losers and the winner. Then one suggested they take the row outside, afraid that if their commander heard them they would be in trouble. They walked out of the house and followed the school wall, still arguing, and into the graveyard.

Zhong said he had followed them at a discreet distance. The soldiers stumbled on, reaching an area called the mixed graves land, where the poor were buried in unmarked graves. Bodies had been dumped here for over 2,000 years.

John takes up Zhong's story: 'Suddenly, the men who lost the money jumped on the big man, grabbing his arms and legs. They had ropes and tied him up. To stop him from yelling and screaming they tied a noose around his throat and choked off his voice. Then out came the knives. They were plunged into his body repeatedly, stabbing him until he stopped moving. Then they stripped him of his clothing, took his papers away so he couldn't be identified, gutted his body open, and left. Zhong hurried home. He was a witness, and if they spotted him, they would have chased him down and killed him as well.'

Whatever the truth of Zhong's account, John never forgot what he had seen that day: 'To see that man's naked skeleton, shimmering and shiny, left a graphic, indelible image in my mind that has plagued me to this day. Somewhere far off in Sichuan province, there was a mother whose son went off to war and never came back. She must have gone to her grave wondering what happened to him. Was he killed in battle, did he get sick, did he get shot? He never came home.'

Zhong's house was the scene of another violent encounter a few months later. A soldier had absconded, taking a rifle with him. Troops had closed the city gates and were conducting a house-to-house search for him.

'During the pursuit, the soldier ducked into Zhong's house and ran into the kitchen. It was very dark there and he hid under the stairs, near a water tank. The soldiers pursuing him rushed in, and finally found him. They bound him and took him away, straight toward the graveyard...

'We all watched at a distance as the group marched across the field... He knew they were taking him to a death by bayonet.'

28 PEARL AND MILDRED TOGETHER, THE LONG MARCH DRAWS NEAR

Everything was looking good for Leslie Pacey and Mildred Button. In February 1935 Les was able to return from Tung Chuan to Kunming, and they were reunited. His diary for February 1 reads: 'Met by Mildred on arrival... Glorious time' and, two days later: 'Mildred and I engaged'.

They were delighted to find that they were both to be posted to Kunming, which was unusual with unmarried but engaged missionaries. They expected to be together permanently from April, with Mildred assigned to do evangelistic work with women and girls. Les was to have a bachelor flat in a building by the church but, until it was ready, he was given an attic bedroom in the mission house.

Yet, by the end of the year, they would be far apart once again, and Mildred would find herself not with Les, but with Pearl.

In the background, the political situation was deteriorating, and threatened to derail things for all the missionaries. On April 12, Mildred's diary entry covers both the worrying big picture and the little successes of her life: 'On Wednesday there was a report of a Communist army approaching Kunming. Today GLB [Girls Life Brigade] going well, twenty-four girls.'

Five days later, on the Monday before Easter, Les and Mildred joined everyone else on the favourite and familiar trip across the lake, and a walk up to a Buddhist temple. This was to be the last day of quiet enjoyment for some time. Twenty thousand Communist troops on the Long March appeared to be headed for Kunming, intent on passing through to the neighbouring province of Sichuan. They were pursued by government forces, which showed little enthusiasm for catching them.

The British consul warned the missionaries that they must be ready to evacuate at a moment's notice. Leslie wrote: 'Since Wednesday we have been living each with a suitcase ready packed... we have only to get on the railway and go down to French Indo-China.' At the same time, Alf was also under pressure to leave for another, very personal reason. William Grist wrote from London, urging him to take his overdue furlough, while thanking him for 'the fine spirit which has prompted you to stay for so long a term.' The fear in London was that he might suffer another breakdown, and even take his own life.

Alf refused, because of Pearl and John. He replied that delaying his furlough 'enables us to have Pearl in our home for a longer period, and helps us give further personal direction for John, who is [both] too young and too old to be left (thirteen years).' Eventually, he and Bessie did take their furlough, in June, while John stayed on with the Mays.

For a time, normal life went on, but against a backdrop of preparation for violence and terror. Les wrote: 'After tea we went out, riding in rickshaws, to do some shopping. Here and there, soldiers were busy putting up barbed wire, sand-bag barricades and mud walls. It looked very warlike. Gun holes had been made in the walls along the river. The bridge was almost blocked by a mud wall. There were also sand-bag barricades in the centre of the city. Our rickshaws had to wait while a machine-gun squad marched by...

'When Pearl came back from her job at the hospital at about 7pm she told us that Dr Yews had said that the outlook wasn't very good. Then we heard that martial law had been declared. All the shops were shut, and the people were told that anyone found on the streets after dark would be shot... the authorities were afraid that there might be sympathisers inside the city who would raise a riot when the Communist army was close.'

The next day Les wrote: 'We went to bed wondering what might happen. I slept until 1.30am when I heard folk talking. Uncle [Alf] came up to my room to tell me a message had come from the British consul ordering all women, children and men without responsibilities to leave the next morning by train by 7.40am... I hated having to leave. Some of the Chinese were up and watching us as we went to the station. Their faces were all fear and questioning. It was rotten having to leave them. Uncle stayed behind, but he was keen that I should accompany Mildred and Auntie Bess.'

Alf cabled London: 'Situation is critical. There is uncertainty. Kunming women and children have been evacuated this morning.' Pearl, however, nursing at Hui Tian Hospital, stayed.

Les described the evacuation: 'There was a rare crowd and confusion at the railway station. There were French traders, English and American missionaries, and many Chinese and Annamese [Vietnamese]. We got to Hanoi on Thursday after a good trip down. The first night was at Amitchou, where the little hotels by the railway were full... but we managed. In the morning I washed and shaved at a tap in the yard. Refugees can't be choosers... The second night we spent at Laokay, just this side of the frontier. Here there was more room in the hotel.

'Mildred is a bad traveller... the motion of the train makes her sick... The train wandered in and out among the mountains, making the most of amazing bends, crossing deep gorges on thin steel bridges, and taking us through about 135 tunnels. Often I looked out of the window and could see nothing for hundreds of feet below because we were on the edge of a precipice. It is a marvellous railway.

'Laokay was terrifically hot, and we haven't got much cooler since. It was like an oven in the train. The first part of the day was through thick jungle which gradually gave way to cultivated fields... Here in Hanoi we are staying with a Mr and Mrs Cadman, missionaries who Auntie knows. It is strange being in a modern city...

'This is the capital of French Indo-China and there is a big foreign population. The streets are wide and paved, cars and trams are buzzing about, there are big shops and cinemas... Mildred and I visited an Indian silk shop and bought material for her wedding dress. It is a bit early, but there probably won't be another good chance.'

The crisis passed quickly, however. The Communists skirted Kunming and, on May 12, the evacuees got a letter from Alf to say it was safe to return. They were back in Kunming five days later.

'Uncle, Pearl and a number of Chinese friends were at the station to meet us,' Les wrote. 'Then we had a shock. Uncle had received a telegram from Mission House in London, sent via [Will] Hudspeth, which said. "Urgent need at Wenchow. Urge [Mildred] Button to proceed there immediately."

'We were stunned. No details could be given in a cable and so I don't know why they suddenly need a nurse at Wenchow... Coming up on the train, we were discussing our plans, and now they're all gone... everyone is very disappointed, me most of all.'

On May 20 Mildred left by the morning train, seen off by Pearl, Bessie and Alf. 'I went down the line on the train with her for about half an hour, and came back on a slow train an hour later. It was hard saying goodbye for so long.'

Wenchow was on the far side of China from Kunming, and the journey there was a complicated one. Mildred first took a train 600 miles south to Haiphong, on the Indo-Chinese coast. From there she went by ship to Hong Kong, another 600 miles, and then for 800 miles on a P&O liner to Shanghai.

She booked into Beaman's guest house at 382 Avenue Joffre, which was regularly used by missionaries. In Shanghai she was met by Lilian, newly-married to Leslie's college friend Roy Hooper. They were living in Wenchow and Lilian had come to Shanghai to accompany Mildred back with her. The town was sixteen miles from the sea, and her doctor had told Mildred sea air would be good for her health, but Wenchow had a hot, moist climate, with temperatures of 86f by day and 90f by night, with frequent typhoons.

Only on arrival at the Methodist Blyth Memorial Hospital did Mildred find out why she was needed: the matron had gone on furlough and her replacement had not yet arrived. Mildred was to deputise for her, but her role was wide-ranging. At times she stood in as theatre sister, midwife and sister-tutor. She and Les wrote to each other daily, and he told a friend 'She has been doing too much and spoke of having operations in theatre every afternoon one week. On one day, she nearly fainted during an operation through exhaustion.'

Mildred must also have been writing regularly to Pearl, because they were about to meet up. In October, the matron Mildred was covering for returned to work, but it was decided she should stay on at the hospital. Mildred was, however, allowed a holiday. In the same month, Pearl left her job in Kunming. She and Les celebrated the occasion with a trip to the cinema to see *Madame Butterfly*.

Leslie wrote: 'Pearl has got a bit run-down and hasn't been very happy at the hospital. She did not get on very well with one of the other sisters... She will leave here in a few weeks to take up a post at our Methodist hospital in Hankow, in central China, but first she will call at Wenchow to spend a Christmas holiday with Mildred. These two – Chutney and Pan-yan – were great friends and I also get on well with Pearl... I shall miss old Pan-yan.'

Mildred recorded her delight in being reunited with Pearl in her diary: 'Pan-yan arrived on the Haean... and I went to meet her. The tide was out and water so low that we had to go out to the ship in a sampan. It was good to be with Pan-yan again, she is staying with Lilian and Roy.' Mildred had a flat in the nurses' quarters.

Pearl and Mildred got busy preparing for Christmas. 'Christmas puddings, cakes and mincemeat finished (except for icing) thanks to Pan-yan. Cook was working very hard yesterday, so in the evening I said, "You have been very busy today, Na-Shi". he replied: "No, small busy."'

On January 2 Mildred and Pan-yan left Wenchow together, sailing to Shanghai. Here, she and Pearl 'spent the week shopping to prepare for the wedding and for furnishing a home; shopping and more shopping.'

I wonder if Mildred was aware of the irony of her situation: shopping to furnish a home with Les while spending intimate time with Pearl? Or am I reading too much into what was no more than an intense friendship?

They were together until mid-January, and then Mildred helped Pearl book train and boat tickets for Nanking and Hankow, where the following month she would take up the post of deputy director of nursing at the Pu Ai Hospital. Mildred wrote: 'Today she has another day in Shanghai, but I left for Wenchow on a coastal steamer called the Yi Li.'

Back in Wenchow, Mildred went on another shopping trip: 'I've just arrived back after buying rugs, and all sorts of things for our home. It was marvellous selecting saucepans, pudding basins etc.'

While Mildred busied herself preparing for her wedding, Pearl was bereft at parting from her friend, as two surviving letters written by her at the time reveal.

29 LETTERS OF LOVE

SS Siangtan
January 19 1936

Dearest Best Beloved Chutney,

After you left Beaman's I was very sad and lonely, no more Chutney to talk to for a long time. I did not like saying goodbye, I smiled and waved you *au-voir*, but at the bottom of my very heart I could have wept, as I sat alone in the dining-room, a nasty lump kept coming up my throat. I decided I better write to Les and thank him for those pretty green mats. So I finished that and went upstairs to collect my goods and then had a bath and so to bed.

No one to wrap up together with, only my hot water bottle and guess what I did, have left my bed socks in bed at Beaman's. I shall have to knit another pair or take my green ones out and christen them.

It's been lovely to be with my Chutney all that time. Thank you best-loved for that wonderful holiday and Xmas at Wenchow. I loved making all the pots and pans dirty for poor old Naishu to wash. That's two Xmas now we've spent together – is it not? And they have been marvellous. Pan-yan is really thrilled to think that she has found such a best beloved as her Chutney and also Les being the lucky man. Don't forget to write, eh? I shall forgive you sometimes, but not always.

I'm writing now, because I shall have too much to tell you when I get to Hankow. Don't you go and slave now best beloved, you mustn't look tired when Les sees you? Bye-bye my Chutney. Thanks awfully again. Hope to see you soon, so *au'voir* but not goodbye for the present.

Lots of love and kisses
Pan-yan XOXO

Five days later, Pearl wrote again to 'My Dearest Marvellous Chutney', mainly about how she found her new hospital. It's a lively, chatty letter, full of indiscretions about the people there, and the line beneath her address reads: 'Don't read aloud and not tell others what I think of Hankow folks at present.'

The letter is full of the sort of gossip two close friends would share if they were together. Although it doesn't have the more direct intimacies of the first letter, it illustrates the close affinity between the two young women.

She begins: 'It's your old Pan-yan again. How are you my dear? I wish you were here with me and my flat... I have a very nice room, quite enough for a little person like me, and also a bathroom and a stove you may be glad to hear. I had been looking forward to making my dumpties [cushions] up beside an open fireplace but now I have them on the two straight chairs as cushions or something warm to sit on instead [of] the cold seats, any rate I'm thankful to see a fire, a boy and anna [an anna or ama is a female servant] share the work doing my room. I nearly got smoked out yesterday when I was still in bed.

'The room contains a dressing table, bed, screen, chest of drawers, wardrobe, two cane chairs and two stiff ones, a nice round table and a small square one, the bathroom is something like yours, but much smaller. The room is done up in pink curtains, screen and cushions. You know how much I adore that colour – don't you? But not too bad,' which sounds as if she hates pink and Mildred knows it.

Pearl shares her impression of the staff. Sister Gladys Stephenson, she says, has been reluctant to lend her an iron to use on her uniform on the grounds that it uses too much electricity. When Gladys finally relents, Pearl finds 'the darn thing won't get hot anyway, so that's no good.'

Of the other staff: 'Mr and Mrs Heady, [he is the] chairman, are very nice. Dr and Mrs Bolton, you missed a good sight. I wish you could see them, he wears Chinese clothes and a very heavy solid sort of man, she is very fat, and just so you know has two boys, rather pretty but could do with a spring clean.... Then another couple, Mr and Mrs Frankens ... they have two children ... The father, Oh my dear, I don't know how he managed to produce such nice kids, taken after the mother, I'm sure.'

She compares the hospital unfavourably with the one in Kunming.

'Hospital!!! It doesn't come up to my men's ward. I was really proud of that, I may say. All the wards have a stove! And the inside hasn't that smartness as I expected... you and I are too wonderful for this world. I have not yet seen all the women's wards and maternity, the children's ward is about the best, very sweet, could be made A1.'

I learn from the letter that Pearl cannot read and write Chinese. I'm puzzled, because Alf and Bessie were both fluent in the language. Can they really have neglected such a key part of Pearl's education? But then, perhaps she lost her Chinese in those nine years spent in England. She writes:

'I shocked Gladys because I didn't read [Chinese]. She thought: "fancy coming here and not knowing her language"... Afterwards, *madame* spoke to me and said "How could I lecture them if I didn't know the words?" "Oh well," I said, "I know some, but not very good." My! She did have a shock. I suppose there again I'm not so wonderful as I thought I was... Whatever it turns out to be, a year will fly – won't it? Especially if I don't have a holiday this year and leave at the end of Dec. and then what happens – but here I shall do my best to help the old girl. It's quite certain this is a Christian hospital and I marvel at those who carry it on, and think they are real martyrs.

'Well my Chutney, Pan-yan does miss you and those good old gossips beside the fire, eh my dear. It isn't long since I left you, but my little heart longs to see her best-beloved again.

'Won't it be great when I see you next time as Chutney but not as Mrs Pacey by name.' This suggests to me that Pearl believes Mildred can be Chutney to her, and Mrs Pacey to Les.

'It's time to dry up now and soon will be tiffin time. I'll write again soon, give everyone my love and kind regards to the Wenchow friends.'

She signs off: 'Bye bye my Chutney, keep well – don't overwork
With tons of love
Yours as ever
Panyan
XOXO'

Pearl, photographed by Les Pacey

It was Arnold Pacey, Mildred and Les's son, who sent me copies of these letters. I had asked him if there was any correspondence between his mother and Pearl, and he discovered them among his family's papers. He hadn't read them before, and was shocked at their contents.

He wrote: 'I find these letters rather surprising. They suggest something close to a lesbian affair. I wish I knew how my prim and proper mother reacted. She must have been fairly startled by the intensity of Pearl's language, and I can't help wondering if the lack of further letters in 1936 is because Pearl was told off for writing like this. Or, maybe, the letters are lost.

'When we were choosing words for my father's gravestone, one suggestion was the text from the first Epistle of John that begins, "Beloved, let us love one another, for love is of God". My mother was insistent that the word 'Beloved' should be left out as inappropriate, even distasteful, and certainly liable to be misunderstood. I wonder if Pearl's excessive use of the word had left its mark!

'I can identify with Pearl, poised between two cultures and consequently quite lonely, then getting over-emotional about "Chutney" because friendships had otherwise been so hard to form...

'I'm sure my mother would have been embarrassed by Pearl's tone in those letters, and would probably have asked her not to write in these terms again. I have discussed it this week with my mother's sister, thinking perhaps that they were different when young, before I knew them, but she agrees, Ma would have found Pearl's letters embarrassing...

'One has the impression that if Mildred had not been about to marry, she and Pan-yan might have developed a deeper friendship, mutually supportive of their nursing careers as well as personally.'

Something else very significant happened in Pearl's life in Hankow. She doesn't mention it to Mildred or anyone else until much later, but she meets a woman who will become her companion in later life, and into whose house she will move when she retires from nursing. She is a gynaecology and obstetrics doctor called Norah Li or Lee. But that is a story for later on...

30 JOHN IN TROUBLE

John was in trouble. Because of the civil war between the Kuomintang and the Communists, pupils at the Methodist Middle School in Chaotung had to undergo military training. A small Kuomintang garrison guarded the town and, for an hour during the school day, soldiers had the schoolboys perform drills and exercises, and introduced them to army discipline. But John, a strong-minded, hot-headed 13-year-old, didn't take well to discipline. He writes: 'One day they asked students to work levelling a field as part of training. I went to Mr He, who taught social studies and literature, and questioned the decision, asking him if it was necessary. I told him I wanted to learn, not level a field.

'He suddenly got extremely angry, which was not unusual for him, but to an extent I never anticipated. He shouted for the custodian to get the bamboo cane. It was two and a half inches wide and three feet long. He told me to put out my hand, and swung with all his might. The impact watered my eyes. It hurt so much I withdrew my hand, [so] he started hitting my arms, my body, my back, just swinging away... He kept flailing on me, again and again, until I could no longer bear the pain. I ran from the classroom and walked home sobbing... I couldn't move my hand for days. It was black and blue. I'm amazed it wasn't broken.'

This was the second serious beating John had received and, as with the first, administered by Li Shuang-mei, who looked after him when Alf and Bessie were on a previous furlough, he was incensed at the indignity, brutality and injustice of such treatment. Next day, he found that the beating was not to be his only punishment: John was told he had been expelled. He would not be graduating, which he knew would be a profound disappointment to his foster father, who was so keen to see that he got a good education.

It fell to Ken May, whose family John was staying with while he attended the school and Alf and Bessie were on furlough in England, to seek to defuse the situation. 'Revd May went and talked to the principal. It was decided I would go to the teacher and apologise profusely... Mr He said something like it had been a misunderstanding.'

This was a great reprieve, but not the end of the matter. Ken May had written to Alf, who would soon be back in Kunming, telling him what a close call John had had. At the end of the summer term he would have to travel home and account for himself to his foster father, who he both feared and respected. 'Revd May said I had two choices – I could take a [sedan] chair or ride a horse. I said I'd walk. I knew three students going back to Kunming, and we could walk together.' A soldier joined them, offering some protection against bandits.

This was a far tougher option than the two Ken had presented to John, and I think his choice offers an insight into his character. John seems to be saying: however tough you can be on me, I can be tougher on myself. It also promised to be a great adventure.

The journey proved very challenging for a thirteen-year-old: walking twenty-five miles a day for twelve days. It gave John his first experience of primitive Chinese inns: 'I was not prepared for the bed bugs and fleas. All the inns had bed bugs, so you learned to live with them. They lived in cracks in the floor, holes in the bedding, places like that. You didn't know they were there until you felt them under the sheets. By then it was too late. And they always hunted at night...

'The smoke, noise, and smell from the inn also kept us awake, but after a long day of walking, we were exhausted and slept like rocks, unmoved even by biting bedbugs. The next morning our legs would be covered with red spots from the bites. I forgot to mention the mosquitoes and flies. They were everywhere. For these, we travelled with a round net, suspended from the ceiling, to spare us from these winged assassins, but a mosquito or two always managed to sneak inside my netting.'

This was also John's first immersion in the Chinese countryside. They walked for hours without seeing any sign of human habitation, through wild country and wilder weather. 'The windstorms were truly memorable. They came out of nowhere. Sometimes the wind was so strong it lifted you off the ground. I was not a fully-grown man and the wind certainly had its fun with me.'

Along the way, they had to cross the Golden Sand River, via a rickety suspension bridge over the deep river gorge at Jiang Di, a point at which there had been a crossing for at least a thousand years. 'At each end, steel cables holding the bridge were anchored into big rocks, held in place by gigantic steel nails that were bent so they wouldn't slip out. The rocks were the size of small cars. Over the centuries thousands, maybe millions of people had crossed that bridge. It spanned 200ft, with a 300ft drop into the river below... It wasn't the safest bridge in the world.'

Wobbly wooden planks spanned the 6ft wide walkway. 'One slip and you'd end up plunging to the bottom. We were told not to look down at the roaring river below, because we'd get dizzy and fall off... that happened to people. Everything crossing the river was hoisted, dragged or carried across including horses, baggage, people walking, pack horses with loads. Anything moving on the open highway between Chaotung and Kunming went across that bridge. Sometimes people had to wait. It took time for one group to cross before another could climb on.'

John was glad to have the soldier walking with them. 'One day we glanced back and saw a small group of men approaching us... they didn't look proper. In those times, Chinese who travelled had a big cloth wrapped around their possessions, made into a pack across their shoulders. These men, in addition... had long, curved knives sticking out behind their backs, ready to go.

'We got scared really fast. I remember my heart was pounding. These were times in China when highway bandits were frequent and almost ruled the road... When bandits got caught they were executed, so when they robbed people, they usually killed them to leave no living evidence. In Chinese that's called Huo Ko, or Living Mouths. These men were clearly a gang, and they moved pretty fast [and passed us]. We slowed down, and they faded into the distance. It was a temporary reprieve. A few hours later we saw them ahead of us, lying down in a grass patch beside the road... My heart was pounding and my throat was dry. I wanted to turn and run.

'As we walked past, one of them suddenly said "Let's go," and they jumped up. That scared the hell out of us, so we walked extremely fast, as fast as we could without running. I whispered to the soldier: "What should we do if they come after us?" He said in a terse voice: "Run like hell, and don't look back."

For some reason they walked fast at first, but then slowed down, and we stayed a discreet distance ahead. We could see them behind us. I knew we might have to outrun them – a race for our lives. We couldn't prove they were bandits, but they looked extremely suspicious. I've often wondered why they didn't attack. I'm not sure. Maybe they felt they couldn't catch us if we ran, or that we weren't worth the effort... Maybe there were too many of us. Or, maybe they didn't think we had possessions worth stealing. Regardless, all of us considered it a close call.'

A few days before reaching Kunming the other students peeled off to their home villages, and John walked alone with the soldier. On the final day they were still miles from Kunming when John spotted a familiar figure approaching on horseback. It was his foster father, who had ridden out to meet him.

31 MILDRED WITHOUT PEARL, THE BATTLE OF SHANGHAI, THE RAPE OF NANKING

What did Mildred write in response to Pearl's impassioned letters? We don't know. Did she ignore them? Did she tell her not to write in such terms, as her son Arnold Pacey suggests? If there were letters, they may have gone up in smoke when, in 1977, Les piled many of his personal papers onto a bonfire at his allotment in Ilkley, his retirement home.

Letters from a few years hence do survive, but for the immediate aftermath of their times together, we have only Mildred's diary to go on. It is clear from it that Pan-yan and Chutney remained friends, but Pearl is mentioned only in passing, as a footnote to the big events in Mildred's life: her marriage to Les, the birth of their first child.

In June 1936 Mildred left Wenchow and travelled via Shanghai to Hong Kong, where she met up with Alf and Bessie, who were returning from furlough. The three of them travelled together to Kunming, where Mildred would be reunited with Les, via boat to Haiphong and then train via Hanoi. On June 2 Mildred wrote: 'Last stage of the train journey to Kunming. All the morning was spent counting the hours to 2pm, when Les and I should meet... what joy!' The next day: 'Words cannot express my happiness in being back again with the Laddie I love... to be with Les is for me a greater experience than life has ever shown me.'

This comes just five months after what, from Pearl's side at least, was a hugely emotional parting. How confusing had Mildred found her feelings for Pearl, in light of her presumably equally strong feelings for Les? Given the times, her background, and her role as a Christian missionary, it would have taken phenomenal courage to defy convention and commit herself to a life with Pearl, rather than Les.

Pearl, for her part, seems to have completely understood this, and was prepared to settle for being a friend to Mildred and to Les. I also wonder if Les had any suspicions about his future wife's closeness to Pearl? Mildred and Les were married by the acting British consul on August 1. If Alf had not been away from Kunming on mission business, he would probably have given Mildred away. As it was, Roger Arnold, an American who ran the YMCA, stepped in. Alf sent a message: 'I am looking forward to the work you both will be able to do in Kunming with us in the future. We should have great times at the church... and God's blessing upon you.'

The civil ceremony, which took place before the religious one, was perfunctory, 'little more than a written declaration and a spoken confirmation that we knew of no impediments to the marriage,' Les wrote in his dairy. 'Then we signed, followed by the witness, and that was that.' But the celebrations had begun three days before. 'We could not afford to invite all our guests to a feast, and we felt it good not to give a feast for another reason. The Chinese often spend so much money on the wedding that the married couple are in debt for ages afterwards, and though many would like to break from the old custom, it is difficult to do so. We therefore arranged for a simple tea and cake 'do', but also planned one or two other events for special friends.

'Last Wednesday I took a party of thirty mostly English-class students to the cinema to see *A Midsummer Night's Dream*. Coming during a wedding week it seemed too good an opportunity to miss. It is a glorious film and everyone thoroughly enjoyed it. Isn't it encouraging to know that such a film is drawing full houses. I wonder what Shakespeare would think if he could see people in a Chinese city scrambling for tickets.'

After the civil ceremony they went on to a church service at which Bessie played the organ. 'My best man was Ch'en Shun-I, one of the fellows I have been on outings on the lake with... The service began with a hymn during which Mildred came in on Mr Arnold's arm.'

The church had been elaborately and colourfully decorated; the couple passing through a series of bamboo arches as they walked down the aisle, the floor strewn with fresh green pine needles. Beside the altar were two scrolls, each bearing one large, Chinese character meaning joy. 'The service was in Chinese, but otherwise like the wedding service we usually have in England. We cut out the bit about "who gives this woman away".'

Afterwards, over a hundred guests crowded into the schoolroom where they were given slices of a wedding cake which had been baked in the Pacey family bakery in Spalding and transported all the way to China. Telegrams and messages of congratulation were read out. If there was one from Pearl, neither Mildred nor Les mentions it. Then the couple took a boat across the lake to a newly-built bungalow, a holiday home for staff of the Church Missionary Society, where they were to spend a few days honeymoon.

They returned to some sad news: one of their two young bridesmaids, Chao Mei-Lien, had died. The little girl had been ill before the wedding, but was desperate not to miss her chance to be a bridesmaid, and seemed to have recovered when the day came. Her death was a terrible shock. Mildred wrote:

'The most tragic thing of all is that... the Church Missionary Society doctor (an Englishman) attended her and wanted to have her in hospital. But Mei-Lien's sister had died in hospital about three years ago. This and other things kept her people from letting her go.'

Mildred's only mention of Pearl all that year was the line, on her birthday, Saturday November 7: 'Birthday telegrams from the Wenchow people, and from Pan-yan. Celebrated the day by attending feast at YMCA.'

In 1937 the couple moved from Kunming to Chaotung and, in April, Les wrote to his parents with some happy news: 'Mildred is pregnant... We are looking forward to a baby towards the end of October. We have been wanting to tell you for some time, but as letters are so slow, we decided not to say anything until the good news was absolutely definite.'

On August 1 Mildred writes: 'A year ago today was our wedding day. We have had a gloriously happy year. I'm not sure whether I described Chaotung as I saw it for the first time four years ago, but it is now vastly different. Then I came to take charge of the hospital here. This time I have come as a wife. The hospital then was a poor little place, dark, cold, very small and with few conveniences for nursing. In spite of all its drawbacks, though, many sick folk had been grateful that it existed and had found comfort and healing here. During the three years since I left, miracles have been worked... the new hospital is just a ten-minute walk outside the city. It isn't finished yet but the outpatients' department is in full use and there are some patients in the wards also. There is one Miao doctor and several nurses, some from the Miao and Nosu tribes as well as Chinese.'

Later that month, Mildred learns that war clouds darken the horizon, and her diary mentions Pearl and her plight, for only the second time since they left each other eighteen months before. 'There has been terrible news of a Japanese invasion of northern China, although detail is slow to reach us. Japan already occupied Chinese territory in Manchuria and Shantung, but on July 7, the Japanese made pretext to take more territory, and serious fighting began.'

In September she writes of Japanese military action close to Shanghai, and that they have started taking a Hong Kong newspaper to try to get more accurate information on the unfolding conflict. In that paper she finds her old friend named in a report, and writes in her diary, on October 3: 'Pan-yan, Pearl Evans, is now nursing in Shanghai. A few bombs have been dropped there and one day 400 people were admitted to her hospital with injuries – she was one of two or three mentioned for the good work they did.'

Such news seems almost inconsequential, mentioned among Mildred's domestic concerns. It is anything but. Pearl is living through the terrifying three-month Battle of Shanghai, in which Japanese forces fought to overcome the Chinese and take control of the city. It marked the start of the second Sino-Japanese War, and lasted from August to November 1937.

As a nurse in a major hospital, Pearl was in the thick of it. She had been in Shanghai for just two months when the Japanese occupied the city, and she would stay eight years, until May 1945, working first at the city's Lester China Hospital, then the Hong En Hospital, as nursing director. Not until Japan had been defeated would Pearl be able to return to Kunming, and be reunited with her step-father.

The Battle of Shanghai was one of the most vicious, bloody onslaughts of the whole conflict, involving battle by land, sea and air. It can be seen as the first battle of the Second World War, and has been compared with the Siege of Stalingrad for brutality, body count and suffering. The Chinese were fighting to stall a Japanese advance that threatened to sweep across the country, and to win time to move vital industries into the interior.

Pearl will have lived through fierce fighting in the city centre, the Chinese vastly outgunned by the Japanese. Despite this, the defenders put up huge resistance, and the Japanese, who had a hitherto unshakable belief in their military superiority, were shocked to find that the city did not fall within days, as they had expected.

Not that Pearl was in any position to relay any of this to Mildred, Alf, or anyone else. She was living in fear. Alf later wrote: 'When the Japs took over it was a bit awkward for her because of her connection with us. Some folk tried to stir up trouble for her. But after some years, she was appointed as matron of the biggest government hospital there. And then the end of the war brought further complications, for there was the danger of being accused of helping the Japs.'

While, for Pearl, life could not get much worse, for Mildred it was about to get even better. On October 9 she writes: 'Our baby is expected a fortnight today... Carpenters have screened a veranda this week, so the baby can sleep in the fresh air without flies or mosquitoes.'

The baby actually arrives on October 30, and Mildred writes a couple of days later: 'The infant arrived at 11:40 am eight and three-quarter pounds and is a boy. Having been taught about natural childbirth... I had so looked forward to having a normal labour and producing the infant on my own, so it was an awful blow to realise that I couldn't and that I would have to have an anaesthetic. The great consolation was that Les was with me all the time. Forceps had to be used during the birth, there is a small injury to the infant's head, but we are hoping it isn't serious.'

The baby's English name was Arnold, perhaps after Roger Arnold who walked Mildred down the aisle at her wedding. His Chinese name, suggested by friends, was Pu-ai, which means universal love. 'This is a name with deep resonances in China. On the gateway to the Sun Yat Sen mausoleum in Nanking, which commemorates the founder of the Chinese republic, his hope for the nation is described in terms of love for all, and the words 'Pu-ai' are carved in stone above the gateway. Some hospitals, especially Christian foundations such as the one in Hankow, where Pan-yan worked briefly, have the name Pu-ai Hospital.'

Two months later comes an entry about an event that was to change history:

'Terrible news from the war zone. The Japanese have attacked Nanking and are reported to have massacred half the population. We are wondering how Pearl is in Shanghai.'

While this horror was unfolding, John was on this way to school in Hong Kong. In later life he wrote: 'They call it the Rape of Nanking... The massacre started on December 13, 1937, four months after the day the Japanese captured that city, which was then the capital of China. The Chinese had surrendered, but the Japanese general told his troops: "Kill them all". Four Japanese divisions entered the city, a combined force close to a million men, armed, hungry, extremely dangerous, with a green light from the commander to plunder and pillage, take, rape, and kill everyone in town. They wanted to rip the heart out of China.

'The carnage began twelve days before Christmas. In the ensuing four weeks, an estimated 300,000 people were brutally murdered, and 30,000 women abducted at sex slaves... The stories are sickening. To this day, they evoke shock, dismay, and disbelief. Old people, women, children, and little babies were kicked, stabbed and stomped to death – executed in a mad frenzy. Each and every day, bands of armed Japanese soldiers would enter home after home to rape the women, while making the men watch, forcing fathers to rape daughters and sons to rape their mothers. Those who refused were slowly and painfully killed. Then [they] sliced up the men while the women watched and screamed. The women were raped, slashed and gutted.

'The 'lucky' Chinese women, after being gang raped, were stripped naked in freezing temperatures, their hands tied tightly with ropes behind their backs, nooses put around their necks and yanked like mules into large, penned areas. They were later dispersed throughout the Pacific as sex slaves for Japanese troops, a historically incredible event, that even today is denied [in various ways by some in Japan]'.

32 JOHN IN HONG KONG

Alf had not given up on John after his near-expulsion from school in Chaotung. Instead, he doubled down on his efforts to see John got a good education, by enrolling him at a smart boarding school in far-away Hong Kong. Would his faith be misplaced?

Bessie escorted John there. 'It was a most memorable trip. I was fifteen, full of great expectations, and heading off to the city of cities: Hong Kong! It was very exciting.' The journey was long, and complex. He and Bessie travelled by train, first class, on the three-day trip to Hanoi. 'The cars had elegant, private cabins and the seats were soft leather. In contrast, riding third class you were forced to sit on hard wooden benches near the engine where it was noisy and smoky.'

The train rolled through a China that had not changed for centuries. John saw peasants toiling in the fields, great wide-brimmed hats protecting them from the beating sun; markets where a chicken might be bartered for a shirt, corn for a saddle. On the third day they entered French Indo-China where the train threaded through scores of tunnels, skirted mountains, crossed gorges and rivers. 'A wave of tropical humidity suffocated the train. The windows were open, but the heat was extreme. We disembarked in the coastal city of Haiphong and waited for a ship to arrive. Two days went by, and finally, The Canton floated into harbour: a small, French vessel of just 2,000 tonnage. We all clambered aboard.

'The boat trip to Hong Kong took two days. It's two days I'll never forget. We almost didn't survive. The first day out we smacked right into a typhoon.' The ship was rocked, tossed and rolled by huge waves which broke constantly over the bow. 'I got terribly seasick. I vomited two entire days, hour after hour, long after the dry heaves emptied my stomach. It was unrelenting. I was on my hands and knees. When I went to the bathroom, the toilet went up and down with the waves. For two days I ate nothing: I couldn't keep anything down. It was the most horrible experience of my life. I thought I was going to die.'

It was the same for the other passengers. They stayed in their cabins. John's was next to the dining hall, which remained empty for the entire trip. When they went ashore at Hong Kong John felt the ground was going up and down, and the one-hour bus trip to his new school was pure torture. 'I was still woozy, and with each bounce of the bus I felt worse. I never felt so weak or terrible in my life.'

St Stephen's College stood on a hilltop in Stanley, overlooking the harbour. It had been founded in 1903 by the Church Missionary Society, responding to requests from prominent Chinese businessmen that they establish a school for their sons. 'I didn't know at the time, but the school was famous, considered the finest high school in Asia. The students were mostly children of wealthy Chinese families living in Hong Kong and southeast Asia.'

The views from the substantial school grounds were breath-taking, and particularly enchanting at night, when the many hundreds of fishermen hung lanterns from their boats. 'We saw the twinkling lights below, magical and beautiful, as boats circled the little islands dotting the harbour.'

Bessie stayed for a few days, to see John settled. On their first night in Hong Kong, the typhoon that almost sank their ship reached the city. 'A 20,000-ton ocean liner, the Queen Elizabeth, ten times the size of the ship that brought us to Hong Kong, was lifted by the surging waters and blown from the harbour onto the street nearby.'

Once the storm had passed, Bessie took John shopping for his uniform – blue blazer, grey trousers – and everything else he would need at school, but disaster struck. 'It was drizzling all day, and my mother slipped on the sidewalk, fell and broke her arm. We spent the rest of the day in the hospital. She had a sling on her arm for months. A few days later she went back to Kunming by herself.'

The school day was a demanding one: breakfast at 7am, classes from eight until five and, after dinner, two hours prep from 7-9pm, at which teachers supervised the boys in the study hall. At weekends John would go into the city, the St Stephen's insignia on the breast pocket of his blazer identifying him as a child of privilege. The curriculum at St Stephen's was strongly Euro-centric. Only one class in Chinese literature was offered, but the trips into the city offered him a chance to soak up Chinese culture.

'The most popular street in Hong Kong was Central Queens Road. On one side was The King's Theatre and across from it was The Queen's Theatre. Both showed a steady stream of good movies from Hollywood. One was by Pearl Buck, a famous writer born in China, called *Good Earth*, that starred Paul Muni and Luise Rainer. *The Good Earth* was about Chinese peasant families. In one bookstore I bought *Red Star Over China*, written by Edgar Snow, who was with the Communists on the Long March. Years later he contracted cancer and went to China for treatment, where the Communist leader Zhou en-lai helped him quite a bit. Zhou was the Communist I liked the most, a level-headed man who didn't let things go too far left. He demonstrated self-control, fairness and leadership.' Zhou would serve as premier of the People's Republic of China from 1954 until his death in 1976.

John also took opportunities to absorb American culture, at the cheaper cinemas in the fishing village of Stanley, at the foot of the hill beneath St Stephen's. He enjoyed Laurel and Hardy, and Disney's *Snow White and the Seven Dwarfs.*

Despite his privileged position, John was not well off. 'I needed to be frugal. In those days, most Chinese provinces printed their own money, and the value of the Yunnan money was very depressed, ten-to-one to the Chinese national currency. My money didn't buy much. During the war, all China's provinces unified their monies into a national currency.'

All went well for John at St Stephen's until, when he had been at the school for two years, he fell foul of a teacher called Mr Ash. The familiar pattern was repeating. 'For some reason he didn't like me. He taught chemistry, not easy for me, and maybe that's why I was on his bad boy list. My marks in Chemistry were not stellar. One time he came to my room to check up on me.

'When we went into town we needed a green slip stating what we were going to buy, and the reason. We took this paper to the cashier to get money for the purchase. One time I went to town to get a tennis racket, but ended up not buying it. Ash was suspicious, and he showed up at my room to see the tennis racket I supposedly bought. Luckily, my roommate had one. He looked at it, didn't say much, and left.

'He kept trying to find fault with me and watched me like a hawk. Eventually I had a problem, an argument with another student, so Ash had the excuse he needed to expel me. He said I was wasting my parents' hard-earned money, and I wasn't fit to stay in school. I called a Methodist missionary friend who knew my parents and he arranged my return to Kunming. Sadly, I was a junior – only one year away from graduation. But I was leaving Hong Kong.

'The return trip was depressing. I travelled Third Class on the boat ride to French Indochina. We stayed below the main deck with cattle and other animals above. It smelled horribly. Our space was a large room where we sat and slept next to each other. There was one public bathroom.'

When the ship docked at Haiphong there was another potential flashpoint for John. 'Haiphong seaport was run by the French and the customs process was long and arduous for Third Class passengers. When the French officials went out to lunch they locked us in a big room, where we sat for hours waiting for them to return. Finally, they stumbled back and started checking our bags, one by one. They went through everything. If they liked one of your shirts or ties, they put it aside and it was gone for good: Confiscated. They basically stole it, and if you protested you were making a big mistake. I saw a Chinese traveller with a beautifully handmade cotton blanket. The French inspector used a knife and sliced it open to see if anything was hidden inside. There was nothing, but the blanket was destroyed. The traveller didn't say a word.

'The French were very mean to the natives. If they caught a Vietnamese person breaking the law they'd put him in a water cell. He would stand there for hours, even days, shivering in the cold. The water level was at chest or neck. If your legs became weak, which they eventually did, you slipped under the water and drowned...

'During my inspection, the French official liked an Arrow shirt and tie I had bought in Hong Kong. He took them both and put them aside.' John was about to protest, but managed to keep quiet. He could have been fined, detained, or even imprisoned.

'Once I got through customs, the train ride back was even more sobering. Another Third Class experience – hard wooden seats instead of soft leather ones, smoke, noise and confusion everywhere. Coal smoke is particularly nasty. It gets in our eyes, nose and hair.'

In Kunming, John had once again to face Alf and Bessie. 'My foster parents were very disappointed. They felt I had let them down after all the effort they'd expended on my behalf. But I was about to become a businessman.'

33 MURDER AT STONE GATEWAY

On Monday March 7, 1938 Mission House in London received this cable from Alf: 'Stone Gateway station has been looted. Goldsworthy and some scholars killed. Mr and Mrs Moody were not hurt. Evans.'

It was a devastating blow. A Western missionary presence had only just been re-established in Stone Gateway. For fifteen years, they had been forced to keep away from what, in the words of Ken May, was 'perhaps the most lonely and isolated mission station under our society, it being too dangerous to send anyone there.' Yet, in their absence, Miao and Chinese ministers, teachers, doctors and nurses had kept the mission not just alive, but thriving, with 18,000 in their congregation.

The first westerners to return were a young couple, the Revd Edward Moody and his wife Beatrice, a nurse, in 1936. Heber Goldsworthy followed them, a year later. At the time of Goldsworthy's appointment, Ken May was full of optimism: 'this will make it easier to cope with the incessant calls that are coming in on every side. If it were possible to put a little more strength into this work, we might speedily have a Miao church of 40,000 people.'

And then, just a year on, this: brutal, cold-blooded murder. At the time, Heber's wife, Ida, had been preparing to join him from England.

Edward Moody wrote an eye-witness account: 'On Saturday night March 5 about 12:15 my wife and I were awakened by shots and almost immediately our boy came to us with the news that Mr Goldsworthy's house had been attacked... Before we could get into dressing gowns there were shots outside our house, and the crashing of wood and glass as doors were broken down. We made for the loft and managed to haul up the ladder, close the trap door, and pull heavy boxes onto it as the bandits entered the house. The time that followed was the most anxious we have ever known, we are quite sure we were led by God to go into the loft, for it was a thing we had not planned to do in case of such an attack.

'There was the noise of shots and broken glass, as the house was ransacked. Soon, the noise died down, and then the smell of burning reached us. We were afraid, but the smell passed off. And later we learned that a student dormitory had been burned down. A bugle sounded the bandits' retreat, and we came down from the loft, soon meeting groups of Miao also emerging from their hiding. Mr Goldsworthy had not been seen and so we went to the bungalow, eventually finding him lying by the side of a path, some twelve feet below the house... He had already been dead some time, and my wife inferred from the position of the wounds that death had been instantaneous.

'Before we returned home, a stream of burned students began to arrive. A tin of paraffin had been taken from Mr Goldsworthy's house and used to set light to a dormitory. Students were in the upper part, and the bandits had probably been annoyed by the absence of a ladder to the upper sleeping quarters. As the building burned, the students jumped from a window and were then slashed with knives. Some have bad wounds and most of them are seriously burned.

'The rest of the night was used in attending to those who had been hurt. There were gunshot wounds, knife wounds, broken bones and burns to attend to. The work was very difficult because both the hospital and dispensary (a room in our house) had been thoroughly ransacked. Broken glass, bottles, boxes, and other things were strewn over the floor. Of dressings there were hardly any, and drugs were difficult to find among the confusion; we tried to make them up and then found that the scales were broken. It was an awful business. Dressing the wounded kept us going most of the night. The next morning it was necessary to change the dressings, so that it was 3 o'clock in the afternoon before this was finished.'

The Moodys, having done all they could, sent a messenger off to Chaotung, asking for a doctor and two Chinese nurses to be sent. They didn't reach Stone Gateway until 9.30 that night, but 'it was a tremendous relief to see them, for by then our nerves were just about gone to pieces.

'The main object of the attack seems to have been the bungalow and the money that was there. When daylight came and we went down, we found that the place was wrecked. Little other than books and tinned food were left. The gramophone and other things had been hacked with an axe, apparently in the search for money. We did not suffer so badly, and the impression is that the visit here may have been somewhat in the nature of an afterthought. Our studies were not entered, but the dispensary and kitchen and store cupboard suffered badly and were thoroughly ransacked. Our bedroom was entered. Drawers were turned out, clothing and bedding were taken, but strangely enough, no cupboard was opened. This meant that our clothes and over 1000 nickel dollars were not taken. Several dormitories were entered and bedding and cooking utensils taken. There are no witnesses of Mr Goldsworthy's death, so facts are difficult to obtain. It seems, however, that Mr Goldsworthy attempted to talk with the robbers and was shot. Evidently the shots were meant to kill for the wounds are on the left side and in vital places.'

In the Methodist mission's journal, *Kingdom Overseas*, the cause of the attack was laid out: 'The repercussions of the Sino-Japanese war are being felt even in this remote part of the country, nearly 2,000 miles from the actual fighting. The National Government has been obliged to withdraw its troops from these south-west provinces in order to meet the invaders, and this has given the bandits a new opportunity to assert themselves.'

The attack did not come out of the blue. The threat posed by bands of men who prowled the mountains had been increasing over the previous months. Yet they had felt safe in Stone Gateway. 'With a great bodyguard of 18,000 devoted Miao Christians scattered on the mountains around, and ever watchful and ready to give the alarm at the slightest approach of danger, our missionaries seemed to be in no actual peril.'

Travelling between missions had been shown to be perilous, however. Ken May and family had travelled from Chaotung to Stone Gateway for the Christmas just gone. While Ken travelled on to Universal Spring, another mission centre, Heber Goldsworthy escorted Cathie May and children back to Chaotung. On the way they were attacked.

In the last letter received from Heber before his death he wrote: 'We had a military escort of four men, but about 30 li (10 miles) from Stone Gateway our carriers with their loads were waylaid and attacked, and led away across the mountains by about ten or so robbers. Seeing the situation, I urged the escort to follow them, but though they made some pretence at this, nothing really happened and they were quickly back again, the robbers meanwhile making good use of their advantage.

'After a hurried consultation with Mrs May, I decided to get on my horse and go with the escort after the brigands, and this action did give them a little more courage to pursue. So on we went up the mountains to the north, Mrs May and the boys continuing on to Chaotung. Conditions were against us in actually tracking the robbers, for the higher we got into those unknown mountains the thicker was the mist and cloud enveloping everything, and though at times we followed their footmarks, these would suddenly disappear as we came upon harder earth. After an hour or two in pursuit, I decided to spend the night where I could, though in the absence of both food and bedding! Just then I saw the carriers coming towards me.

'They had been robbed, one or two of them had been beaten, and they were just carrying the salvage. The loads had all been turned upside down on the wayside, the brigands had helped themselves to what they wanted, and the rest had just been pushed anyhow into the boxes and cases, now sadly broken and of little use. So I was with the carriers until we got out of the danger zone, then made a push for the city and managed to reach it in the evening in pitch darkness and very cold and hungry, for I had had nothing to eat since leaving Stone Gateway. That same night the mandarin sent out twenty or thirty of his special men to investigate, but though they were scouring around for two nights, they discovered nothing.'

This was of course a personal tragedy for Heber Goldsworthy's wife Ida. She had been pregnant when she returned to England, and the little girl she gave birth to there would never see her father. The murder was also devastating for all the missionaries, and had an impact on their working lives. With Goldsworthy gone and other senior missionaries on furlough, they were spread very thinly across the vast region they covered. The Moodys were so shaken that they immediately departed on furlough for England, where they would remain for two years. In their absence, the mission at Stone Gateway was closed. When they did return, Beatrice Moody suffered such terrible nightmares, convinced that they were once again under attack, that they could not stay.

Mildred and Les Pacey learned of the atrocity at Stone Gateway while they were five days into a journey along the new motor road from Chaotung to Kunming. There, they were to have joined Alf in mission and hospital work, but that plan had to be abandoned. Instead, they were diverted to another posting, at Tung Chuan, where Alf and Bessie had spent their early years in China. Here they were to run a very busy mission and dispensary, at which they treated 5,000 patients in the first four months.

Alf wrote to them about Heber's death: 'Life in China is like living on the edge of a volcano – every now and then there are terrific upsets which change all our plans… It will be a terrible blow to Ida, but how fortunate she's not now on her way here.'

The murder at Stone Gateway led Les to question the role of the western missionary in China. He had become increasingly disenchanted even before it, and had told Alf he would not return to China after his first furlough. Now he told him he wanted to leave sooner, just four years into his seven-year term, and sent a resignation letter to Mission House in London.

'It may have been a turning point in his attitude to missionary work,' his son Arnold believes. 'If Christianity had flourished among these Miao communities for fifteen years, without any visits from missionaries, what was the role of missionaries more generally? What should it be?' He came to believe that the Miao and Chinese ministers ought to lead mission work, not foreigners.'

Les appears to have had these concerns from early on in his life as a missionary. Two years before he had preached a sermon in which he said: 'The structure of society does not help towards producing Christian servants. Even the humblest of us regard some people as below us, and we find circumstances where we feel free to be master rather than servant. Missionaries' work,' he went on 'is a dangerous trade' involving the temptation of 'overlordship over others if we are not careful.' He quoted from an article, written by a Chinese person, headed *Why I am Not a Christian,* in which it was said that 'missionaries come to lonely places so that they can lord it over others.' Leslie added that, while not many come with that purpose, all were 'in danger of seeking compensation that way.'

The lives of their actual servants also troubled him. Every time they travelled, a team of porters had to carry the missionaries' belongings, and often the missionaries themselves in sedan chairs. This was punishingly heavy labour, was poorly paid, and shortened their lives.

His son writes: 'Every journey involved Leslie in qualms about whether they should be asking men to do this kind of work, and when he learned that one porter who had worked for him had become a Christian he agonised about whether he had treated him fairly.'

Another concern was Mildred's health. She says little in her diary, but it seems her symptoms were debilitating.

We can get a sense of the isolation Les and Mildred felt at Tung Chuan from someone who came across them during their time there. Richard Dobson was the representative of a cigarette company, visiting the local agents in remote areas of China. He wrote a book, *China Cycle,* in which he said: 'At length we came to a place where the road apparently died… Grass and weeds grew all over it, and no wheel-marks scarred its surface, yet still it wound on and on.' He struggled up a long valley until he came to Tung Chuan. 'I paid a swift call at the Methodist mission, where I found a kind, but tired young couple with their baby.'

Dobson could see Les was 'much worried' over the health of his wife. He went on to Chaotung, then turned back towards Tung Chuan. On the way he bumped into a group of missionaries who had been staying there with the Paceys. They talked about Mildred, Leslie and their baby and shared their impressions about the seriousness of Mildred's ill health.

In November, Mildred wrote in her diary: 'Have been feeling poorly now for some time, today closed the dispensary. From now on it is open only for the sale of medicines (and emergencies).' Concerns over Mildred were passed back to Mission House in London.

A report landed on the desk of Harold Rattenbury, a veteran Chinese missionary now in charge of the administration of Methodist work in China. He had been struggling to decide how to respond to Les's resignation letter. Now, with the added issue of Mildred's illness, he sent a cable to Alf Evans: 'Advise Paceys move Kunming immediately.' He followed up with a letter, making the point that there were doctors in Kunming who could investigate Mildred's illness and decide whether she would respond to treatment if she stayed in China. 'If medical opinion is Mrs Pacey cannot stay even in Kunming they should come home as a family.'

Arnold Pacey comments: 'Rattenbury also thought that Leslie's doubts about continuing his missionary work in China were due to the strain of loneliness. If he were to work in Kunming for a while, he would have more colleagues around him, which would help him see things in a different perspective. Rattenbury seemed to think Les could be persuaded to change his mind and said 'I myself want a good talk with Pacey when he comes home… Before I am willing to throw up my hands and say his work there is done.'

When Les and Mildred returned to Kunming they found a city much changed by the war. A mass movement was taking place, as many thousands moved from the war-torn eastern provinces to the safety of the mountainous country to the west, including Yunnan. The government had transferred to the neighbouring province of Chengdu, industrialists were being encouraged to move their factories to Kunming, and the major universities were also being uprooted.

The missionaries saw an opportunity for evangelisation in all this, with Alf and Bessie at the forefront. A report in *Kingdom Overseas* noted: 'Several hundred eager students walked the distance of 1,000 miles in order to resume their studies. Five hundred of these splendid young fellows are actually in Kunming and today, as I write, they begin lectures... all these have received a real Methodist welcome and already feel very much at home, both in the home of Mr and Mrs Evans, and in the church... Our Methodist church in Kunming, under the understanding, leadership and chairmanship of the Revd Alfred Evans, is fully alive to the fact that the Christian church now has an opportunity which it never has had before, which it may never have again.'

Les and Mildred would not be part of this. Mildred's headaches were such that she was advised to leave for England immediately. Les also became ill, stricken with appendicitis. He too was told to go home, for an operation. In March 1939 they left for England, never to return. Arnold Pacey writes: 'Mildred may have left China, but the people and the landscape had entered deeply into her imagination, and were to be part of her thoughts, conversation and language for the rest of her life.'

34 KUNMING: REFUGEE CITY

Among those who came to Kunming in the summer of 1939 was a missionary teacher called Leonard Constantine, dean of the Hua Chung University, which had relocated to Hsichow, near Kunming. He travelled here by train from Hanoi with a group that included students from Yale University, who seemed driven by a desire to experience life in a refugee zone.

In his book *The Bitter Years*, he wrote: 'Each night after puffing its way up the mountain slopes, the train came to a halt and passengers had to sleep in nearby hotels or bungalows. At Kaiyuan, half way between the border and Kunming, Chinese police came round to the bungalow to examine our passports. The two Yale [students] had Japanese visas upon which the police pounced. They were convinced that they had caught two spies, for why should anyone else want to visit Japan? It took all my best Chinese to convince them that it was perfectly natural for travellers from America to call at Japan on their way out and therefore have Japanese visas. Reluctantly, the police let them go.

'Kunming was experiencing the first rush of refugees. Formerly a dignified old city, the Beijing of the south west, with its massive walls and stately gates at the four corners of the city. It was now submerged beneath the great wave of people who had come crowding in. The few hotels had catered for a leisurely tourist traffic and were unable to cope with the present influx. Every room in the city was rented out.

'Kunming was now one of the most important cities left in Free China, but it was unable to fulfil its destiny or speed up its tempo. The streets were dirty and unkempt. One hurried out in the morning to find the shops closely shuttered until noon. Only at night did the city come alive, when crowds thronged the pavements, wandering aimlessly through a city which had few attractions to offer. People spoke of the three 'pu's of Kunming: pu hsi chao, pu ch'i chao and pu ch'i pao: never take a bath, never get up early, never eat a full meal. Already refugees were sighing for the fleshpots of Shanghai.

136

'Our little group found accommodation among different families in the city. On our first morning in Kunming we were hardly surprised to hear that our Yale friends were already in prison. They had confidently set out to explore the city and photograph all the strange sites. One of the city gates attracted their attention, and they had just got their cameras into position when a policeman arrived and demanded explanations. As they had not the faintest idea what he was saying they were hauled off to jail, where they were kept until their host, the YMCA secretary [Roger Arnold], could get in touch with them and bail them out. Their films were confiscated and they were warned not to flourish their cameras again. It was something of an achievement to land in jail on one's first morning in China.'

Another visitor arrived at around the same time: one that Alf probably had no desire to see. His boss in London, Harold Rattenbury, had decided to take a tour of all the districts and missions in China, perhaps to show solidarity with the missionaries who struggled on under war conditions. He had clashed many times with Alf over the way he ran things in the Kunming district, and relations were to get even worse between them.

Rattenbury arrived in August, with the threat from the Japanese invaders growing ever stronger, and noted in his diary: 'Evans thinks that Kunming is due to be bombed unmercifully as soon as the monsoon clouds roll away. So they are not anxious for fine weather. The city is three or four times its normal population, the government advising evacuation, but the people will be reluctant to go till there has been a first-class disaster.' The day before he arrived, twenty-one Japanese bombers had reached the outskirts of the city, but dared not risk an attack while heavy cloud screened the treacherous mountains surrounding it.

Rattenbury came via India and Burma, flying in to Kunming on August 22 with an extremely distinguished fellow passenger: Jawaharlal Nehru, a key leader of the Indian nationalist movement who would become India's first prime minister in 1947, after winning independence from the British. Nehru was on his way to meet Chiang Kai Shek.

Rattenbury wrote: 'We had a clear view all the way and I think the mountain scenery we came over was the most striking and beautiful of the entire trip from Southampton. There were enough clouds on the mountains above and around us and sufficient overhead to make us confident the Japanese wouldn't get us. "The cloud of the protecting love" takes on a new meaning under the circumstances. After all, Nehru came with us: a slight, slim, intellectual figure in a dark suit and congress cap, his hair going silver grey.'

Rattenbury adds: 'I certainly have come into a land and province of problems.' One of those problems was knowing what was going on in the outside world. The alignments that would bring about the war in Europe were falling into place. Two days after his arrival he writes: 'There is no newspaper here, nothing but a typed sheet published by a group of missionaries, from wireless and other sources. We realise that Germany and Russia have reached some sort of accord, that Parliament meets today, and that anything may happen. This may or may not bring changes in one's plans, but as for me I am inclined to judge I had better press on with my visitation... Meanwhile, the sun shines, the birds sing, the mosquitoes bite, and God is over all.'

Leonard Constantine was also following what news he could glean from Europe. He writes: 'Now we knew the aftermath of the Russo-German pact. The radio told of the gathering storm in Europe, mobilisation, evacuation of children, air raid precautions. Still most people were hopeful. There had been alarms before and a settlement had been patched up. One good sign was that the Japanese soldiers on the borders of Kowloon have suddenly started fraternising with the British sentries [guarding Hong Kong]. We set out on the Burma Road, not unduly worried.'

They do so on August 30 in a truck owned by Constantine's university, headed first to Chaotung and accompanied by Rattenbury. Two days later, on September 1, Germany invaded Poland and, two days after that, the United Kingdom and France declared war on Germany.

The Burma Road had only just been opened to traffic, and they are unsure what driving conditions would be like. Constantine wrote: 'Side-by-side with the road, hundreds of coolies were working on the new railway which was to connect China with Burma. Already the road bed was taking shape. The third track which we constantly saw was an old stone-flagged trail, the Marco Polo Road, over which that great traveller had ridden to Burma with Kubla Khan's soldiers.

'We passed through magnificent country, climbing over mountain tops until we seemed to be on the roof of the world, with the vast plateau of Yunnan spread out below us, but gloom descended on our party. At one halt, Mr Rattenbury was observed with an anxious look on his face, going through his pockets, and then emptying his suitcase.

"Have you lost anything?" we asked

"Yes, I can't find my wallet."

"Anything important in it?"

"Well, rather, it contains my passport, return ticket to England, all my English money and a letter of introduction from the Chinese ambassador in London."

'He could not think what he had done with it, or where he had last seen it. We were all sorry for him, but sorrow was tempered with satisfaction that such a catastrophe had happened to a visiting secretary from London, and not to a humble missionary in the field. We could well imagine the sort of letter London would have written to a missionary careless enough to lose such a valuable possession.' It turned out he had left it under his pillow at their overnight stop two days before. Rattenbury would travel on through China, reaching Shanghai in the following February, 1940.

Alf was probably glad to see the back of him. Beginning in 1938, there was rising conflict and tension between Alf and mission headquarters in London about how he administered the district, of which he was chairman. Alf had written to Rattenbury several times over many months before his visit, defending his failure to file the accounts on time: 'My inability to supply these returns and schedules at the stated times have long been a sore point with many. In this matter, I have failed to satisfy the folk at home and the folk on the field. My excuse has been that I have had too much other work to do to give the time required for these things.

'At the same time, as regards finance, it is the simplest thing in the world for the committee at home to examine the grants and the bills that I have sent, for them to see that I have not drawn money beyond what has been granted by the committee. Furthermore, I have asked that someone be appointed to act as assistant to the chairman, and to receive instructions from him as to schedules, letters etc etc. This has not been granted.'

By this stage Alf was quite ready to give up the chairmanship of the South West China district and, by implication, his life's work. In February 1939 he had written: 'I have no desire to spend time seeking to justify my actions (or inactions). I have previously stated that this seeming neglect is not due to intentional flouting of the wishes of the finance department... It is very possible that the work... has been held up by my negligence, but the Kingdom of God has been helped along by my failure to do my own work. Since September 1937, there has hardly been a time that I have not been called upon to render assistance to some other mission. If I had refused, their work would have suffered. Our mission at Kunming is now known all over China and letters of appreciation from very, very many folk are an offset to the dissatisfaction expressed by our home committee.'

London recognised Alf needed help, and it had been intended that Les would provide it. Rattenbury was concerned that Alf's relentless pace of work might trigger another breakdown: 'With all that is upon Mr Evans' shoulders, I have been fearing seriously for his health... The crux of the matter is that no one can do all that Mr Evans is trying to do. He must delegate some of his tasks.'

It was decided that Alf should pass on responsibility for the primary and middle schools in Kunming and cease to be the chairman of the district, handing over to Ken May. Alf would be appointed as local representative of the committee in London, which oversaw the work in South West China. He would, however, still act as the financial agent for the whole district. May was in England, so another missionary, Frederick Cottrell, would act as chairman until his return.

35 TASTING BITTERNESS

John returned from school in Hong Kong to a cool reception from Alf and Bessie. Nothing was said; they didn't directly accuse him of squandering the opportunity St Stephen's had offered, but their displeasure was clear and the mood in the house was glum. There were many awkward silences.

What would John do next? With Alf reluctant to waste any more effort and money on his education, John had to rely on his own initiative. Perhaps that was Alf's intention. Help came from a curious and unexpected quarter.

The Evanses often put up people who were in difficulty in their home. When John returned two American missionaries, Lester and Beatrice Van Meter, were staying in the second-floor box room. The Van Meters were not part of an organised church mission group. They had come independently, at their own expense. They simply told those close to them that they had been called by God. They arrived in Kunming, their second stint in the city, in July 1939. The Van Meters relied on donations sent from churches in America to fund them and their work but, with the war, those funds were not consistent.

John writes: 'When the money stopped flowing, the Van Meters needed help, so mother and father took them in. Father told us they had a different interpretation of Christianity. They were southern Baptist, and "got carried away, sometimes,"' he said. It was through Lester Van Meter that John got a job.

'In 1940, as soon as Hitler moved into Paris, the Japanese immediately took French Indo-China, which today consists of three countries: Vietnam, Cambodia and Laos. Vietnam, with its long east coast, was the first to fall... They used Hanoi as a base to bomb cities in south-west China that were strategic and large, including Kunming.'

Faced with an expected Japanese invasion from the south, using the railway from Vietnam, the Chinese tore up the tracks on their side of the border. This caused a major logistical problem for the universities that had moved to Chengdu, in Sichuan province, banding together under the title West Union

University. Many of their supplies came via Kunming, reached up that railway line, including those for the dentistry department. With trains now halted at the Vietnam-Yunnan border, university supplies were dumped beside the line.

John writes: 'Someone was needed to handle the transfer of the supplies through Kunming. In those days, Yunnan was under the French Indo-China sphere of influence, and the French controlled customs in Kunming. West Union, founded by Canadian missionaries, offered Van Meter US$300 a month to serve as the intermediary. He jumped on the job. But, over time, the load increased and Van Meter's health started deteriorating. He couldn't handle the workload, and asked me to help.'

John, the businessman

John quickly mastered the system: taking papers to customs, getting permits, waiting in offices, taking the goods home, finding trucks for the 54-mile, five-to-six-day trip, negotiating prices, and then shipping the goods. 'After paying a large duty fee, because we were supplying a foreign university, we'd hire coolies to carry the boxes back to our house, find trucks, get the right price, reload the supplies and have them shipped to Chengdu.' A lot of money was involved: 30,000 to 40,000 Chinese dollars for one to two tons of cargo.

They split the income fifty-fifty but, with Lester's condition worsening every day, John took on more and more of the work until he was handling everything.

141

'In fact, I became an agency, running my own business.... Father Evans would look over the paperwork I filled out, to make sure it was satisfactory. He had a good business sense.' John found that his ability to charm worked wonders: 'I was a frequent visitor to the French customs office. The processor had a big stack of papers on his desk, and he always put new applications on the bottom. Usually you'd have to wait one or two days to have them reviewed. If the official liked you, he put your papers on top and you'd be out in minutes. He liked me. I learned ways to grease the system, so I wasn't waiting forever.'

In Kunming, Lester Van Meter was unable to get a clear diagnosis for the cause of his sleeplessness and cold night sweats. Doctors sent him to Hong Kong, where he was told he had cancer. His two children were pulled out of boarding school and the family returned to the USA. Lester died a few weeks after arriving home in Riverside, California.

John had become increasingly conscious of the privileged life he had been brought up in, and decided he wanted to make his way on his own account, without help from Alf. Also, he seems to have wanted to undertake some form of penance. He called it Du Chi Ku: 'tasting bitterness.' He decided to return to Hong Kong. He had a schoolfriend from St Stephen's, Yang, whose family owned a business there, shipping Tung oil, which is obtained from the tung tree and used in oil paints, around the world. He asked Yang if he could fix it for him to work as a simple labourer there, and he did. Alf and Bessie knew nothing of his plans.

'I'd asked my friend to show me no favours, to treat me like a hired hand, and that's what I got. I was raised in privilege and I knew it... I was itching to taste the life of the common man, despite my education and upbringing.' John loaded huge vats of Tung oil onto freighters all day for little pay, before returning to a tiny shack with a tin roof which he shared with three other workers. The tin roof made the shack as hot as an oven in summer. When it rained, they stayed inside and sweltered. Meals were cooked outside, in a hole in the ground. The only toilet was a roofless hut 50 yards away, shared between hundreds. Mosquitoes infested the area, too many to keep at bay with nets, and John's arms and legs were covered in itchy wounds.

Such privations were exactly what he wanted: the sort of suffering he believed he deserved to endure. He even managed to enjoy the work for a while: 'At first, it was great... the pay was bad and the work dangerous... We had to walk across slippery gangplanks to load vats of oil into the hulls of huge ships. There was oil everywhere and it was very slippery. If you slipped, you fell into a huge tub of oil, with no way to be rescued. You would flounder for a few seconds, and then sink to the bottom, drowned in oil. You can't swim in oil. There were many stories of people slipping, falling and being swallowed alive in the thick liquid. I almost lost my footing many times... I will never regret what I asked for, although I didn't expect anything quite so drastic. My nights were sleepless, my days long. I ate, slept and worked. Time moved slowly, it was tortuous.'

After four or five months of tasting bitterness John fell sick with a fever. 'I was sweaty, delirious, and seeing stars. I could barely walk and, with the help of a fellow worker, stumbled to the Queen Mary Hospital. After a long wait a British nurse came to assess his condition. He started to tell her but she interrupted angrily: 'Don't you know to stand up when an English lady speaks to you?'

'I suddenly realised I was a third-rate subject. I was Chinese in a British colony. I was embarrassed and stunned. I was so upset, I got up, walked out, and took a taxi to a smaller clinic in Kowloon for treatment. I had a bad fever, my throat was sore, and I was immediately hospitalised.'

When, after several days, he was well enough to leave the clinic, John did not return to work. Instead he went to downtown Hong Kong 'on a lark'. There he unexpectedly met another St Stephen's schoolfriend, Lu Guo Liang, the eldest son of a warlord, Lu Han, who was related to Yunnan's governor, Long Yuin. Guo owned a smart hotel, popular with foreign businessmen, and John stayed with him for a few days. Finally, Yang, the friend who had got him his job, tracked him down and asked why he hadn't been coming to work. John told him he had decided to return to Kunming, but that he had enjoyed the opportunity to taste bitterness. He bought a third-class ticket, again travelling via Haiphong.

'Looking back, the experience was invaluable. I learned about life outside the comfort of my existence. I learned about suffering and hardship. It was the best education of my life.'

36 A HAVEN FROM WAR

Terrible things are going to happen to Bessie and Alf, some of them related to the war that is about to engulf Kunming, others are more personal. Bessie is becoming increasingly frail. Walking is not easy. Alf is overworked, in conflict with his bosses and some of the younger missionaries, and in danger of another mental collapse; but for now I just want to paint a picture of the happy life they led, despite all their adversities.

The retirement house Alf and Bessie built across Lake Danchi

Over the years, Alf and Bessie had numerous visitors and guests staying with them, at the mission house in Kunming and in a retirement house they built for themselves across Dianchi Lake, the 40-mile-long expanse of water to the west of Kunming. A number of those guests write warmly about the couple, giving me a vivid impression of the homes they made together, and a comforting picture of the bedrock that sustained them: their love and their sense of duty to others.

The Van Meters' daughter Edith at the Evanses' city home

To Lester and Beatrice Van Meter, who had stayed before their return to America: 'These two were golden threads in the weaving of our lives as missionaries in China.' In their book, *If Only One*, they say Bessie was 'a loving hostess,' the city house and garden a haven: 'When one visited the Evanses, the Chinese city outside disappeared... peace and serenity reigned as she played mother.'

The house was protected by a 12ft high enclosing wall, topped with shards of glass to deter burglars. There was a gatehouse, with stout, wooden double doors guarding the entrance. The wall enclosed a garden 50yds square, planted with many eucalyptus trees and palms, and laid out with wide borders of flowering tropical plants. There was an extensive grape vine, raised on a trellis, a fountain and a tennis court.

The Van Meters took many photographs there, and I am looking through them now. I see a very English, white-rendered brick house with angled bays and sash windows, under a steeply pitched roof. The ground floor is surrounded by a wide verandah.

In one picture Alf stands in its shade, wearing a suit and homburg, patting an Alsatian, one of many dogs they owned over the years. In another he sits on a tiny donkey, a Van Meter pet, lifting his feet up, and grinning. He could easily stand astride it. The donkey was named Honker after the wild hee-haw that it gave when roused, ending with a frenzied flapping of its loose lips. In a third picture the Van Meters' daughter Edith, wearing a sun helmet, sits in the garden on a dining-room chair, clutching three puppies on her lap, the mother dog looking on. There were numerous cats, and a flock of chickens, bred by Bessie from fertilised eggs she bought in.

The house, the Van Meters write, had 'a vast library, each book treasured', a formal dining room and a cosy sitting room. 'Uncle had a fine organ they had carried with them for many years. Its sweet tones were mellow with age. When Auntie played, it was a little bit of heaven.'

Outside those protective walls, things were far from idyllic. To get to the house you had to turn off the wide main street, Jinbi Lu, and on to Shulin Jie, a very narrow alley alongside an open sewer that ran in a steep-sided ditch, 20ft deep and 30ft wide. They called it the Stinking Brook, or Stinking Water River. And stink it did. Rubbish and sewage sat in its semi-stagnant waters, and on occasion dead bodies were found there. Stinking Brook is in the pictures too.

In one, Bessie stands on a wooden bridge that spans it, one of their dogs at her side. Only when it rained really heavily was the filth in Stinking Brook washed away. Visitors pressed perfumed handkerchiefs to their faces as they were pulled in rickshaws, with their two cart-like wheels at the back and shafts between which you would think a pony ought to be harnessed, but which were hauled by a man. Bessie had to travel by rickshaw even for very short journeys, because of her weakened legs.

As the threat of bombing raids by the Japanese grew, Alf decided to build an air raid shelter just beyond the tennis court. He had a trench 20ft long, 10ft wide and 6ft deep dug out, roofed with corrugated iron, the earth piled back on top, and a thick matt of ferns and ivy planted over it. There is a picture of the Van Meters' three children, David, Dolly Be and Edith, standing in the entrance, David shielding his eyes as he looks to the sky. In another image a group of friends are lying on the long grass of the lawn, also looking skyward and, the caption says, waiting for Japanese bombers.

Come they would, but not quite yet. There were false alarms of an attack. Once, in the middle of lunch, they heard the faint sound of an air raid alert, which meant that planes had crossed the Yunnan border and might be over Kunming in a matter of minutes. Beatrice Van Meter remembered that, while

Lester took their children to the shelter: 'I hurried up three flights of stairs to get things we might need. It would be cold and damp in the dugout, so I got blankets, coats, oil sheets, sleeping bags and a medical kit and dumped them down the stairs. I heard a shout because I almost caught Auntie under the deluge... Somehow it seemed funny even then.

The Van Meter children at Alf's air raid shelter

'Dear Auntie! She wouldn't dream of being caught anywhere overnight without her many curlers for her snow-white hair! She ran back in the house to get them... They had quite a good size dugout, one of the few in the city, and by sitting close together many pushed in. Uncle stood at his open gate inviting inside neighbours, church friends who had no safer place to go. Many strangers also came inside the gate and waited quietly, feeling they were more secure with Pastor Evans.

'To while the time away and calm the frightened children, we pretended we were rabbits and this was our cosy little nest away down where it was cool and dark.' They sang and Beatrice played guitar. 'After several hours we were astonished to see the Evanses' cook come creeping in, his arms loaded. He said we had hurried too fast with our lunch, he had cooked some dessert and he expected us to eat it! We obliged.... we heard later that the Japanese planes came within ten minutes of our city. Then they became confused because they couldn't find their target. We were hidden under the storm clouds.' Yunnan, she notes, means Cloudy South.

Among those that Alf and Bessie took under their wing were a young mission couple, Ted and Isobel Harrison, newcomers to Kunming. Their house was a few doors down from the Evanses. Isobel wrote a letter home that gives a wonderfully warm portrait of Bessie and Alf. It shows them planning a future beyond their work as missionaries, building that retirement home across the lake, a place where they could live out their final years. They must be painfully aware the war is a threat to that future, but Isobel's letter shows them doing all they can to cling to normal life. The Harrisons are invited to travel with them to the lakeside house on a number of occasions in July and August, 1940. Alf and Bessie tended to cross the lake each Monday, their day off.

To get there they take rickshaws for the 20-minute journey to the canal that leads to the lake. Isobel writes: 'Mrs Evans has her own rickshaw, and it is quite a superior vehicle – she looks like a grand duchess as she glides along the street in it.' At the canal they transfer to a small boat, a sampan, and Alf and Bessie always hire the same one. 'For most of the sampan owners, their sampan is their only dwelling – most are born in it, live all their lives and die in it. Over the middle third of the sampan they have a bamboo awning which is all that protects them from the elements.'

It takes another 25 minutes to reach the lake, the sampan steered by the men while the two women row, standing up and facing forward, arms outstretched as they plunge the oar into the water then haul the boat forward. They do this without pause for the two and half hours it takes to cross the lake. Out on the water there is a splendid panoramic view of the mountains that surround the plain on which Kunming stands.

Out here they see how fishing is done. 'Some sampans were stationary in the middle of the lake. Perched on one side of these boats were about a dozen cormorants. When a cormorant sighted a fish it dived into the water, but if successful it was unable to swallow its catch, for a metal ring was around the bird's throat. Choking on the fish, the Cormorant sought relief by approaching its owner. He turned the bird upside down and shook the fish free. After the seventh catch the owner removed the ring, so when the Cormorant made its eighth catch it had its reward, and swallowed the fish.'

Alf and Bessie's retirement home is built on a spur of land jutting into the lake at a place called Hsi Shan. On three sides they have an uninterrupted view over the water, on the fourth of the wooded slopes of the mountain. Because foreigners are not allowed to own property, the house is held in the names of Pearl and John.

The Van Meters also came here: 'The nights across the lake were especially lovely. We walked through Auntie's fragrant garden where the lavender, jasmine and gardenia grew. We looked over the wall towards Kunming where the city twinkled across the water. Above, the Milky Way spread its lace.'

High above the house are sacred Buddhist temples tended by monks, which the Evanses, Isobel and other guests climb to, up a thousand steps. The entrance to the main temple is guarded by two fierce looking idols, as large as elephants. In the temple itself are 500 figures, the Lohans or disciples of Buddha, each unique. In the temple courtyard is a pond full of goldfish, and sacred lotus plants. Lotus leaves are much bigger than water lilies and their flowers are like pink tulips when in bud, but open out to resemble huge pink roses. Buddha is often depicted sitting cross-legged on a lotus flower, in contemplation. Some devotees will visit annually, others just once in a lifetime.

What Isobel describes is in some sense Alf and Bessie's escape from reality: reality being Kunming, a city not just of well-heeled refugees but also of people who represent every segment of the global conflict into which the world has been plunged. Len Constantine's account shows that side of things. He writes: 'To be in Kunming in the summer of 1940 was a curious experience. In the one hotel catering for foreigners there lived together, in very close quarters, British and Americans, German Nazis (mostly pilots connected with the Eurasian Airways and not yet expelled from China) and Jewish refugees. In the hotel lounge they separated into small groups, discussing the news in low whispers and ignoring each other. The Germans were on top of the world. They had boisterous celebrations in restaurants and came back to the hotel rolling drunk in the middle of the night. The other nationalities gave them a wide berth.'

The Battle of Britain, in which the Royal Air Force successfully defended England's skies from Nazi Germany's Luftwaffe, brought hope in the summer of 1940, but also disbelief among some. Could the figure of 195 German planes shot down in one day be true? 'Some Americans openly said the BBC was telling lies: it was trying to bolster morale. We wondered and hoped. As day followed day and the expected invasion did not materialise, we knew the figures must have been true.'

Yet successes over Southern England had no bearing on the threat to Kunming from the planes of the Japanese.

37 THE DAY OF DEATH

September 30 1940 was a day of terror in Kunming. Twenty-seven Japanese planes flew in low. The sky seemed full of these gleaming silver instruments of death. Scores of bombs were dropped right across the city, and the accompanying fighters machine-gunned people in the streets. Beatrice Van Meter remembered: 'There is no word to describe the barren feeling of absolute nakedness when enemy planes were swooping overhead dropping their bombs. The only true shelter was under the very wings of God.'

Because of so many false alarms, many did not leave the city, as they were ordered to, when the alarms sounded. John was among those who stayed. Usually the planes came no nearer than the airport, which they blitzed, before turning back. John was sitting in the living room with two friends. Suddenly machine-gun fire from enemy planes ripped across the garden. The three rushed toward the shelter but, frightened by the gun-fire, dashed instead towards a small outhouse.

'Then came the terrible sound of bombs exploding. I ran to hide in the corner of the building. I could feel and hear my heart pounding as hard as it could, fully expecting a bomb would hit near me at any second. The moment of death was at hand.' Mercifully, he was spared. As the sounds of bombing ceased and the roar of the planes receded, he stepped out beneath a sky pitch black with smoke and dust. A horror confronted him.

'I saw a dead body, lying face down on the ground. I thought it was Paul, one of our servants, but then Paul showed up. A dead man had somehow been catapulted into our garden. As we searched for more victims, we first found the body of a young child near our front door, then the body of a woman lying not far away under a hedge, and finally another unidentified girl, seven or eight years of age.

'We later found out that these bodies were those of a poor peasant family of four who lived next door to us, just beyond the compound walls. Their house had scored a direct hit. The entire family was wiped out, and there was a hole 50ft deep where the house once stood... If that Japanese bombardier had pushed the release button one second earlier, I would've been among the dead that day.' When night fell, the entire city was dark, the only sound that of wailing. This was the first of a series of terrifying bombings.

Alf and Bessie were not at home when the raid happened, and Alf's report to Mission House in London is more detached, but itemises the damage caused: 'During the first raid, Number 67, our house, was badly damaged, roof and windows; and three dead bodies [rather than the four John remembers] came flying into the garden, two of them over the top of the house; a large stone also crashed through the roof.... The second crash brought damage to Harrison's house, Number 47, and also to the church premises.'

Ted Harrison was at home when the bombs fell, but his wife, Isobel, had gone into town. Her account vividly captures the terror of the many hundreds forced to flee the bombs: 'I shall never forget the date of the first air raid. It was the longest day I've ever lived through.' Isobel had gone into the city with a Canadian nurse, Miss Gay, who had to visit the British consulate to get her passport and other papers dealt with. They were sitting in the consulate, just within the North Gate at the opposite side of the city to the mission, when the alarm sounded.

The consul told them to go outside the gate, where a car would be waiting to take them out into the safety of open country. They were caught up in a great flood of people fleeing the same way, but they found no car waiting for them. They joined the crowd: 'I'd never seen such a sight in all my life. The trail was miles long; a real target for the machine guns of the Jap fighter planes.' About a mile out they met Mr McGeary, a secretary at the American consulate who they knew. He took charge, and led them away from the crowds and into the fields, where he said they would be safer. Yet, as they tramped across the fields, 'Chinese soldiers bobbed up, seemingly from nowhere, shouting wildly at us as though we had committed some unforgivable offence. Mr McGeary got really hot and bothered. He could do nothing but swear at them for he couldn't speak the Yunnanese dialect.'

They realised they had stumbled across a military camp, and turned to leave, 'but as I hurried away, I found myself confronted by a soldier with a bayonet pointing towards me, and that weapon was too near my tummy to be pleasant! Miss Gay, fortunately, could converse with the soldiers, so she came to the rescue and assured them we would do whatever they commanded us to do.

'By this time, McGeary was being marched off between two soldiers, and I fully expected they were going to put the three of us in prison. We were marched off too, and as we went Miss Gay explained to me the reason for their conduct and anger. McGeary was dressed in white from head to foot, even shoes which were mostly white. A few days earlier the government had ordered everyone to wear dark clothes and certainly not white. The soldiers must have decided that here was a foreigner who was disobeying orders in order to attract the Jap airmen to their camp area.' Isobel threw her green mackintosh cape over McGeary and they were led to the shelter of a clump of trees, and told not to move. They plucked grass and spread it over McGeary's white trousers as he sat on the ground. Two soldiers kept guard over them.

Forty-five minutes later, they heard bombs being dropped on the city and saw great clouds of dust rising. Then, those twenty-seven departing planes passed overhead. Isobel was terrified for her husband, Ted. She was desperate to get back to see if he was safe. It was two hours before the all-clear sounded and they had got back to the North Gate, but as they arrived the alarm sounded again. They were turned back with a group of German Jews, and it was another hour before they could enter the city.

There, Isobel learned that 'a house in the Church Missionary Society Hospital compound had received a direct hit, as had houses in our area. I've never had such a fright in my life; our garden adjoined the hospital compound.' They managed to find a rickshaw: 'On the ride, I didn't seem to notice anything or anyone until I suddenly saw a Chinese girl, a friend of ours, who waved to me. She must've seen I looked anxious, for she called in a loud voice "your husband, he's waiting for you." I was so relieved I wept for joy. I was still weeping when Ted met us in the main street from which ours branches off. Both roads just looked as though there had been an earthquake.'

Ted had had a very narrow escape. He was in the garden, running for their dugout, when bombs dropped all around him. He was hit by wood and stones flung into the garden, which gave him a bloody nose, but was otherwise unharmed. At 8:30am the next day, they had to trek out into the country following another air raid warning. There were to be many more.

Alf decided it was time to leave the city, and took as many people as he could across the lake to the relative safety of the retirement house. He told London: 'The day after the first bombing, the Harrisons came across to the lake residence, and since that time we have been here, going to and from the city each day to attend to work, and to keep up the morale of the servants left in charge of premises.' For the next fortnight Alf and Bessie sheltered thirty people, after that around twenty. Alf said: 'If this place had not been almost completed, I do not know where we should have gone.' By now, neither the Harrisons' nor the Evanses' houses in the city were habitable: windows blown out, ceilings down, holes in their roofs.

On October 17 the Methodist church was badly damaged, but left standing, and services continued every Saturday and Sunday evening.

Kunming was a particular target of the Japanese for two reasons: it was the only entry point to free China accessible to the outside world, and the Chinese air force had relocated here after Japan took the former capital, Nanking. It wasn't much of an air force, equipped with just a few planes of World War I vintage – old, slow, and virtually useless against the new Japanese fighters and bombers. They could offer little resistance. John writes: 'We were sitting ducks, thousands of people being used as target practice.' It would not be until the following year that the Chinese gained the means to fight back. John would play his part in that endeavour.

38 JOHN GOES TO WAR

For the next year, Kunming was at the mercy of Japanese bombing raids. It was not until December 1941, with the arrival of a new fighting unit, the American Volunteer Group (AVG), that the fightback began. The AVG was led by a remarkable man called Claire L. Chennault, known as Old Leather Face, who, after his retirement from the US Army Air Corps, had been recruited by Chiang Kai Shek, initially to lead a small group of American civilians training Chinese airmen. Later he took command of the Chinese Air force and was sent to America to buy hundreds of fighter planes.

He was a hero to John: 'Chennault was a daredevil pilot as a young man. He started off doing circus stunts. He would tie off the joystick, jump out of the cockpit, and stand on the wing of his aircraft in a move called the Flying Trapeze, while the plane performed diving, looping, breath-taking feats, before gasping onlookers.'

The American President, Franklin D. Roosevelt, recognised that if China did not halt the Japanese advance, the whole of Asia would fall to them. John writes: 'FDR agreed to form the AVG – and that involved giving planes to China, and forming a fighting force. First, the president signed a secret executive order, allowing active pilots to fight in China as volunteers. Officers in the army and navy could quit their jobs, go into the AVG, and were guaranteed their old spots back when they returned.'

Chennault commanded this force and, in 1941, moved with it to Kunming, where they fought to repel the Japanese advance north-east from Burma. Their P40 Warhawk aircraft bore Chinese colours, but flew under American command. In Kunming, they needed interpreters, and looked to the newly-formed Southwest Union University, an amalgam of institutions that had had to move to Kunming. Many students were studying English there, and John was among them.

'My foster parents heard about this recruitment and training, and told me I

John the soldier

should join up. My foster father got a letter from the British Consulate to introduce me, saying I was fluent in English and Chinese, that I'd just returned from St Stephen's, and that I'd be very useful.'

John was accepted as one of fifty trainee interpreters. Then came a key turning point in the Second World War.

'During my six-month training, we heard the news that Japan had bombed Pearl Harbour. It was December 8, 1941. We all jumped for joy when we read the news in the Kunming daily paper. We knew we now had a very powerful ally to fight Japan: the United States of America. We were no longer alone against the genocidal Japanese imperial forces... We all had a patriotic feeling we were helping repel the invaders from our land.'

Len Constantine wrote: 'The astounding news was received with jubilation. We might almost say the news that the American fleet, Hong Kong and Malaya were being attacked was received with cheers. What the Chinese had been hoping and praying for over four years had happened. America was in the war. Smiles lit up every face that day. "How long will Japan last?" It was generally agreed that in three months all would be over. That was even a conservative estimate. Didn't America have thousands of the most modern types of aeroplanes which could smash Japan to atoms?'

In fact the optimism proved to be premature: the war would grind on for another four years but, throughout that long struggle, Kunming would never again succumb to an air attack from the Japanese.

39 BESSIE'S FINAL DAYS

Maybe it was from the sick soldier she was nursing that Bessie caught typhus, or perhaps she got it from a dirty public rickshaw she rode in on her way to church in Kunming.

Either way, Bessie did not live to see Kunming's change of fortunes. She died on June 10, 1941, at the house across Dianchi Lake where she and Alf had hoped to spend a peaceful retirement. She had been sick for ten days, but it was only by chance that John came to visit on the day she died. He was aged twenty, in the middle of his training to fight with the Americans, but used the opportunity of a rare day off to take a sampan across the lake to see his parents. He knew Bessie's health was fragile, but was shocked to learn that she was suddenly so close to death.

'When I entered the room, I wasn't sure if mother recognised me. The English nurse, Miss Tingdale, said she didn't have much time. I was at her bedside, staring at her old, wrinkled face. Time ticked by so slowly. She was very weak, and could not speak. As I stood there – sad, bewildered and helpless – my mother finally stopped breathing. It was very quiet in the room. The nurse asked us to leave so she could attend to her. Father and I slowly walked down the stairs, and suddenly we both burst into tears.'

Five days after Bessie's death Alf wrote to Harold Rattenbury, the mission secretary, in London. His letter has all of Alf's formality, and stoicism, but also a profound sadness: 'You will have received my telegram, giving the news of Mrs Evans passing to higher service. She was ill for about ten days, with what proved to be typhus. It was hoped it would prove to be the milder type as usually found in Kunming, but this is getting worse each year, and by the tenth morning, her temperature had gone up to 105.

'Mrs Evans had gone into the city on May 31 with Mr Pratt [a missionary who was staying with them at the time] for the Sunday services on June 1. I stayed here as I had had some tummy trouble. But on the Sunday morning the [air raid warning] alarm sounded early, 7:30am, and they had to get off to the country and did not get back until the afternoon. Mrs Evans came across here by boat, but upon arrival was in collapse...

'We had the funeral yesterday, and a large crowd gathered at the cemetery, and also many friends at the house here... Mrs Evans had been thirty-eight years in China and her life has been one of complete love and loving service for all who came around her. I have told friends that it was better that she should pass to her higher service from China, where she was surrounded by friends who loved her very much, rather than she should return to England and be among strangers in her homeland.'

Bessie was buried, John writes, at a small English garden cemetery for foreigners in Kunming. 'On her tombstone, father chose the words: "For those we love within the pale, who once were comrades of our way, we thank thee lord".'

What of Pearl? She couldn't be at the funeral, or at her foster father's side when he needed her most, cut off as she was in Japanese-occupied Shanghai. This pained her very much, as one of her few surviving letters to Mildred Pacey makes clear: 'Yes, it was a great shock to me when I heard of mother's death. I was not at all well at the time. I felt sorry for father more than anyone. They were planning to retire to the little house across the lake and now mother is gone. I was glad that mother had her wish [to at least spend some time there]. The house was nearly finished and she also planted the flowers in the garden. It seemed that was the end, she had been very tired. She was looking after a soldier in the village at the time...

'As you know one cannot get through [Japanese occupied] Haiphong now, and it is a very long journey up the Burma Road, and for one thing I have not the money myself as I only went home last year. I feel it is my duty to go but what can I do? Father has written to say that he does not wish me to alter my plans and that he is alright. The only thing I can do now is to wait until the war is over and see what can be done.'

Pearl is relieved that John is with Alf, but reveals that he is still a worry to his foster father: 'I hope before father leaves us that he can make him a good man, from other sources I heard that he was not such a good lad as mother thought he was, so I am hoping that he will improve within these few years.'

Pearl's own health was not good. For some months she had found it hard to stand up, or to walk, and feared she might have tuberculosis of the spine, but tests showed it was actually arthritis. 'I had electrical treatment and massage for a long time and I am now only on seven hours duty. The doctor has injected Novocaine into my leg three times but it has not done much good. I still have some pain at times... so there is not much hope of my becoming matron in my life, as I have to take great care and rest as much as possible.'

Pearl tells Mildred that the matron, Miss Taylor, has made a vague promise to help her get a Florence Nightingale Scholarship to study administration, for which she would travel to England. 'It will be very nice if I do. In that case I would see you then, but I'm not building very much hopes on it. Miss Taylor can be very sweet when she wants you to do something.'

Pearl makes a passing reference to Dr Norah Li, the close companion she met in Hankow in 1936, and who seems to have filled the gap left in her life after Mildred's marriage. They are working in the same hospital, where 'they want her to teach the midwifery students,' but Pearl says no more. She signs her letter 'yours lovingly'.

When he sent me Pearl's letter, Mildred's son Arnold picked up on her reference to John, saying that it 'confirms my suspicion that Uncle Alf was disappointed in him and did not like to talk about him. My parents didn't talk about him, either, though they spoke much about Uncle Alf and Pan-yan, so I know almost nothing about John.'

Yet Bessie's passing seems to have brought John and Alf closer together. John writes: 'After my mother's death, I tried to spend as much time with father as possible. He was still across the lake, but I made the trip frequently. I helped out more around the house as well, cooking dinner and the like. I helped with house chores, because he was always so tired. He worked like a dog his entire life and was getting old...

'With the American Volunteer Group I worked twenty-four hours straight and then was able to take two full days off. I liked to spend those two days with father. It was always very relaxing and peaceful, and we felt mother's presence. We both liked to read Chinese or English books, and listen to music or the news on a crystal set [an early radio]. I enjoyed cooking dinner for him and listening to classical music on the gramophone. He always looked after me, and wanted the best for me.'

Becoming a widower strengthened Alf's determination to retire from his post as committee's representative at the end of 1941, two years before the scheduled end of his term of service. The complaints about him had continued, and he had had enough. He told Harold Rattenbury: 'I hope to serve the mission as best I can for the remainder of my time, and I had hoped to carry on until some one of the next senior men could relieve me... I'm sorry that I have to write this during this time of stress. I would have preferred that we on the field and you at home would both carry on under the assurance that each was trying to do his best, but it is evident that my efforts are not giving satisfaction, therefore it were better for you to appoint someone else in my stead. Please don't think this is said in a huff.'

At least Alf was not alone at the house across the lake. The bombings in Kunming meant that there were always mission staff and others in need of accommodation. The mission formalised things by paying Alf 500 Chinese dollars a month, so that he was not out of pocket. Ted and Isobel Harrison were among many who remained ever-grateful for the sanctuary with Alf during the months when the city held so many perils. They also felt Bessie's death profoundly. Isobel wrote: 'It was a great blow to us, for we had a great affection for Auntie Bess. She really was a dear and mothered me from the very beginning. I personally feel that I have lost my first friend, and best friend, in China. Like most folk who are getting on in years, she lived very much in the past, but it was such a glorious past that I did not tire of hearing about it.

'The Chinese folk in the village in which their retirement house stood loved her and went to her with all their aches and pains and sick babies – even though they were not Christians they had complete trust in her. I've known mothers come miles with their sick babies for her to treat. I feel extremely sorry for Uncle, because they were absolutely all in all to each other – just like a newly married couple.'

40 THE FLYING TIGERS

John was in the thick of the fight-back against the Japanese. The American Volunteer Group (AVG) arrived at Kunming's only airport, seven miles from the city, on December 21, 1941, thirteen days after the attack on Pearl Harbour.

'The day after the AVG arrived, the Japanese came again to bomb Kunming. This sortie was small – ten bombers from Hanoi with no escort. They knew Kunming's anti-aircraft guns were useless, but apparently they didn't know the Americans had arrived, and were waiting for them. Chennault got the information – the enemy was on its way – and sent his squadron of eight aloft with thirty minutes to spare. The planes climbed rapidly and circled high above at about 15,000 feet, with all eyes glued to the southern horizon, eight men with a thumb hovering over the radio button, looking for that speck in the sky, ready to sound the final alarm. "Bogies sighted at 11:30" came crackling over the air. Everybody's blood pressure jumped.

'The Japanese had no idea. For months, with impunity, they had dropped thousands of bombs on defenceless Chinese people. It was a turkey shoot, a duck hunt. They just blasted away. But on this day, it would be different. It was my day off, and I happened to be in Kunming. I was in the front row of a deadly, living production. I was lucky I wasn't killed.'

John remembered a bright, sunny day. The third and final air raid warning had been sounding for several minutes when he heard engines, straining in the distance, and saw planes zipping across the sky. Suddenly, from high above, a Chinese P40 Warhawk dived straight down, guns blazing, and scored a direct hit on a Japanese bomber. Black smoke billowed from the plane as it spiralled to earth.

'Everything happened so quickly. The images are still imprinted on my mind. The roar of plane engines. The smoke in the sky. People cheering and screaming with unexpected joy. The Americans had come.' When a second bomber was downed the rest turned to flee, back to their base in Vietnam. The P40s pursued them, chased and eliminated all but one that managed to limp back to Hanoi. 'When the sun set that night, the streets of Kunming were filled with light – merriment, laughter, and excited chatter. The next day, the paper printed the joyous news. The Chinese were almost delirious. All day, the city enjoyed excited talk and bustling, hopeful people.'

This was a truly historic day: it marked the first occasion in the Second World War that the Japanese were defeated by a force inside China, and the first time an air engagement had been won by China. In Kunming's daily paper the next morning it was said that these American pilots were so good, they looked like tigers flying in the sky. 'The AVG guys saw this quote, and so did their commander, Chennault, who said: "That's good, let's name this group the Flying Tigers".' Pilots painted the face of a tiger on the noses of their planes, mouth open in a roar, sharp white teeth gleaming.

At the same time as the Japanese were bombing China from the south west, their armies were plunging into the country from Hong Kong, in the south east. Less than eight hours after Pearl Harbour, the Japanese launched an invasion with 52,000 troops against 14,000 British and Canadian defenders. The battle of Hong Kong lasted two weeks, ending on Christmas Day, 1941. The missionary Kenneth May wrote: 'The storm has broken over us in the East. At the moment we are full of anxiety for the fate of our fellow workers in occupied China, and now of Hong Kong and our friends there. We are fully aware that if things go badly in Malaya, at Singapore or in Burma, we are in a precarious position, but our faith is in God, who is our father, and we are calm. In Russia, and in Libya, the main theatres of the war, there is much to rejoice over.'

There were practical implications for the missions, too. Their payments from London could no longer be made through Hong Kong, leaving them scrabbling for other routes for the transfer of funds essential to their work. Inflation was soaring: 'Prices are rising with leaps and bounds. We are therefore threatened with a cut in our income of about 50 per cent while prices have doubled in the last three months.'

John's old school in Hong Kong, St Stephen's College, was at the heart of the fighting. It had been converted into a hospital for wounded allied troops. A fierce battle took place before it succumbed; one of the last defensive positions to surrender to the Imperial Japanese Army. John wrote: 'Japanese soldiers burst into the college and murdered hundreds of the wounded, stabbing and shooting them in their beds. It was known as the St Stephen's College Incident. It was actually a massacre. The Japanese later merged the college with part of Stanley prison to form the Stanley internment camp.'

With America fully committed to the war, Chennault's position, and that of the AVG, needed to be formalised. The volunteer force was disbanded, replaced by the US 10th Air Force, which transferred its headquarters from India to China to become the US 14th Air Force. Some AVG pilots and personnel stayed on, as did Chennault, who was promoted to Brigadier General. Had Kunming fallen to the Japanese, the course of the war might have been very different. 'At a minimum,' John wrote, 'the Tigers saved thousands of innocent Chinese lives. At the maximum, they may be credited with saving China.'

In 1943, his training completed, John was assigned to fighter control as a translator. 'It was a 24/7 job. We were on site twenty-four hours straight, on-call and ready to go. Occasionally we took short naps at night, but always fully dressed and ready to bounce up at the slightest alarm. If something happened, a Chinese soldier would call us. All our waking moments were in the control room, where we worked directly with top brass.' Translators performed a vital role. 'American officers and enlisted men were on duty daily in the control room, and verbal exchanges were constant, as Americans, with no Mandarin, needed translations of all information pertinent to the war. I was talking constantly, using English and Mandarin almost every minute, processing a lot of information.... the work was very tiring.'

The control room monitored the movement of China-based fighters and bombers, as well as the 'hump' pilots, who flew transport planes over the hump of the Himalayas from north east India. The transporters performed a critical role: bringing war supplies – Jeeps, guns, gasoline and anything else that could be flown. 'One day when I was going to work, I saw a transport plane coming from India. It was flying low and circling to land when, out of the blue, the plane suddenly burst into flames and crashed. I was stunned. Then, as all of us stood staring at the sky, it started raining Chinese money. It was like a scene out of a movie.'

American pilots commanded the skies above Kunming from the day they arrived until the Japanese surrender on September 2, 1945, almost four years later. 'The number of Chinese lives saved is uncountable. Even today, the bones of many all-American boys lie scattered around the hills of Kunming, a lasting tribute to US-China relations.'

In June 1944 John received an order that would take him away from his homeland for forty years: he was being posted to America, as chief translator for a group of eighty Chinese air force cadets being sent there for advance training. The move would also tear him away from Alf. The pain this caused suggests that, perhaps with John's success serving the war effort, relations between the two had improved. Was Alf impressed at the application John was now showing? Another thought occurs to me: hearing about Alf's clashes with authority, his determination to do things his way, makes me think that perhaps he and John had more in common than Alf might once have liked to admit.

John sought Alf's advice before accepting the posting. 'Foster-father Evans agreed it was my destiny and, emotionally, he bid me farewell... it was painful to leave him. He had lost his wife and soulmate just three years before. And I would be leaving soon.'

41 THE FREE AND THE INTERNED

As the war ground on, the missionaries in Yunnan were relatively better off than those in areas of the country under Japanese occupation. But only relatively. Even here, in Free China, they lived under constant threat, and continued their work with great difficulty.

While Kunming was no longer being bombed, in the summer of 1942 the Japanese crossed from Burma, now Myanmar, into Yunnan. Len Constantine wrote: 'There seemed to be nothing to stop them, they could come right on to Kunming. It was difficult to know just where they were. Rumours flew thick and fast... people have seen them just the other side of the mountain.' The only reliable information came, faint and crackling, over the radio from England: 'Nightly, we listened to London to know whether we must run away or not. When people said the Japanese were just around the corner we quoted what London had said the previous night. "Don't believe the radio" we were told "the Japanese will be here while London is still telling you that they are 100 miles away."'

In fact the Japanese never did come to Kunming. However, the plight of missionaries in the occupied provinces became dire. At first, they had been interned; confined to their own compounds, but allowed to continue their work. In 1943 the policy would change. From then, it was determined, all British and American influence must be eliminated. The Japanese decided to ship missionaries to Portuguese East Africa, and large numbers were taken to Shanghai, where they were held in internment camps to await shipment.

However, there were no ships to spare, and so they remained there. Over half the China missionaries were in enemy hands, the Methodists had seventy staff interned, including thirty men and twenty-three wives. Pearl was in Shanghai too, fearful that her connection with the Methodist mission might cause her to be interned.

Among those who lived through all this was a man who was a second-generation missionary within his own family. Kenneth Parsons was the son of Harry Parsons. Ken had become a candidate for the Methodist ministry in 1937, and was due to travel to China in 1940. He asked to be stationed in Yunnan, in Free China, where he had spent the first ten years of his life.

Harold Rattenbury, mission secretary at London headquarters, had other ideas, insisting he go to Hankow in Central China, which was under Japanese occupation. Ken writes: 'I protested that war was imminent, but Mr Rattenbury assured me there was absolutely no prospect whatsoever that there would be a war. After several delays, I eventually said a very difficult goodbye to Peggy, my fiancée, and sailed from heavily bombed Liverpool on Christmas Day.'

When Ken had reached Rangoon, Rattenbury was again being warned by missionaries on the ground that Ken should fly instead to Free China. Yet, Rattenbury insisted he go to Hankow, which he dutifully did. While other missionary societies had pulled their people out of the city, the Methodist mission staff, fifty-two men, women and children, were still there, despite three increasingly urgent warnings from the British consul that they should pull out.

The inevitable happened. Ken writes: 'Early on December 8 1941 a Japanese soldier banged on the compound door with a letter saying war had been declared. All the British and Americans were immediately put under house arrest until [two years later] we were taken down to Shanghai and interned in prisoner of war camps... Being single, I was herded with 1,070 other men – British, Americans and Dutch – into an old, disused, bug-ridden BAT [British American Tobacco] warehouse in Pootung on the other side of the Hwang-poo river facing the Shanghai Bund', or waterfront.

'We were better off than the men in the forces in that we were not forced to work, but living conditions were very rough and we were always desperately hungry... The whole of Pootung was heavily armed, with hundreds of anti-aircraft guns, land mines, pill boxes etc and thousands of Japanese military crowded into adjoining buildings. In 1945 the Americans started dive bombing, shattering our windows. The air raid shelters we dug flooded immediately. The Americans planned to carpet bomb us later in August and we knew perfectly well, if this happened, we had very little chance of survival.'

They were saved by the American atomic bombing of Hiroshima and Nagasaki, which brought Japanese surrender, and the end of the war.

Meanwhile, the war years were an increasing struggle for Alf, despite his living in the relative safety of Kunming. After the loss of Bessie, his clashes with Rattenbury and the other missionaries became more profound. Was that because Bessie's calming influence was now gone? Or had he just grown angrier? Rattenbury thought Alf should not be allowed to retire across the lake to his house at Hsi Shan, but be ordered to move to another mission town. Better still, go back to England. If he were allowed to stay so close to Kunming, Rattenbury feared, Alf was bound to interfere with and undermine the authority of whoever replaced him.

Kenneth May did not see why Alf shouldn't live where he liked, and said:

'Were I appointed to Kunming the fact that he was living so near would be one of the attractions of the appointment. Hsi Shan is sufficiently distant to prevent undue influence in the work, and yet it is near enough to place the ripe wisdom of a man of such long experience at the disposal of the younger man.'

It was acknowledged that Alf had been a great asset, but Rattenbury to a great extent, and May and others to perhaps a slightly lesser one, found his way of working very frustrating. Alf never filed the financial schedules and accounts for his district either in full or on time, and made decisions unilaterally that should have been referred up. He was a maverick.

It transpired that, when Harold Rattenbury was on his China tour, Bessie had told him how upset she was at the way Alf was being treated when switching roles from district chairman to committee's representative. Rattenbury had since told Alf what Bessie said to him, and Alf replied: 'You mentioned that Mrs Evans was troubled about the change of administration made when you were round on your visit. I am not aware that such was true of her... From what I know of her at that time, she would support my retiring from that office, but she was upset at certain rumours and innuendos that were floating around of which we need not now trouble ourselves. It was natural and right that she should feel upset over these, but my reply was "that my service in South West China was quite able to take care of my reputation, but if it were not so, then the reputation was not worth fighting about".'

We don't know what those rumours were, but perhaps they involved hints at financial impropriety. At other points in this correspondence it was stressed from all sides that, while Alf might not tell people what he was spending and why, there was no hint that he was acting in anything other than good faith, and in the interests of the mission as he saw them.

I conclude from this that Alf was a proud man, and headstrong. He believed his way was right (and it probably was), but the bureaucrats wanted procedure to be followed, and Alf didn't do that. I find I like him all the more as I read into his conflicts with authority. The more I learn about his life, and as conditions for missionaries in China become worse and worse, the more I feel a wonderful sense of vindication as he is proved right time after time.

There are several further rows with Rattenbury. One comes when Alf, acting on his own initiative, has his old, bomb-damaged house in Kunming repaired and rented to a British military mission. Rattenbury tells May 'it is not surprising that Evans went ahead, I believe without any word to you, and clinched the matter. That is his way and it is no use questioning it now.'

Another row is over lorries. Rattenbury tells May that Alf 'is a good deal upset over what he thinks is a misunderstanding about the purchase of trucks, and the way in which generally I am dealing with him as committee's representative... He is evidently much aggrieved.'

In July 1942 Alf becomes desperately needed: not by the Methodists, but by the Anglicans, as superintendent at their hospital, keeping the accounts and managing the business side in support of the medical director.

Characteristically, Alf has accepted the post without consulting his bosses, who are annoyed. Grudgingly, Rattenbury says that if this is an emergency, Alf can do it for a few months, not more than twelve, 'but we simply do not contemplate anything more permanent.'

There is sniping from other missionaries, too. One, James Heady, writes: 'I have a feeling from what I have observed that Mr Evans is tolerated rather than welcomed at the hospital. The doctor heartily welcomes him because he takes a tremendous load off his shoulders, and it was at his urgent request that Evans took up the job [but they] would be very much happier if they had an Anglican doing the job.' Alf does a good deal more than twelve months at the CMS hospital, eventually working there for three and a half years.

James Heady gives an insight into Alf's daily life during this time: 'Mr Evans is at present receiving from the hospital a sum which enables him to keep his house at Hsi Shan going with servants in there while he is away, to pay his fares to and fro and so on. While in the hospital he gets his food there. But he is not receiving anything like the amount he would be getting if he were simply employed on a business footing.'

In addition to keeping the accounts and managing the business side of the hospital, Alf 'exercises a good influence on the staff, takes part in leading prayers, and so on. He also often preaches on a Sunday at a chapel near his house at Hsi Shan.'

In some ways the Methodists are glad to see the back of Alf. With a new man, Edward Moody, doing the mission accounts, Rattenbury says: 'It really begins a new epoch... I feel at last we are getting straight and thank God for it.'

In other ways they still need Alf, and work out a role for him in his retirement. He becomes a paid supernumerary, meaning he will continue to do some missionary work after his retirement in 1943. They do this partly because they fear Alf will not be able to make ends meet once his salary at the hospital ceases.

Meanwhile, the circuits within Yunnan are increasingly being funded by their local congregations, rather than with contributions from English parishes funnelled through London. British missionaries are stepping back from positions of power in favour of Chinese, Miao and Nosu ministers.

Alf seems to be happy with his life, or as happy as he can be since he lost Bessie just three years before. One missionary, Paul Jefferies, who goes out to China in 1944, finds Alf living in retirement in his lake-side house, where he had made a fine garden and was growing his own vegetables. On his first Sunday in China, Jeffries went for a restaurant meal with Alf, who tells him that he spends time tending his garden and occasionally preaching.

Many others find sanctuary from war in the house across the lake.

42 A GUEST IN 1944

In 1944, as the Japanese advanced across China, women missionaries, wives and children were evacuated to Kunming from Wenchow, Hunan and Kukong, and Alf took some of them in.

Jean Moore was one. She stayed for four months in 1944, and found a house that had become very much a bachelor pad. Bessie's high standards of housekeeping had not been maintained. Jean had been living in Kukong, and was evacuated with her three young children, Margaret, Dierdre and John, and two other mothers with young families. She wrote: 'It was a two- to three-hour flight to Kunming and for the three of us and the children our first journey by plane... Each child was handed over to a serviceman as his particular charge. The idea being that he would hold the child if it was necessary to jump... Halfway through the trip, through skies of cloudless blue, the radio officer announced "the Allies have landed in Normandy!" It was D-Day June 6, 1944, a day I shall never forget.'

Driven to Alf's home on an ammunition carrier, they find a comfortably furnished house 'patterned on a half-timbered English style.' They saw little of their host: 'He was acting as business manager of the Church Missionary Society hospital, where he lived for most of the week, only returning to his home by bus at the weekend to work in his garden. Here he successfully grew flowers and enjoyed the views of the lake and the surrounding hills.'

The housekeeping, Jean felt, left a lot to be desired. 'Uncle's staff consisted of a Miao tribesman, who shopped at the market and acted as cook, and a young lad who watered the flowers and wielded an ineffectual broom both indoors and on the clay paths. To complete the menagerie were two rangy dogs, which were thin, underfed and completely untrained, though not bad tempered.'

Bessie's presence was still felt in the house, three years after her death: 'The main bedroom, allocated to me because I had three children, was still full of Mrs Evans' belongings, the wardrobe and drawers being filled with clothing which I did not like to move. The kitchen was primitive in the extreme with open cooking holes in a brick shelf on which one placed pots over wood and charcoal fires.

'The cook, who wore trousers and a filthy vest, sported long, grime-encrusted nails and clearly took a dim view of our invasion of his territory, because his life has been one of ease and non-interference till then. He could cook rice and vegetables, which were abundant in Kunming's fertile soil and temperate climate, but his European menu consisted of roast leg of mutton and pancakes, these a mixture of flour, water and sugar, fried in oil and the consistency of rubber.

'We wondered if we could hire any women servants as there were three of our brood wearing nappies, but there was none to be had. Before two or three nights had passed, we found the children with huge bites on their bodies, though there were mosquito nets in use, and we realised that the beds were infested with bedbugs, which scuttled out at night to feast.

'Uncle was a most hospitable man and frequently welcomed members of the Friends' Ambulance Unit. Unfortunately, in their journeyings the men stayed in local inns and so picked up the bugs in their packs. We boiled the mosquito nets and used kerosene on the wooden parts of the beds, but we did not easily rid ourselves of these creatures, whose bites raise lumps which itch for several days.' Jean realised that if they wanted to live in a clean place they would have to get to work themselves. 'We began to clean uncle's house, beat his dusty carpets, wash and polish. He owned some French porcelain figurines, and when we heard their value we gasped and gave them a careful soapy bath.'

Jean's companions soon flew on to India, but she remained. She had little company, other than Alf on his weekly visits. 'He would open his storeroom, bring out an occasional tin or some coffee and regale me with tales of the Yunnan tribespeople amongst whom he had previously worked... As time went on, I received unexpected guests, either men from the Friends' Ambulance Unit or members of the British Army who required rest and recuperation. They would arrive, sent by uncle, with a leg of mutton and a loaf of bread and stay from a few days to two weeks, usually recovering from some illness. Once several Red Cross nurses came, but I found the men much more helpful. They would carry the children to the nearby lake where we would swim or row around in an inflatable rubber boat. The Burma Road passed uncle's house and US army jeeps driven at speed rushed past, so it was impossible to allow the children beyond the confines of the garden.

On several occasions, a Chinese woman who attended to uncle's washing and mending could be persuaded to watch the children while I walked three miles to the cottage hospital to borrow some books from the English matron.... I welcomed the exercise and the books were a Godsend. Kunming's climate was pleasant and the green hillsides were beautiful. However, owing to the proximity of the airfield the noise of aircraft was constant, for this was the vital link between beleaguered China and India by which military supplies were ferried. During the months I lived there, no Japanese planes attacked the airfield, although flying over enemy-occupied Burma could be hazardous.'

After four months, Jean and her children flew in a British RAF Dakota over the mountains of Burma to Calcutta. As she left, she reflected that: 'The house was now clean and a routine had been established. Even the cook accepted us, though without any great enthusiasm. The army friends who visited and our excursions to the lake had relieved the monotony. As we went through the village on the way to the lake, the local children rushed out to call [in Chinese] "army very good" and were used to us as neighbours. The vast lake where the weeds below the surface stroked our bodies as we swam was a constant delight. Kunming was beautiful, with its hills, temples and temperate climate. We had accommodated ourselves to the lifestyle there.'

The fact that the house has been so useful pleased Alf enormously. I believe it was a great comfort to him that, even though he could not enjoy it with Bessie, so many others were able to find peace, safety and sanctuary here.

He later wrote: 'This house has been a blessing to very many folk. I came over about once a week, but there was always someone having a vacation here, or convalescing from illness, and during the years, I have had folk of many places and many nationalities staying. Missionaries who had to evacuate their stations have been here for several months together, several families with many children, Americans, Canadians, Australians, Germans, Norwegians, many of the Friends' Ambulance Unit from England and America, and Chinese from Canada, Australia and elsewhere, besides those who live around here. So the house and garden has served a very good purpose.'

43 WAR IS OVER, WAR HAS JUST BEGUN

The defeat of Japan may have ended the Second World War, but in China the key conflict was still unfolding: that between the nationalist forces of Chiang Kai Shek and the Communists. And while the province of Yunnan had escaped direct involvement in the war against Japan, it would not be so fortunate in the three years leading up to the Communist takeover, and in the profound upheaval that would follow.

In the Methodist publication *The Kingdom Overseas*, tribute was paid to China: 'If there is one flag that deserves to fly above all others in victory celebrations, surely it is the flag of China. This war did not begin in Poland in 1939, or even in China in 1937, but in Manchuria in 1931. China stood alone in her heroic struggle from 1931-1941. She has fought aggression longer than any other nation, and has come between the world and Japan's dreams of conquest.'

The report quotes Harold Rattenbury, saying: 'The four foundations of the world to be, our statesmen have declared, are America, Britain, China and Russia... not the last or least of them is China. She isn't just a market, she's a great nation. There can be no hope of a settlement in the Pacific, or in the world, without her goodwill and cooperation. I myself believe America, Britain and Russia can never of themselves, together, establish the new order. We made that sort of mistake the last time [after the First World War]; don't let's make it again... Now Japan has surrendered and left China with two countries: Occupied [China] and Free China face a problem like that of the home in which husband and wife have been separated by years of war service. The two must get to know each other before they can begin life together again. The Methodist churches from Occupied and Free China need time to share the experiences and discoveries of the war years before plans can be made for the new life.'

In October 1945 Kunming saw fighting in the streets between Chiang Kai Shek's forces and those of Yunnan's governor, Long Yuin. Under the headline: A CHINESE GOVERNOR DEPOSED, FIGHTING IN KUNMING *The*

Times reported: 'Long Yuin was the only important figure of the war-lord era who was not eliminated or brought under control when the Nanking government, under the Generalissimo [Chiang Kai Shek], began extending its authority to the four corners of the country.'

Chiang Kai Shek issued an order, ousting Long Yuin, who did not give up without a fight. The report goes on: 'Widespread street fighting broke out in Kunming yesterday as soon as General Chiang Kai-shek's order was made known. The order divested Long of his military command and placed the Kunming garrison and the police under the authority of Chungking's Central Government. Troops under General Tu Li-ming marched into Kunming at dawn yesterday. Yunnanese troops resisted their entry, and the casualties are reported to be heavy.'

The report notes: 'there is likely to be little regret at the governor's departure.'

This local battle was a side skirmish to the main struggle taking place in China. With the Japanese gone, Nationalist forces, the Kuomintang under Chiang Kai Shek, and the Communists under Mao Tse Tung, raced to occupy as much territory as possible.

As Geoffrey R. Senior writes in *The China Experience*: 'In the end the Kuomintang controlled the greater part of the country with a population of about 300 million while the territory controlled by the Communists in so-called Liberated areas held around 130 million people.'

Very late on in the Second World War, the Soviet Union had joined the fight against the Japanese, occupying most of Manchuria in just a week. Under the peace agreement, the Japanese handed over their arms to the Soviets in Manchuria, and to the Kuomintang in China itself. When the Soviets left, the Communists took over in Manchuria. 'Battle lines were therefore drawn between rival Chinese forces, and the stage was set for a new destructive war, as if the sufferings of China over the past eight years had not been sufficient.'

On paper, the Kuomintang should have won. They had overwhelmingly superior forces, with three times the soldiers of the Communists, and an air force of 1,000 American planes funded with $6 billion of US aid. However, partly through better military leadership and tactics, but also 'because they had won the support of the people,' the Communists would be the ultimate victors. The Kuomintang had alienated its traditional support base – intellectuals and the middle classes – through its corruption, and the implementation of reforms which redistributed land to the peasants.

Peace talks were held between the two sides in Beijing, the new headquarters of the Chinese Communist Party, in April 1949, but ended without agreement. In response, Mao moved to achieve final victory. Within days the Communists had occupied Nanjing, the Kuomintang capital. A month later Shanghai, the heart of Chinese industry, also fell. By the end of the year the whole of China was in Communist hands. Chiang Kai Shek and the remnants of the Kuomintang fled to the island of Taiwan, then known as Formosa. On October 1, at a mass rally in Beijing's Tiananmen Square, Mao Tse Tung announced the formation of the People's Republic of China. He said: 'Ours will no longer be a nation subject to insult and humiliation. We have stood up.'

Throughout it all, the missionaries in Yunnan struggled on, with control increasingly being handed to the Chinese, Miao and Nosu. The minister now in charge of their Zion Methodist Church in Kunming was from Central China and, the 1945 annual report noted, 'the Miao tribespeople have a great Christian leader in Chu Huan Chung, who has been appointed the first headmaster of the new Middle School in Stone Gateway.'

The refugees who had flooded into Kunming were gradually returning home, on dangerous journeys hampered by rough, unrepaired roads, preyed upon by bandits, destined for towns devastated by the ravages of war. 'The people left in Kunming were largely non-partisan,' the annual report concluded. 'They just wanted to be left in peace to live their lives.' That, sadly, was not going to happen.

44 PEARL COMES HOME

The defeat of the Japanese meant that Pearl was able to leave Shanghai and return to Kunming, and Alf. From February 1946 to June 1948 she was back at the city's Hui Tian Hospital as deputy nursing director. She and Alf were in almost daily contact. Pearl came across the lake once a week to see him, and wrote twice a week, and Alf went into the city once a week. I know how much Pearl wanted to be with her foster father when Bessie died, and I can imagine how she and Alf had longed to comfort each other. Now they could.

Two letters from Alf to his sisters, Lucy and Annie, written in 1947, give a tantalising glimpse of their times together in those two years. Alf writes of Pearl's time in Shanghai, about how she was first an object of suspicion because of her adoption by English missionaries, then, after the Japanese departed, faced the danger that she would be accused of being a collaborator. However, he writes, 'that trouble passed and she was able to come along here last February, and so has been here for nearly one year.'

The house across the lake held many memories for them both: 'Bess and I used to come across here, with Pearl and John, for summer holidays, and so all the village folk know us.' It had also kept Alf busy in the lonely years following Bessie's death. He had painted the house and wired it for electricity: 'The electric light is not here yet but it may be brought along within a year or so, and I am getting ready for that time. Then I also walk about four miles to one of our schools.' This is T'ien Nan Middle School, established seven miles out of the city in the premises of an electrical factory that had moved back to the east with the end of the war. Alf taught English here twice a week, and had some of the students staying at his house.

He was also running a pharmacy: 'I have to carry on some of Bess's work of giving out simple medicines to the village folk, and just now they are coming to me for smallpox vaccinations.' Visits for this and a range of ailments meant he dispensed to between forty and seventy people a day.

'The folk come here before I have finished my breakfast in the morning, and continue at all hours until it is dark. It is my policy, at present, to see them when they come, because many of them have walked from three to five miles and some even ten miles, and then they have to go back again. But, latterly, it has been such strenuous work that I am thinking I shall have to fix certain days in the week for this treatment, so as to leave me free for other tasks. There! I have just been called to a case of a lad, who lives more than a mile away, and had fallen on a stone and nearly gashed his eye out. He walked the whole way here for me to treat him. That is how it is day in and day out, so I am seeking to be of use to them all.'

Alf doesn't mention it, but he has other responsibilities: the Methodists have taken over a church from the Anglican mission near the school where Alf teaches, and he is pastor there.

He tells Lucy and Annie that he has thought about retiring to his homeland: 'It is now over ten years since I last left England, but I hesitate to return, because of the shortage of accommodation, and there are so many needy folk wanting houses, but chiefly because if I leave China now, I shall not return here again, and I am more of a stranger in England than I am here.' He also expects his foster-son to return to China, so perhaps envisages a future in which both his children are with him: 'John is at present in America, acting as interpreter for the Chinese Air Force students. He expects to be back here again soon, but there is little prospect of work here for him at present.'

Alf also gives an insight into how China is suffering. 'When the Americans first came here, their $1 US could get $20 Chinese currency, now it is about $8,000 Chinese for the $1 US. And everything on the street has of course jumped up to similar extravagant figures. The poorer people get their value for goods sold, so they have not suffered too much, but people who have money in the banks find the value of it getting less and less as time goes by, and theirs is a very heavy loss.'

With Alf no longer involved in the administrative work at the mission, there is a growing recognition that he was actually doing a very good job, despite his maverick tendencies. Administration is faltering, payments are not being made. Ken May complains to Harold Rattenbury: 'Very unfortunately my wife has been greatly upset and disturbed by the report of a debt of £300 on my personal account at the Mission House, which is entirely the result of delayed payments on the part of the Mission House representative in the field... the deficit was almost entirely due to Moody's failure to send home my allowances on time. I do not blame Moody. The fact remains that we have all of us about three times as much work to do as we ought to have... it was the same when Evans was there.'

Edward Moody responds by telling Rattenbury that he is struggling to get the annual schedules together on time, just as Alf always did. It is, he says 'a very time-consuming business; I wonder if there is any way of simplifying them... it is not an easy matter finding the time necessary for dealing with the annual schedules.'

45 BACK TO STONE GATEWAY

Once he is released from internment by the Japanese, Ken Parsons is able to return to the province his father, Harry, had served. For Ken, Chaotung and Stone Gateway are places with many childhood memories, as with Pearl and Kunming.

Ken and his twin brother Keith were born in Chaotung in 1916, and lived for the first ten years of their lives in Stone Gateway. Ken loved his life there. In his *China Diary* he writes: 'Our nearest English neighbours were in Chaotung, 25 miles – a whole day's journey – away. My brother and I spoke Miao fluently and had many Miao friends. Indoors with our parents we had to speak English. Amid all her other pressing commitments, mother did her best to educate us. We had a wonderful childhood!'

On his way back to Stone Gateway in 1947, where he is to continue his father's work, he visits Kunming, and Uncle Alf, for whom he has great respect. Alf, he says, 'had a wonderful gift of sharing his long experience and wise counsel with us younger folk without in any way appearing to interfere. He was retired, but it was so good to know he was always there.' At the house across the lake he and his wife Peggy and baby daughter Christine find: 'All sorts of delicious fruit and veg growing in the well-kept garden; peaches, apples, plums, pomelos, pomegranates, and grapefruit. We had happily arrived at strawberry time!' Pearl was with Alf at the time and 'it was a great joy to meet her again.'

At Stone Gateway, Ken would not only be returning to the place where his father and Sam Pollard did so much ground-breaking work, and gave the Hua Miao a written language. He would also be extending the reach of the mission into an area and to a Miao tribe that Sam Pollard and Harry Parsons had been able to reach only fleetingly. They were the Ch'uan or River Miao. Ken remembered, as a boy, his father trekking for seven days just to reach them. When he returned, he said that something must be done to take the Gospel to them immediately, but the demands of the Hua Miao at Stone Gateway made that impossible.

Harry Parsons' breakdown while on furlough in 1926 meant he and the family could not return to Stone Gateway, and the murder of Heber Goldsworthy in 1938 again meant work there suffered greatly. Now Stone Gateway could be fully staffed again. The hope was that they could now achieve the sort of mass conversion of the Ch'uan Miao as they had with the Hua Miao in 1906.

From Kunming, Ken and family travelled by truck via Weining, where his twin brother Keith (also a Methodist missionary) was stationed. Keith was to travel with them to Chaotung, where his wife Doris had given birth to a baby daughter, Helen, two months earlier. In Weining, Ken learned of the grave dangers missionaries faced in the district, and saw the awful strain a life of relentless toil under the constant threat of death put upon them.

He wrote: 'Keith, hearing the truck, came out to meet us. I was shocked. Admittedly we had not seen each other for over six years, but he looked so gaunt and thin.' Ken could tell his brother had suffered some sort of crisis.

After dinner, while Peggie was settling the baby, he got Keith on his own and the story came out. About ten days previously, bandits armed with spears had raided the compound. The Chinese girl who helped in the house was badly cut, and the cook and odd-job man received far more serious injuries. 'Keith had only escaped the thrust of a spear by stepping forward quickly. Even so, the waistband of his trousers was ripped at the back. It was as near as that. I noticed his hands shaking as he talked. He stayed up to the early hours every night reading, in the vain hope he might be able to sleep. The good news was that the bandits had now moved out of the area.'

Despite such traumas, Keith had got a great deal done in Weining, which was the centre for work among the Nosu. He had built a brick church, a dispensary and schools, and had a multi-ethnic staff: a Hua Miao dispenser, a Nosu minister and a Chinese headmaster.

The brothers quickly moved on to Chaotung, where Ken met his brother's wife for the first time. Next day they baptised the baby, and the day after that Keith and family returned to Weining. 'Peggie and I were very sorry that we did not have more time with Keith and Doris after all the long years of separation, but that was the way life was.'

Ken had been instructed to build two semi-detached houses in Stone Gateway, one of them to be his family home. The road there was little more than a bridle path, and crossed a river which, after heavy rain, became a torrent. It was safe at the time the family travelled, but Ken recalls with some relish that Harold Rattenbury had an upset here. 'One of the six men carrying Rattenbury's mountain-chair slipped and he was almost dropped into the roaring water... it could have been very serious, with the London head of the China mission swept away.' Given the profound danger that Rattenbury placed Ken in in sending him to occupied China and internment, he can be excused a chuckle at the man's discomfort.

As he neared Stone Gateway the childhood memories came flooding back. Passing through a gap in the mountains: 'I dismounted and stood enthralled. Never had I realised that the mountain on the left towered so high nor how lovely were the hillsides covered with rhododendron and azaleas. Beside tumbling streams grew maiden-hair and other ferns. In the distance far below was Stone Gateway, a number of whitewashed buildings just as they were when we had left 21 years before. The fir and other trees that father planted had grown, covering large areas of the hillsides. I walked slowly down towards the copse of oak trees that we used to climb when we were boys, and rounding a bend, surprise, surprise, there were two long lines, on either side of the road, of school children and adults. They must have seen me coming. They immediately burst into their song of welcome. I could have wept. At last, after so many years, we had arrived.'

Ken was greeted by Charlie Steel, the superintendent of the Stone Gateway missionary circuit, based here with his wife and two daughters, and together they walked down, crossed the stream on stepping stones and up the steps that gave Stone Gateway its name.

Next day was Sunday, the Miao came to church in their best clothes, and a welcome had been arranged. 'It was with very mixed feelings that I sat in the church where father and mother had preached so often.... One old man stood up and spoke of all the things mother and father had done – introducing potatoes, building schools, the orphanage, and the leper home, making a new road through the gorge and so on. He spoke of mother's very great influence among women and men alike, of how women even now copied the hair style that mother used! It was obvious that the Miao continued to hold them in high regard and great affection. And I, their son, already had a blessed inheritance of real affection. I was so glad that I remembered enough Miao to reply.'

Ken visits the site of the £5 House, the little three-roomed hut where his mother came as a bride and where she, his father and Sam Pollard saw the beginning of the great mass movement of the Miao to Christ. In his parents' day, men, women and children would crowd into the yard at the side of the house after church, where Ken's mother dispensed medicines. 'She had not trained as a pharmacist but experience had taught her a lot. Now, providently, there was a clinic and a Miao dispenser who had had a certain amount of training.'

He walks past the house Heber Goldsworthy built, and where he was murdered, then on for half a mile up the hill beyond the compound, at the top of which lie the graves of Sam Pollard, who died of typhoid in 1915, and of Heber. He stands bareheaded beside them.

Before Ken could build the two houses at Stone Gateway, the ancient kiln used for making bricks had to be restored, and supplies of wood and stone identified. He also tackled a project that was to have profound consequences when the Communists took over in Chaotung. He can have had no idea that there was anything significant, let alone dangerous in this at the time but it was to cause two missionaries, Vernon Stone and Elliott Kendall, huge problems in 1949.

Ken had brought with him an electricity-generating device called a wind charger, a Lucas Free-light which he had bought in England for £25. It consisted of a propeller which fitted directly on to a dynamo and which he mounted at the top of a 12ft pole strapped to a chimney. 'The hot air over the Chaotung plain rose each afternoon and drew in cold air through the gap in the mountains in the north. This created a strong wind which turned the propeller at a sufficient speed to charge up the two large 12-volt batteries. We were not only able to run our wireless set and get the English news, but we also had a 24-volt reading lamp downstairs and lights in both the children's bedroom and ours.'

As soon as he could, Ken set off on his first visit to the Ch'uan Miao. Ken May, the chairman of the district, came with him along with Charlie Steel. This would be the first time three foreigners had been seen together in this remote region. 'We knew that the Ch'uan Miao tribe was even larger than the Hua Miao and that they had been asking for the Gospel for over 30 years. There was obviously a tremendous opportunity awaiting us. We were sure that there could well be a mass movement to Christ, as there had been among the Hua Miao.'

The hope was that they might eventually station two missionary families among the tribe. The help the missionaries offered was by no means solely spiritual. Along with Bibles and hymnals they carried drugs and dental forceps and 'a mountain of other essential supplies and equipment'. They were away for five weeks, the first of many trips.

While work on the two houses went on, Ken's family stayed in Chaotung. It was not until February 1949 that they could be together again in one of the new houses in Stone Gateway. By then they had a second child, John. The weather was bitterly cold as the family rode on horseback to their new home. When they could no longer feel their hands and feet Ken and Peggie had to dismount and walk until their circulation was restored. They managed to keep the children warm by tucking hot water bottles within their many layers of clothing.

The house had been prepared for them by their newly-hired Miao cook: 'I had asked him to light huge fires in every room... and as we went indoors, it was beautifully warm. A welcome cup of tea kept us going until we had unpacked and made up the beds. John was happy in his playpen and Christine excitedly explored every room. The cook put on a hot meal and we got the children bathed and into bed in good time.'

After saying prayers and settling them, Ken took Peggie on a tour of her new home. None of the rooms had been whitewashed and seemed a little dark, but that could soon be put right. Ken had a surprise for Peggie in the fitted wardrobe of the spare bedroom: 'Instead of shelves I had hidden a little staircase leading up into the roof space which had been boarded over, making a wonderful place for me to do carpentry and the children to play.

'"Now look at this," I said as I opened the door. To our absolute horror we were enveloped in clouds of smoke and could hear the crackle of fire at the top of the stairs. Providentially the children's bath water had not been emptied and the large 'kuo' – an earthenware pot – in the bathroom was filled to the brim. Peggie rushed bucketfuls of water along the passage and, standing halfway up the stairs, I was able to pour the water right on to the centre of the blaze.

'Smoke and steam choked us but again, providentially, there was enough water for us to get the fire put right out... we dared not go to bed until we were absolutely sure that the chimneys had cooled down and there were no smouldering timbers left. I started to apologise to Peggie for bringing her to China and these awful situations. She immediately shut me up. "Didn't God bring us together and love us both?" When we eventually got to bed we just couldn't get to sleep. Another five minutes and the fire would have got such a hold that we could not have possibly put it out, and both houses would have burnt down. Oh God, what a thought.'

Next morning Ken found the cause of the blaze. There had been violent earthquakes the previous October which had disturbed a rafter that was anchored in the bricks lining one of the chimneys. The roaring fires had ignited it.

While things were peaceful at Stone Gateway, bandits were active on the road to Kunming. They had dug up the road, which meant it was hard to get supplies and cash to Chaotung and Stone Gateway, including funds for the Hua Miao and Ch'uan circuits. Bandits threatened Weining and, on Good Friday, a band a thousand strong laid siege to Chaotung. It was five days before government forces could drive them off. However: 'A few days or rather nights after the lifting of the Chaotung siege, we heard that another big band of bandits, who had been looting and raping not far from us, was on the way to attack us. Somebody, and it didn't require a very clever person, had put two and two together – the arrival of the mission truck and the fact that teachers and preachers in the Chaotung area now had money to spend – and surmised that a lot of money had come over the Yunnan horizon!'

They had to prepare for an assault. Ken had substantial sums in cash: 'It would have been unwise to have hidden all our money away, but we must do something. It was already dark and I opened up a brick drain that ran down through a newly dug flowerbed, pushed about fifteen [packets of notes]... into the drain, replaced the bricks and finally raked over the soil. We took the children out of bed and, in the pitch darkness, scrambled up the mountainside behind Stone Gateway. It was very rough going and we couldn't get very far. John was sleepy and quiet, but Christine, wide awake, would talk and only keep quiet if she could ride on my shoulders. We eventually put a rug down on the bumpy earth and waited.

'Of course, we hadn't got that huge amount of money which the bandits were expecting to find and I wondered what, in their disappointment, they would be driven to do. No doubt they would have been drinking before they arrived and any appeal to reason would be useless. It was on such a night as this that Heber

Goldsworthy had been murdered. We waited and waited and at about 1.30am there came a panting runner with the wonderful news that the Chaotung militia had scattered the bandits and the danger had passed. We got home just as it started to rain heavily and not even Chris minded the party being over!'

However, Ken and his family were not to be left in peace for long.

46 ENEMIES OF THE PEOPLE

In June 1948 Pearl suddenly left Kunming and returned to Shanghai. Why? It seems most likely it was because the Communists were coming. The pattern across the rest of the land they had conquered saw every individual held to account, and severely punished if they were considered to be counter-revolutionary, or tainted by association with foreign powers. Pearl could face a long period of re-education, sentenced to what would effectively be hard labour in the countryside.

Alf too might face sanctions for his role in raising Pearl as his own, in a British household. It could be judged that the baby rescued from a rubbish tip had been brought up in error, and would be seen as irremediably corrupted, and corrupting. So Alf lost his daughter once again, and she her father.

Pearl had to get away, to obscure her connection with Alf. And so she fled, back to Shanghai. There was another element, perhaps, in this decision. Her companion Dr Norah Li, who she had been with since 1936, was in that city. In a letter to Alf, Pearl said she hoped to be able to return in a year or so, but that was never possible. Alf stayed on until the bitter end, only leaving Kunming when all foreigners were expelled in 1950-51. He saw the final days of the old regime.

Following the failure of peace talks between the Nationalists and Communists in April 1949, Mao Tse Tung's forces swept across China, mopping up the last remnants of opposition. Yunnan held out until, in September, resistance began to crumble. There was a coup which, *The Times* reported, 'if not specifically pro-Communist is certainly directed against the authority of the Nationalist Government.' The provincial governor, General Lu Han, issued a statement saying that eight regiments had revolted and proclaimed their independence of the Nationalist Government.' However, there would be two months of uncertainty in Kunming, as remaining Nationalist forces battled with those that had declared for the Communists.

181

Elliott Kendall and Alf Evans were among the few missionaries left in Kunming. Alf, having given up missionary work, was now needed again. He took over the duties of Kunming circuit superintendent, responsible for the churches. Both were in post when the Red Armies surrounded the city. Having been glad to see him take a back seat, it was now seen that Alf had a vital role to play, apart from the work he had taken up. Edward Moody writes: 'There is also the point that in negotiations with the Communists Mr Evans is best suited for this than any of our staff for he is so widely respected.' Alf had moved back to Kunming from across the lake and 'he is now living with us and like ourselves is giving the maximum service within his powers, considering his advanced age.'

In the second week of December the provincial government under General Lu-han broke with the Nationalist cause and announced its allegiance to Mao Tse Tung. Elliott Kendall wrote: 'For several days there was a very strict curfew and some days no one was allowed out of doors at all.' However, this did not immediately bring peace. 'There were still two Nationalist armies in the province, their commanders being in Kunming, and it was obviously hoped they would follow the local lead and break with Chiang Kai Shek.'

In the week before Christmas, Kunming was the scene of nightly battles as Nationalist forces within its walls, and Communists surrounding it, fought it out. Barricades and trenches blocked the entrances to the city and dotted its streets. 'An exceedingly stubborn defence was put up by the provincial boys, which excited everyone's admiration, particularly those who were on the inside. However, it was very much a touch and go affair. As the bullets whistled around the houses, and the fighting seemed to be creeping up the streets, we felt that it was all over at times.' The surrounding armies were in a very low state of morale, short of several months' pay, and bent on wasting the city. 'It would have been a nightmare if they had got in and at the worst times it looked as if they had succeeded.'

Then came a lull over Christmas. The attacking forces moved back into the country. 'In this lull we were able to enjoy some very curtailed Christmas festivities. Then the new phase began: a sustained bombing campaign. Elliott writes: 'Many houses were wrecked and a number of people were killed.' In the face of all this, Alf and Elliott tried to help, organising relief packages and a first-aid squad, with Elliott driving an ambulance. The bombing continued for two weeks; thousands scattering across the countryside to hide among the dykes. During this period Alf's house across the lake at Hsi Shan was damaged by a stray bomb.

It was a great relief when, in February 1950, the full Liberation Army reached Kunming and drove out the final Nationalist resistance. The Communist troops: 'made a triumphant entry into the city, receiving a bigger welcome than any similar arrival in remembered history. Our schools, church and we ourselves joined in the welcome and in the general festivities. The new regime has finally taken this place over and we may now expect that there will be some real changes and a new revolutionary programme put into effect.'

Kendall still hoped that it would not be necessary for him to leave: 'Perhaps they would be better than we had feared and it might well be that they would bring law and order and new development, we must wait and see.' What he saw was a mixture of long-needed reform and horrific retribution. The Communists 'established their power of control in a very short time. One saw the process whereby even in this remote city at the end of the Burma Road in far off South West China, they immediately assumed absolute control and with very careful planning, with very able people, they began to administer and control the place.

'One couldn't help but admire their sheer ability to govern. They knew what they were going to do, their policy was clear and directions were given. In a nutshell, what one saw in the next few months was this Communist power take over and then, one by one, begin to dismantle all the previous institutions in society or to mould them anew. Everything had to be dismissed and ground down to nothing... It was really rather exciting but at the same time one began to be fearful. Some of our friends were people who were high up in society, in administrative positions, and such people had to be re-educated and so, without any choice in the matter, they were taken away for intensive re-indoctrination, and that was a pretty fearful experience.'

For decades Chiang Kai Shek had been vowing to rid China of opium. The Communists did so swiftly, but with great brutality. A deadline was given, by which opium smoking must stop. After that, the Red Army rounded up anyone still smoking it and took them away in trucks. They were never seen again. 'And so, in the first year, opium-smoking as a way of life and culture had ruthlessly been stamped out.'

The Communists also came for the landlord class. Party members would visit every village, gather the peasants together and drill into them the extent of the exploitation they had suffered. 'So when, after many weeks of indoctrination they asked the peasants what they should do with the landlords the answer came: "kill them". "Who should do it? Not the army, not the police, you should do it. You are the oppressed."' So the landlords were arrested and brought for public trial. 'There were plenty of peasants who could stand up and relate horrifying accounts of the cruelty and exploitation they had suffered. And then finally and fearfully the peasants joined in the execution of the landlords. That is typical of what happened in village after village, and China is a land of villages, right across the country... and the landlord class was exterminated.'

In the area of the South West China mission a hundred thousand could have been executed; across China, millions. The Communists cracked down on the free press, too. In October 1950 five Kunming newspapers were closed down and seventy-seven journalists jailed. The Communists also oversaw education. Eleven middle schools were closed, and there was strict government supervision of the remainder.

Not all the changes were destructive. 'They began to organise things that needed organising, cleaning up the streets and organising education and fixing rates and standards for remuneration for the working classes and so on. And then the immense input of energy and resources into the development of social services such as medicine at the local level, hospitals, clinics, and training.' In short, in this respect you could say that the Communists were doing all that the missionaries had done under the previous regime: a regime that was happy to neglect its people's welfare and have foreigners come in and make up for their lack.

One further gain was 'the wiping out of brigandage after much very sanguineous campaigning, so that I should say that Yunnan is clearer of bandits than it has been at any time in the last ten years. This is a very great achievement with limited resources... but with unmitigated harshness.' Elliott was impressed at 'the quite miraculous way in which the revolution reached out to touch people at every point in their life in the cities and the villages.'

In Kunming 'the Party began to organise the people for re-education. Every street had to form a committee.' No one was excused, all had to attend weekly meetings at which they would be taught about the Communist revolution.

There was a good deal of bloodletting. People who had been prominent under the old regime, and who were judged to have done wrong, were brought to public trial. 'There were public executions twice a week. It was a fairly fearful experience to live through this time and you sensed the ruthlessness and power of this new government.'

The missionaries did not escape scrutiny. Running their schools became increasingly fraught. The boards that had funded and overseen them were made up of wealthy merchants, representatives of the old order. They could no longer help financially, and resigned for fear of retribution. The students and teachers represented the new order, and seized control. The Communists, seeing that the missionaries could no longer run their schools, took them over.

The main Methodist church in Kunming also suffered, because it was led by foreigners. The missionaries themselves faced severe restrictions on what they could do. Elliott writes: 'There was no possibility whatever of travelling... We had to remain where we were. As the Communists dug in, it became obvious that one had to keep one's head down, certainly not travel outside the city very much and, on the whole, not be too prominent. The churches were still functioning, although under pressure, having to have re-indoctrination courses and such like.' The missionaries, like all Europeans, were considered enemies of the state, indelibly tainted by the history of colonialism and foreign exploitation of China.

Kendall and others realised that the days of foreign missionaries running things were over. They found a Chinese minister, Wang tsi-hsing, the general secretary of the YMCA, who agreed to lead the church in Kunming. They elected a Chinese chairman, Chu Shui Kuan, Kendall noting: 'It was really an historic occasion and it may well be that from now on, in the new China, we may be able to stand by and work with, not lead. From the prevailing atmosphere it appears to us possible, if not probable, that the time when a foreigner was in the chair is for ever gone.'

Alf was finding life hard. In July he was still waiting to hand over the church to Wang-tsi-hsing, who was at a conference in Shanghai. Kendall wrote: 'Mr Evans has become increasingly dissatisfied with his position and with things in general and, indeed, has really found the effort required, both mental and physical, rather more than he could stand. I do not think it will be long before he lets go altogether... he has been feeling it would be a good thing for him to wash his hands of commitments here, give up his accumulated property and retire to happier climes. He finds it extremely difficult to reach a decision, and it may well be that he will still be here when we want to go; on the other hand, it is not impossible that he may decide to leave within the near future.' In September he added, in a further report, that Alf 'is exceedingly anxious to leave and would do so now, if loyalty to his younger colleagues did not restrain him.'

While this was going on the Korean war broke out, with America, Britain and the United Nations fighting alongside forces in the south, the Chinese with those in the north. As a consequence, says Elliott, missionaries from those nations were seen as China's enemies.

'Within a year; it became obvious that we could not stay [in Kunming] and that there was no future for us. We couldn't really do any work. We could not be of assistance to the church. We might indeed be an embarrassment to it... So the right thing was for us to make preparations to leave.'

By December 1950 all British Methodist missionaries had left or were awaiting permits to allow them to do so. They were leaving a Kunming Christian community of 17,925, now served by seventeen Chinese ministers.

47 ESCAPE FROM CHAOTUNG

Ken Parsons was facing the same crisis as the other missionaries. In 1949 he had a tough decision to make: should be heed the instructions of the British consul and leave Stone Gateway, abandoning the Miao, or stay to see what Communist rule would bring? Ken writes in his *China Diary*: 'To be quite honest, we knew, and our Miao friends knew, deep down in our hearts, that things couldn't go on as they had been. We foreigners were so conspicuous – we stuck out like sore thumbs! Although we lived very simply, people thought we were very rich.'

The mission compounds they lived in were vastly superior to the thatched huts of the Miao, and very different to most Chinese houses in the cities. Because westerners were prone to dysentery, typhoid and typhus, the missionaries had to keep their homes scrupulously clean and eat carefully prepared food. The Miao fertilised their crops with human sewage, which could transmit diseases fatal to Europeans. Sam Pollard and Bessie Evans were among those who died of typhoid, and Ken's father Harry, having had typhoid and malaria in Stone Gateway, suffered from fevers and severe migraines all his life.

'There was no question about it. We must start packing and quickly... We were terribly disappointed. Having just settled, Peggie and I were now doing the missionary job that for years we had longed to do. However, we had to face up to the fact that, when the Communists came, our presence would be an embarrassment and even a very real danger to our Chinese and Miao colleagues.' The Communists would see them as stinking capitalists corrupting the minds of the people, and any local Christians associating with them could suffer terrible consequences.

When they got back to Chaotung, Ken tried to sell anything they could not take back to England: tools, safari beds, mosquito nets. 'There were more personal things too, crockery, cutlery, pictures and so on. Having lost all my books under the Japs, I was now going to lose all the replacements I had managed to get. But by far the biggest wrench would be having to say goodbye to our Miao colleagues and friends and the Revd John Li.'

The Miao hurriedly arranged a farewell service. The church was packed. That day Ken and another missionary, Charlie Steel, baptised over a hundred mainly young people. 'We left Stone Gateway the following morning. How difficult it was to say goodbye.'

In Chaotung, Ken learned that there was the possibility of a skeleton staff staying on there. He would not be one of them, he was told, because of his years under Japanese internment, during which Peggie had had no idea if he were dead or alive. The missionaries talked all night, thrashing out the options. Wives and children would definitely have to go, but Charlie Steel and Vernon Stones, who both had young children, could not face being split from their families, under incredibly dangerous conditions, for who knew how long. They felt there was no one at Mission House in London whose judgement they could trust. While everyone in China was certain the Communists would take over the whole country, in London Harold Rattenbury and others thought they might not. 'It was eight years ago that Rattenbury had assured me that there would be no war with the Japs. Was he still living in cloud cuckoo land?'

Peggie had a suggestion: 'We can't trust him but we can trust our Miao and Chinese colleagues. How would it be for you to offer to stay on the condition that you will be able to leave when the Revds Chu Huan Chang and Chu Shui Kwang advise you to go? They would know when, for your sake and theirs, you must leave.'

Then a cable came from Rattenbury: 'Delay evacuation and send mothers to wait in Hong Kong and concentrate rest of personnel at Chaotung and Kunming.'

To Ken and the others it was clear Mission House hadn't got a clue about the situation. 'We treated the cable as a joke, but in fact it was pathetic. Didn't they know that a mass evacuation of foreigners out of China was going on and Hong Kong was packed with families waiting for passages to America, Australia and Europe? Many families were living in tents waiting months for a passage home.'

They decided to rely on the advice of their Miao and Chinese colleagues about when to finally abandon their posts in Stone Gateway and Chaotung. For now, it was decided that Ken would stay on in Chaotung with five others. Lettie Squire, who had retired to Chaotung with her lifelong companion Li Shuang-mei, was not budging. Stone Gateway would have five staff remaining.

A plane was sent to evacuate the others to Kunming, on the first leg of their journey home. As the old Dakota, loaned by the Lutherans, lifted off with his wife and children aboard, Ken's thought was: 'Dear God, should I ever see them again?'

For a while, life for Ken went on as normal: 'I was able to do a lot of very worthwhile travelling in the Miao circuits, riding Prince, the excellent horse I had bought and which we decided to give to the Miao and Chinese ministers when I had to leave.' They completed the rebuilding of the leper home and the large church at Stone Gateway, which had been badly damaged in recent earthquakes. Ken was also able to build a memorial chapel on the site of the £5 House. The missionaries were also busy training Chinese and Miao doctors and nurses to take over running the hospital.

However, as city after city fell to the Communists, it became increasingly obvious to Ken that nothing could stop the Red Army.

Then, three things happened. The first was another warning from the British consul that they should leave while they could. Secondly, the leader of the Miao at Stone Gateway, Revd Chu Huan Chang, told Ken: 'When your father and mother were here and the brigandage was bad, we were able to take you as a family and hide you in the cave and you were safe. Had the Japanese advanced and taken Chaotung, the missionaries would have lived with us in our villages high up in the mountains and they would have been quite alright. But the Red Army is absolutely different and we are sure they are coming. For your sake and for ours, you must go.' Thirdly, the senior pastor in Chaotung, the Revd Chu Shui Kwang, told the missionaries that their continued presence would be an embarrassment to the Church. The two Chinese pastors 'were very highly respected among the Chinese and Miao, and quite independently they had given us the same advice.'

They cabled Ted Moody, the missionary committee's representative in Kunming, to tell him what they had been advised, and ask if they should leave. He agreed and they all began their journeys home. However, while they were on their way, Harold Rattenbury cabled again. He rejected the advice of the two Chinese pastors and instructed Vernon Stones, who was still in Kunming, to fly back to Chaotung to join the other missionaries who had remained there. Stones felt he had to obey orders.

When the Red Army arrived in the city a few months later, Ken writes: 'disaster struck and struck immediately... The fact that there were five hated capitalist enemies of the State, still living in this little remote city of Chaotung, far away in North-east Yunnan, naturally aroused... the immediate suspicions of the Party and brought tragedy, especially for the Christians.'

48 WIND CHARGERS AND A WIRELESS

It was the wind chargers at Chaotung that sealed Vernon Stones's fate. Those and a little radio.

Ken Parsons had installed one charger, on a 12ft pole, in 1949, but in the years since then, other much taller ones had been bought to boost the electricity generated for the mission compound. When the Red Army searched the missionaries' houses they saw those, and then found an ex-army radio that Elliott Kendall had bought in Gamages, the London department store. Their suspicions were aroused because it was possible for a transmitter to be fitted to it. This, together with the cluster of 50ft high poles put up for the new wind-chargers made them suspect they had uncovered a nest of foreign spies. They had not, but their concerns were understandable in the febrile revolutionary atmosphere. As Elliott had jokingly said earlier, those tall masts made the compound look like a Marconi radio station.

Vernon and the others were having breakfast on February 17, 1951 when the soldiers rushed in and searched the house. When they found the radio receiver they interrogated Vernon, demanding to know where the transmitter part was. They refused to believe he had never had one. Poles and radio combined gave the military police cause to accuse Vernon of espionage. Suspicion also fell on the other British missionaries, but it was the three Chinese ministers who worked most closely with them who suffered the most profound consequences.

Vernon and the other British missionaries were ordered on to an open truck. They left their breakfast on the table and hurriedly picked up a few things. They were taken on a five-day journey on that open truck in freezing conditions to Kunming, where I shall pick up their story in a moment. The fate of the Chinese clergy implicated in the supposed spying plot was so much worse.

John Li died after six weeks in prison, on July 15. Shortly afterwards, Chu Shui Kwang hanged himself in his home in Chaotung and Chu Huan Chang escaped from the house where he was imprisoned and hanged himself in a nearby wood, driven to it by the brain-washing and torture he had suffered. Kwang and Chang had been the ones to warn Ken Parsons and the other missionaries when they must leave, but they were unable to save themselves.

John Li had not been accused solely of espionage. Elliott Kendall later reported to Mission House that he had fallen foul of something that came with the revolution: denunciation. A distant relative raised a land dispute, which led the authorities to suspect John was among the hated landlord class. In prison he caught relapsing fever, a tick-born bacterial disease. His wife tried to visit him, and send in medicine, but was refused. One day she was told to come and collect his body. It was the first she knew of his death. She came with a coffin but was made to wait outside while his emaciated, tortured body was put into it and sent out to her.

Elliot wrote: 'The eternal question which will never be answered is: had the Mission House accepted the strong advice of the Chinese ministers and leaders, and evacuated all the missionary staff from Chaotung, would those three ministers have survived?'

Elliott Kendall was in Kunming, 300 miles south, at this time. His role was to try to keep in touch with the small band of missionaries still in Chaotung, and with Mission House in London. He awaited the missionaries' arrival. When the truck carrying them reached Kunming it was stopped by police and their papers examined. Vernon Stones was ordered off and the driver told to proceed. So, Elliott Kendall wrote, 'the vehicle arrived at the house where I was living with these passengers and their luggage, but no Vernon Stones. He had been kept apparently in custody but no reason given whatsoever... we just hoped Vernon would turn up but he didn't... He disappeared.'

It was weeks before Elliott discovered that Vernon was in a large prison in Kunming. 'I went to try to secure information about him, to try to make contact with him, and was turned aside. No relationship whatever was permitted.'

Vernon later told his story. He was kept in solitary confinement for four and a half months, and never allowed out of his cell. The lights blazed all night, and the guards were changed every two hours. 'For the last two months of my imprisonment they woke me every two hours at the changing of the guard because someone had committed suicide in the next cell and they thought it might be infectious.'

They refused to speak to him, meaning that in all this time he had no human contact with anyone. He asked for work to do, anything to occupy his mind, but was refused.

Vernon's Bible and hymn book were taken from him when he arrived at the prison and, despite several requests, were not returned. 'I was, however, given Communist propaganda books in Chinese. I refused to read them at first, hoping they would be persuaded to let me have some English books, but that did not work.' Eventually he did read them, and was glad he did, because he learned the Party line.

With no human contact, nothing to do, and only propaganda to read: 'Under these circumstances my greatest worry was for my sanity... getting up in the morning and wondering how on earth to get through till night without going mad. I knew the fear in which solitary confinement is held by criminals in the West. I had had, in the past years, duodenal ulcer trouble. I had had dysentery last year. I was 10,000 miles from home. I had thought it possible that Mr Kendall had left, but he had loyally remined, though I did not know it... I was troubled at first by the sheer injustice of my imprisonment... I abandoned hope in this life and clung to the other-worldliness of so many of Wesley's hymns... and remembered the dictum... that God is less interested in our circumstances, than in our reaction to them.

'I think this other-worldly attitude saved my reason, and especially at Easter, with all the resurrection atmosphere, I experienced wonderful joy in complete abandonment of this world.'

For all this time, Elliott Kendall waited. Any missionaries who could leave did so, but he stayed on. Then one day the security police ordered him to come to their headquarters. He was interrogated for two hours, then told to go home. The next week, and the week after, he was called in again, for further interrogation.

'It began to dawn on me that this interrogation had something to do with Vernon, although they didn't come clean about it.' Finally he was called in one evening and told abruptly that he was going to be taken into custody. He was sent home but, next morning at 6am, there appeared 'an armed guard – a security officer with a revolver at his hip and four or five men with tommy guns ready to march me off... I was marched down one main street and up another and there eventually, through all the morning traffic, in front of me was the big security police headquarters.'

He was taken into a courtroom before a magistrate or judge, officials and police and told to go into the defendant's box. 'There was Vernon sitting waiting for me. He had been brought from prison. He clearly had been ill, he looked thin and pale. I was sat alongside him and the two of us were treated as criminals; there to be convicted and sentenced.' There was no defence lawyer, just a series of questions fired at them, in Chinese, by the judge. At one point he said directly to Elliott: 'You know that you can be taken out and shot?' Elliott replied: 'Yes, I know that.'

They were charged with spying for Britain, the enemy China was fighting in Korea. 'I denied very strongly that this was so and said that even though you certainly have the power to execute us, I am not a spy and my colleague is not a spy... They were trying to get us to confess and they tried to bribe us that if we would confess the State was very lenient... Eventually the judge said that we were convicted of espionage but... rather than being shot, we would be deported from the country.'

Vernon and Elliott were bundled into a truck with five or six armed guards and driven off. They had no idea where they were going or what would happen to them, but were taken on an extraordinary journey which took several weeks.

They were driven 6,000 miles through Yunnan and on to Chungking. It was here that, on their way into China at the start of their missionary work, they had switched from the Yangtse river to road. Now they were making the enforced return journey. A boat took them downriver to Hankow where they were marched to a railway station and on to a train. 'We were put in a small compartment with the armed guard and the train began to go south. It was a long journey from those cities of Wuchang and Wuhan down towards Canton.' Here they were taken to a prison and locked up for the night.

Next morning they were back on a train which 'rumbled on through south China and then eventually came down to the border opposite the New Territories of Hong Kong.' Here they were handed over to the border guards. 'The guards at the border told us to go forward and... so we walked across this iron bridge. We were moving out of China and out of Communist authority on to the New Territories.' Across the bridge they found a little railway station, and caught a train to Hong Kong.

When they arrived a very familiar figure was there to greet them: Alf Evans. Elliott later wrote: 'What a sublime climax, after such a journey lasting almost a month, to find a friend waiting on the other side, so entirely unexpected, so like Mr Evans to be there.'

49 AT HOME ANYWHERE

Alf had left for Hong Kong in January 1951. The tortuous, delay-stricken journey from Kunming took six weeks, and he finally arrived on February 23. Four months later he was talking of awaiting a passage back to England, which he had previously described as a land of strangers, but in the end he never left Hong Kong. Alf wrote to his sister Lucy on June 9 to say that he was waiting to try to get Pearl out to England with him. Perhaps it was when this proved impossible that he decided to stay in Hong Kong. At least, here, he was relatively close to her.

However, what became clear was that an iron curtain had come down between Alf in Hong Kong and Pearl in Shanghai. For the rest of Alf's life it would only be lifted very occasionally to allow her to leave Communist China and visit him. And when he died, permission to attend his funeral would be denied.

Of all the missionaries, only Alf seems to have stayed and, ever-positive, he created a new life for himself in this then-British colony. I found two people who knew him in the two years after his arrival. Geoff Mauldon, an Australian medical physicist friend of Alf's in those years, told me: 'Around the time I first came to know Uncle, he was living on the first floor of the Sailors and Soldiers' Home in Wan Chai on Hong Kong Island. His room was located behind the stage that was there for occasional use, and he had relative privacy.

'By today's [standards his] accommodation would be considered rather restrictive and limited. Uncle was the strange man who lived behind the stage of the main meeting hall which was also located above the S & S Restaurant where we, as a church group, had lunch after morning service. It was some little time before I had the honour of meeting this mysterious man and coming to know him as a friend.'

The Revd Geoffrey Jones, a Quaker who had driven ambulances during the war and met Alf at his house over the lake, came across him again at this time.

He told me: 'For nearly two years we shared the same meal table with a dozen or so other missionaries and I felt I knew him fairly well. He was a fluent Mandarin speaker but at rather a disadvantage in the Cantonese speaking church in Hong Kong. However, he carved out for himself a distinct avenue of service, gathering together as well as he could other Mandarin-speaking Christians and helping to link them to the church. At the age of seventy-plus he began to learn Cantonese, no small achievement.

'In 1951 I was ordained to the Methodist ministry in the church at Wanchai and Uncle Evans gave the address (the charge as we call it). It was based on Corinthians 5:20 "We are ambassadors therefore on behalf of Christ".

'My wife and I keep a visitors' book and your great-uncle [Alf] visited our flat on May 19 1952 and signed our book. In the address column he wrote "At home anywhere!" Our memories of Uncle Evans are very precious. He was deeply committed as a missionary and had a great love of people. He usually had a twinkle in his eye which expressed a real sense of humour. From what I can gather he must have been rather lonely at the end of his life since so many fellow missionaries, especially those who had known west China, had moved on elsewhere, as indeed we had done.'

One by one the other missionaries Alf had known in Yunnan passed through. Vernon Stones and Elliott Kendall were followed by Lettie Squire, who had finally given up on her idea of retiring in Chaotung. They had all suffered so much, and no doubt reflected on what they had come through together with Alf while they awaited a berth on a ship for England. Some of them were able to find positive results from what they had endured. Elliott Kendall wrote: 'Vernon's particular experience, and our final arrest and deportation, has been a deepening religious experience for us both... We have been driven back on the final realities of life – looked death in the face and finally been unafraid, released our hold on life and with resignation left ourselves in the hands of God. Our release is by grace alone... We give thanks for our deliverance with more than mere light-headedness.

'Vernon is well – pronounced medically fit – his mind completely normal and not suffering nervously or [under] any great strain. An intense religious experience in gaol – the assurance not of deliverance but of a hold on eternal life that nothing could shake – has kept his sanity in four and a half months of solitary confinement, threatening, and dramatic night trials... we have had a wonderful time of fellowship together since leaving Kunming.'

Elliott and Vernon sailed on The Canton, arriving at Tilbury on September 1. During the voyage Elliott was asked to write his reflections about what had happened in China.

He wrote: 'Freedom there is none, as we understand it. Fear is in its place. BUT there is freedom – and this needs to be emphasised – freedom from large-scale abuses of the past, from corrupt officials high and low, and from instability and uncertainty, from inflation, from profiteering, from excessive difference between wealth and poverty, from ostentatious display and parade of wealth and position, from exploitation for private profit, from landlord, from arbitrary oppression by individuals, from the power of money to circumvent the law, from economic insecurity, from the disgrace of foreigners receiving preferential treatment and occupying positions of authority in commerce, from toadyism to things foreign, from a feeling of national weakness compared with other nations, from aimlessness, from the need to think for yourself, from decades of civil war, from brigandage, the press-gang, gangsterism, and even petty robbery.

'All this, and more, means that the people generally, and some classes in particular, are able to find a great deal of satisfaction with what has taken place. Unpleasant features may easily be dismissed as temporarily necessary in the early stages of revolution. The good time is in the future, and if we are going to be a great nation, then it is worth going through this for the sake of it. These people can get things done, and what a new experience that is for China.

'One Christian leader said to me, "Much of this is childish; futile, cruel and unintelligent, but basically the revolution is right." One cannot help feeling that he is correct. The country needed a revolution, and has got a thorough-going one, but violent social revolutions are bloody, odious periods to live through.'

He adds, magnanimously: 'Neither Stones nor I have any resentment or strong ill-feeling because of treatment received; the whole thing is so much vaster than our own small experiences.'

50 PEARL IN SHANGHAI AFTER THE REVOLUTION

I have two accounts of Pearl's time in Shanghai under Communism. One comes from her step-brother, John, the other from Dan Lu, whose mother Mao Ming was a colleague and friend of Pearl's. I also have a series of letters from Alf, which reveal something of the constraints she was living under.

John's account comes from a visit he made to Pearl in the 1980s, after a break of forty years. Dan's is partly from childhood memories of her, but mainly from what his mother told him in response to questions from me. John's is by far the bleaker of the two portraits.

Pearl in Shanghai, 1959

Pearl invited John to dinner at a smart restaurant. John wrote: 'When she came to greet me at my hotel, she was not allowed to come to my room. We met in the public guestroom downstairs. She seemed nervous and scared.'

John had lost touch with Pearl in 1945, and had only learned recently that she had been in Shanghai for almost all that time, working for the Lester China Hospital. In his account, it can be hard at times to know when he is relaying exactly what Pearl told him, and when he is bringing his own interpretation to what she said. At some points it's clear he is talking specifically about her, at others he appears to be generalising.

He writes: 'Despite Communist claims that Shanghai was taken over peacefully, one of the first actions was to clean up the portion of the population who were considered counter-revolutionaries. The undesirables. They were classified as Hi Wiu Nei or The Black Five category. This included anybody who had worked for the Kuomintang, landlords, Christians, or was associated with foreigners.' Mass arrests took place of these 'enemies of the people', and thousands were executed. Places like the Canidrome, a stadium originally used for greyhound racing, were transformed into mass slaughter houses. The so-called enemies were persecuted, and forced to do menial work like cleaning public lavatories.

'It seems my sister Pearl was persecuted as well.' Pearl had adopted the Chinese name Chi Tsang after Liberation, perhaps in order to mask her Western associations. John says she was tormented, and driven to despair. 'And so, eventually, Pearl, the crying baby my mother found in the tall grass, tried to commit suicide by slashing her wrist. But she was discovered in time, and her life was saved.'

Yet, he says, the harassment continued. 'One of the torture methods was to force a person to write essays, confessing their sins and asking for forgiveness. The writing was always unsatisfactory and always needed to be rewritten over and over again, sometimes a hundred times. It was a sick mind-game. They emphasised over and over that the person "needed to be forgiven" so really they were torturing you mentally. The repentance was an illusion, a cheap trick conjured up to make the innocent feel guilty. It was a strategy to brainwash people.'

Dan Lu's portrait is nothing like as grim. I found Dan, who was living in Hong Kong and teaching at the Baptist University, through John, who was living in North America. Dan told me: 'Pearl was a bosom friend of my mother's and in close contact with my family.' Dan's mother Mao Ming was a colleague of Pearl's at the Lester hospital and told Dan that Pearl worked there from 1948, first as deputy nursing director, then being promoted to nursing director, and retiring in 1963.

Pearl retired, Dan says, simply because of her age and poor health. 'No political factors were involved.' He writes: 'Perhaps the sad picture of Pearl's life was exaggerated to some extent. In my opinion and according to my mum's memory, she did not suffer much even in the Cultural Revolution. This is because she had retired [three years] before it broke out, so that she was out of the Red Guards' attention.'

However, her life in retirement was not all peace and harmony. There was one period of punishment and public humiliation, which chimes with what John says. Dan told me: 'She intended to commit suicide during the Cultural Revolution because she was forced to do manual labour in public.' He adds that, because of her age, this treatment did not last long.

'If she had remained in the post of the director of the nursing department, then she would have been severely criticised and even tortured physically and psychologically. To my observation, most of the time she lived peacefully without external disturbance. She was very cautious, never talking about politically sensitive topics. The small circle of friends she kept might also have saved her from the troubles. Otherwise, she would have been involved in the turmoil, for nearly all who had received education overseas were regarded as unreliable.' Their freedom of association and movement was restricted to prevent them infecting others. 'Pearl was not within this category. Not for a single hour did she lose her freedom, nor was she beaten and scolded. She kept a low profile in those years.'

Pearl in 1964

Dan also says that Pearl's lack of written Chinese was not a problem because she had assistants who could write documents for her. 'Though she could not write [it] well, she was able to speak Chinese perfectly'. In any case, he says, most communication at the hospital was verbal. Pearl did not speak about her past, and her connections with foreign missionaries: 'My mother told me that Pearl seldom mentioned her life experiences to anyone. Maybe it was because she felt shame at being an orphan.'

Alf's letters give further insight on the constraints Pearl was living under. From the time he moved to Hong Kong, they wrote every two or three weeks. Pearl also wanted to write to Mildred, but doing so directly was dangerous, so communications were channelled via Alf. Chutney never forgot Pan-yan at Christmas and on her birthday. Go-between Alf signs his letters 'My love to all and Pearl's to you'.

In September 1960, when Mildred and Les sent a birthday card to Pearl via him, he warned them: 'Unfortunately it is still not wise to send letters direct from England to Pearl. Someone did so recently, addressed, of course, in English, and it caused quite a lot of curiosity – I expect from all the [hospital] staff from gatekeepers up. From here I send greetings and make some general remarks about the weather with... [an] envelope written in Chinese. Since they know that I am here, the letter is taken for granted, but may at any time be opened or questioned, so I only write generalities and have been warned not to write too often.'

The following year Alf writes: 'It is not possible to send much in our weekly communications but I do manage to slip in a remark about folk occasionally, although the frequent mention of foreign names of persons may at any time bring trouble. The folk there, of course, know that she received letters from me from HK, and the absence of such letters might cause enquiries or critical remarks, and it is just possible that any such letter may also be the subject of critical remarks at any time.'

Alf writes also in these replies about his life in Hong Kong. He has been keeping well and busy. In a report marking Alf's fifty years of missionary service, the *Methodist Recorder* wrote of one initiative he led: 'This 77-year-old 'retired' missionary was responsible more than any other person for supervising the construction of the Wesley Village, the refugee village which the American Methodist missionary authorities have described as the most outstanding and interesting piece of work overseas in recent years.'

Sadly, Alf's health was failing during his years in Hong Kong. In 1958 he had suffered a stroke and, after a spell in hospital, needed more care than he could receive at the Soldiers' and Sailors' Home. Through the Methodist Mission he befriended two sisters, Jennie and Jane Fung. He had some money saved and offered to use it to buy an apartment with them. Together they bought a third-floor flat at 215B Prince Edward Road, Kowloon. The Fungs effectively adopted Alf and cared for him until his death. Now, for the first time since Bessie died, Alf was living with a family once again.

I have a pile of tiny black and white snapshots that show how happy this new life made him. There are photos of Alf and the Fungs around the dinner table, with Geoff Mauldon joining them; out in the country together on trips; up in the mountains at Sha Tin Pass; and at Lok Ma Chau on the border between

Hong Kong and mainland China; in large extended family groups, Alf with a child on his lap; and at tea parties. In one, Alf is cutting a cake and looking directly at the camera. A caption written on the back reads: 'Well! I'm cutting you a piece aren't I?'

Alf tells Les and Mildred that despite a weakened heart, 'I am keeping remarkably well. Hearing and sight not so good as last year, but general health good.' However, 'It means rest every afternoon about which I often fume, but I know it is good for me and so submit. I am able to go to the morning service at the Chinese Methodist Church, Kowloon, 8.30am and then across to Hong Kong for evening service at the English Methodist church.'

Alf's letters to Mildred and Les reveal that Pearl, too, has failing health. She has always suffered from arthritis and headaches, he says, but in 1960 these

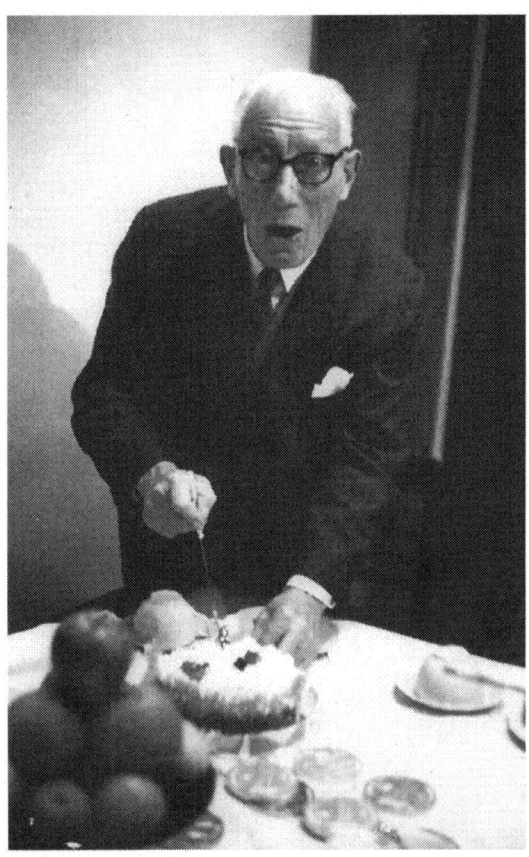

Alf: 'Well! I'm cutting you a piece aren't I?

have been worse. 'She is being given some time off duty, when the pains are very bad and just at present she has been one month off. I get frequent letters from her – just a few lines to tell me how she is. This is the worst attack for quite a long time... I have asked her if I could send her anything, but she replied that I was not to do so – not yet at any rate – for, of course, any parcel received by her would be known by the whole staff from the man at the door to the head of the hospital, so, at least, [this] is my interpretation of the conditions. Pearl is still on monthly sick-leave, and tells me that the heads of departments are all very kind to her, and continue to give her the medical treatment of both Western and old-fashioned Chinese medicines. Both kinds are admitted in Chinese hospitals now.'

Alf's letters also reveal that Pearl is lonely, separated from the second great love of her life, Norah Li. Norah was posted to Outer Mongolia in 1957 or so. She 'came home for a short holiday during July but has returned to Ulan Bator for another spell of duty, so Pearl has been deprived of the one person to whom she could talk more freely than to others. But she has long realised that the less said in conversation with others, the less likely [she is] to have additional troubles.'

In 1961, when Alf is 82, he is unable to go out as often as he once did, but still attends two churches every Sunday, regularly goes to other church meetings, and occasionally preaches 'at some small Chinese gathering of social workers'.

He says the Methodist Church in Hong Kong is thriving, with extensive youth work. Within two years they have raised the funds to build a new church and school at North Point on Hong Kong Island. 'All branches of the Church are represented here in this Colony, including many of the latest, Jehovah's Witnesses, Latter-day Saints, etc, and so Hong Kong and Kowloon is one of the most mixed-up "one Holy Catholic Church" to be found anywhere, and all contained in this small area, where since the war the population has increased from around 7-800,000 to over 3 million.'

Each year a further 70-to-80,000 refugees arrive. 'Imagine, in this small area, a new city of 80,000 has to be housed, schooled and hospitalised every year! An impossible task! Of course, there is poverty and overcrowding, and the fires among the wooden huts on the hillsides where the refugees settle bring untold suffering and demands for further relief and accommodation. Think of it, and let the youth think of it, and the HK Government should receive some praise.'

51 PEARL IN HONG KONG

Pearl was allowed to go to Hong Kong twice before the Cultural Revolution to visit Alf. In 1962 she managed a long stay. I have pictures of her then. She looks thin and frail, dressed in some in what looks like a Mao jacket, wearing half-rimmed spectacles that make her look very studious, but she is smiling. The letters she writes to Mildred and Les from Hong Kong are very different to those sent from Shanghai. Knowing that these will not be opened by the censors, she gives an unvarnished picture of her life there, and also goes into detail about her own long-term illness.

Pearl in Hong Kong, 1962

In her first letter, written eight days after her arrival, she says: 'I am down here again for six months leave. Father was at the border to meet me. The baggage took nearly two hours for the customs to examine, as I was staying longer this time, I brought summer and winter clothes with me, they searched everything, I thought I would miss the tram to Kowloon, as I was the last one to cross the border, Father looks fairly well, getting old like the rest of us, takes his daily exercises, walking around.'

Alf has mentioned in letters to Mildred and Les that Pearl has been taking some time off work, but now she reveals that she has actually not been working for two years. 'I have been off duty since August 1960. I had a slight some sort of thrombosis one night at 10.15. Suddenly the arms and legs went numb, tongue to left side, I was unable to speak for about seven minutes. Blood pressure low usually. I had constant headaches for many years, now getting terrible each time, my old doctor who did the spinal fusion said it was due to cervical arthritis.' Her doctor wanted to investigate further but 'I am not going through all the unnecessary examination, I am old and not young, if I can keep going on my two legs and enjoy life, that is quite enough.'

Despite her inability to work, the hospital has treated her very kindly, she says, only cutting her pay by 30 per cent, despite knowing she will not be returning to work.

She writes about her friend Norah Li's house, which Norah shares with her sister, who suffers from heart disease. 'They live in the former French town, nice and quiet.' Living at the hospital, she says, 'does not suit my head or nerves.' With the communal phone right outside her door ringing at all hours, she was suffering from mental exhaustion. She feels so much better in Hong Kong: 'Now I just eat and sleep.'

It is her birthday while Pearl is with Alf, on July 1, and she gets cards and presents from Mildred and Les, and also from Hilda Thexton, the wife of the late missionary Leslie Thexton, who she knew in Yunnan. The previous year Hilda had invited Pearl to come and live with her in England, and she makes the offer again. Pearl tells Mildred she has said no, because it would be too much of a burden for Hilda to have to look after 'an invalid like myself'. However: 'If I was younger I would consider the question again.' It's not that she doesn't want to go: 'I wish I could have the wings of a dove and fly to come and see you, Les and the family.'

If Pearl were to just get on a ship or plane for England, no one would stop her. She must be tempted at times, but resists. She does however apply, in September, to extend her stay with Alf. 'I have sent another wire off this morning [to ask for an] extension... because the time [to return] is drawing near. The reply came wanting to know the reason why, so I sent a wire saying father's heart is not good and my own illness has not improved.'

In Hong Kong she regains her strength and something of her health. 'I am making hay whilst the sun shines, getting all I can into my stomach.'

Mildred appears to have sent cash, and seems to have asked if there is anything else Pearl needs, because in her reply she writes: 'I do not need any clothing, but to have my teeth repaired and eyes tested for new glasses, they are the two main items on the list during this visit, so when I am eating and reading I shall remember my old dear friends.'

Pearl details the severe food rationing in Shanghai: 'Since I was taken ill in

August 1960, I have been on half a pint of milk daily, extra nourishment including vegetables, because the staff's food is quite ordinary, one of the heads and sometimes the superintendent comes up to my room to see me and bring some little parcels of food.'

Her salary of just over $100 per month is enough to supplement her food ration: 'I really enjoy myself going out eating and buying things to eat: food is very expensive and rice is rationed. Years ago I was put down for 22 catties of rice per month, and at most times one could buy cakes, biscuits, and go to restaurants without a rice ticket, but now it is the other way about.' A catty is about 600grams or 1.3lbs.

'Every time one must use rice tickets so one has to be very careful. If you eat too much at the beginning of the month, then you have to go without at the end.' Most people get slightly more than Pearl's rice ration, 27 to 29 catties, and those doing physical labour get 35, but it is not enough. So there are no longer any fat people in Shanghai, 'all dresses are too big, but one wears them just the same, because the cloth ration is also very limited.' The number of rice coupons is linked to salary, with the higher-paid getting more to eat. 'In the restaurants, one has to give a 2oz rice ticket to start with, then if you want more rice, you pay accordingly. I usually eat 2oz of rice, and make up on the vegetables. One can order more than one dish and bring it home for the family.'

Rations have been reduced over the years. The monthly cooking oil ration was 1lb, then half a pound, then 3oz, and now 2oz 'not enough to smear the frying pan with, eh?' The vegetable ration is 8oz for ten days, meat now 2oz a month. Eggs are very hard to get hold of, so many households keep chickens, if they can afford their feed. Because of all this, there is a thriving black market in food. The one thing Pearl misses is fruit, which is almost impossible to get hold of, so 'you can imagine I am enjoying bananas and apples here in Hong Kong'.

Even writing from Hong Kong she must be cautious, and ends this letter: 'Well Chutney and Les, these bits of comment are for you only, please do not pass anything on [or] it won't be very nice for me, eh?' It is clear from that last caution that Pearl could get into grave trouble with the Communist authorities if they knew she had revealed all that she has about life in Shanghai.

Pearl writes twice more before she returns to China. On July 2, the day after her birthday, she reports 'I am feeling much better in general health, the headache still on and off, heart pains come on sometimes, but I have lots to be thankful for.' The offer of a home in England is still open: 'Hilda has written again asking if I have made or changed my mind, she has my bed ready, waiting for me to arrive.'

Pearl also speaks of her step brother: 'Regarding John, I do not know how much Father has told you, or perhaps he does not want to go into details so do not repeat what I have told you. He is in America, teaching in some high school... I expect you know he was married to an American girl and had a little girl... He married a second time to another American and had a little boy.'

Finally, on September 21, it is clear Pearl's request to extend her stay has been refused. 'Just a line to say goodbye until next time. I shall be leaving here on the 27th... I have been here five months, this time has gone very quickly. I feel much better, and thanks to all the kind friends who have made it a holiday which will not be forgotten... All things come to an end and I must leave and love you and again say thank you for everything.'

Pearl would never see Alf again.

52 JOHN IN AMERICA

It's time to bring John back into the story. When we left him, he was headed off to America as part of a scheme under which Chinese Air Force personnel went to the US for advanced training 'with new aircraft, to learn new skills. I was sent as an interpreter. I was excited to go.'

He was stationed first at Biloxi, on the Gulf of Mexico close to New Orleans, then in 1945 moved to Scott Field, St Clair County, Illinois, where airmen learned to operate aircraft radio communications.

Thus began a rather turbulent time for John, with highs and lows, great happiness and much sadness. It included his first marriage, after a whirlwind courtship which was soon followed by his illness from tuberculosis, which led to him spending six months in hospital. While he was being treated the order came through for all Chinese personnel to go back to China. The training programme was shutting down.

John was desperate to stay, hoping that the fact he was being treated for TB and had married an American might work in his favour. So he appealed: 'I went straight to the top. I wrote a personal letter to President Harry Truman. The White House actually answered, but referred me to the Chinese authorities in Washington. I thought I was dead meat.'

The date for his departure was set. John was to board a ship at 6am the next morning. Then came a stroke of great good fortune. 'At two in the afternoon, the day before our scheduled departure, the phone rang.' The caller was an old acquaintance, Qiu Zheng Huan, who John had met at Southwest Union University in Kunming and had trained with for the air force.

'John, old buddy, did you write a request for a leave of absence?" Qiu asked. "The orders just came through from Chongqing. You can stay and get treatment."

'I was stunned.'

John stayed, and was officially discharged from the military. He continued his treatment until, after six months, his money ran out. Fortunately another hospital took up his care, for free.

Alf sent John money on which he and his wife were able to live for a while, after which they both got jobs; he as a caretaker in a church and she managing a vitamin store. Trouble came quickly, as it often seemed to for John. He was sacked from his job at the church, ostensibly for not working fast enough, but 'the other employees were behind expediting my departure' and then he discovered his wife had an alcohol addiction. One day he confronted her about her problem and she left him, but called some time later and asked to come back. They were able to live in the accommodation that came with their next jobs, at an interior decorator's.

Then she became pregnant and they were told they had to move out. She gave birth to a daughter, but started drinking again, coming home later and later. Sometimes she stayed out all night.

Finally John had a stroke of great good fortune, something he considered a turning point in his life: 'I'd gotten a letter from a Presbyterian minister, Joseph Allen in Kunming, who introduced me to his brother, who happened to be the dean of academic affairs at a local college.'

I can't help wondering whether Alf wasn't working behind the scenes, trying to help John make a success of his life in America. John wrote to the dean, who told him he would try to get him a scholarship. 'And he did. They created a foreign student scholarship for me. I started my studies in the fall.' They even supplied housing for John and his family.

However, there was no living allowance, so John got a job at a Samsonite suitcase factory. But relations between the couple became impossible and his wife abandoned him and their daughter. John filed for divorce and put the baby into care. 'I was forced to put my daughter into a children's home, a place where there's no father or mother. The state runs them. They're known as Christian homes.'

John got divorced, and he also obtained his U.S. citizenship, for which he gained the support from a range of senior air force officers with whom he had worked, including General Chennault. He stuck to his studies, and graduated with a degree in Education and Social Sciences, getting a job in a high school, teaching geography and history.

Eventually he met the woman who would become his second wife.

It was around this time that John learned his step father Alf had had a stroke. 'I took a leave of absence from teaching and flew to Hong Kong to see him. The summer heat in Hong Kong is suffocating. There was no air-conditioning in the hospital. Father Evans was just lying there, staring at the ceiling. He couldn't speak, or even move, and was sweltering in the heat. There was no way I could communicate with him. Maybe he could still hear me but I don't know. That's the last time I saw him. I was there for three days but then had to get back home. Looking back, I wish I had stayed longer.'

Perhaps seeing Alf so ill, and realising that he could easily die, helped John realise the value of the people who loved him. He certainly seems to have become far more settled after seeing Alf close to death. His new marriage represented the first family stability he had known for years. Soon afterwards his son was born. 'I was heavily involved in the parenting process, making formula for the baby because my wife was ill and couldn't produce milk... Compared to my situation before my first marriage, my life was wonderful.'

John continued his studies, completing a masters and starting on a PhD. He was making good at last, and was elected president of the State Council for Social Studies and to the National Board of Social Studies. He was the first to teach Mandarin in the regional school system and worked to improve Asian-American relations. He was awarded a Distinguished Service Award.

However, John's happiness was not to last as, some years later, his wife became seriously ill. After many months in and out of hospital, she passed away. She was not the first person close to him to die. In 1967 he had lost his foster father.

53 ALF'S FINAL YEARS

So, John is in America, Pearl is in China, and Alf is in Hong Kong. Alf would not see the others again; Pearl and John would meet once more. The comfort is that each has a family of their own: Alf with the Fung sisters in their shared flat, John with his second wife and child, Pearl with Norah, who is back in Shanghai.

The last picture I have of Alf is in a group photo, taken on February 10 1964. There were three things to celebrate at about this time: his eighty-fifth birthday, the Chinese New Year, and the fifth anniversary of his setting up home with the Fung family at Prince Edward Road, Kowloon.

When Alf wrote to a relative back in England, Walter Best, (the son of his sister Lucy) and his wife, Hilda, enclosing a copy of that photo, he explained that the party was held on the tenth 'to avoid my eighty-fifth birthday a few days earlier and the Chinese New Year on February 13. We hoped to avoid those two dates so as to emphasise the Thanksgiving Service held in our little flat, but of course, many of the folk had the other two dates in mind. Our thanksgiving was in remembrance of our fifth year now in this home, and the kindness of the friends who look after me so well.'

For Alf, it seems clear, the sisters are the most important thing in his life after Pearl. In his letter he runs through the people in the photo, identifying Jennie and Jane Fung, his friend Geoff Mauldon, the resident nurse who looks after him, and several former missionaries he knew from Yunnan. He ends: 'This was the season of the Thanksgiving for all kindness and God's grace continually received. This is the Year of the Dragon and we are hoping for a more plentiful rainfall so as to cancel our present ration of water three hours every fourth day. The bath tub is our reservoir. A Happy Easter to you all in memory and experience of our Risen Lord.'

Alf looks well in that photo, but nine months later he writes to Walter and Hilda: 'Eyes are not too good, and hands are shaky, but wishes and greetings

Alf with the Fung family

are sincere.' Just over a year after that, on January 28 1966, the Bests get the first of a series of letters from a man who signs himself W. M. Carter, Asia Field Assistant to the Methodist Missionary Society. It reads: 'As according to our records you are one of the next of kin of the Revd Alfred Evans, we are writing to inform you that we have this afternoon received a cable from our representative in Hong Kong saying that your uncle is dangerously ill as a result of cerebral thrombosis. When we receive further news from Hong Kong, we will write to you again.'

The haemorrhage had occurred two days earlier, and Alf was rushed to Queen Elizabeth hospital. On February 2, Carter passes on a little more detail: 'Uncle has not been too well over the last few months, but has retained his mental alertness to a wonderful degree... I have just visited him, and there seems precious little improvement... He is at present paralysed on the right side, leg and arm [but] we think recognises people. He cannot speak. At almost eighty-seven one cannot be surprised that events should have taken this course... The nurse and the sisters, amongst whom he lives are, of course, rallying round wonderfully. So are his many friends, Chinese and Western. He is greatly loved.'

However, Alf is tough, and is fighting back. Five days later: 'He is still very seriously ill but appears to be holding his own and possibly there are signs of improvement. One side is completely paralysed and he cannot speak though recognises friends. Uncle is most lovingly cared for by the Chinese family with whom he has lived for several years.'

Jennie Fung is a registered nurse and has taken a month's leave from work in order to stay in the hospital and help look after Alf. 'Mr Evans is in a private ward in this the most modern hospital in Hong Kong and we are quite confident that he is having the best possible treatment. His adopted son John, now in the USA, and adopted daughter Pearl, in Shanghai, have both been informed and the cables have been acknowledged.'

On February 6, Alf's eighty-seventh birthday, a cake was baked for him by the hospital and he received flowers from Walter and Hilda Best, and a number of cards. The Bests are told: 'We are sure he knew that this was his particular day'.

Alf clings to life for a year. In February 1967 his condition worsens, and 'he is moved to the Baptist Hospital in Waterloo Road, near the foothills below Lion Rock. Jennie and Jane Fung take it in turns to spend the days with him.'

The next communication was a telegram: 'ALFRED EVANS DIED PEACEFULLY 2am FEBRUARY FOURTH'

A newly-arrived missionary to Hong Kong, J. Michael Franklin, also writes to the Bests: 'You will know how very weak and frail Mr Evans had been, these last months especially. His courage remained strong right to the end, but in the early hours of February 4 he was finally released from all the weariness of his long illness. We are sure that although there must be some sadness at the passing of such a fine Christian gentleman, you will rejoice with us that he has now passed into the nearer presence of the Master he loved and served so well.'

Pearl's request for permission to come to Alf's death bed, and attend his funeral, was refused. The oppression of the Cultural Revolution was at its height and there was no compassion for someone like her. John doesn't mention why he is unable to come, but he did write this about Alf in his memoir: 'Something has always touched me strongly about his life. He is a man who dedicated his life to something he believed in: to spreading the gospel far and wide, to always doing what he thought was the right thing. He had helped all the people he could, especially those in need, building bridges of understanding. He was a man who had done so much good, and for him to suffer such a painful end was certainly against the laws of Karma, or justice.'

Two days after his death, on what would have been his eighty-eighth birthday, Alf's funeral was held at the Chinese Methodist Church in Kowloon, his coffin carried by his ministerial colleagues, followed by burial at the Chinese Christian cemetery, close to his last home.

But that's not the full story. The procession to the funeral was highly eventful. One of the mourners, Margaret Gardner, sent me an account of how Uncle Alf managed to be late for his own funeral.

Margaret wrote: 'His funeral ride was the most hilarious I have ever attended: indeed, I cannot remember having been to an even mildly funny one before, and I like to think that Uncle, with his delightful sense of humour, was highly amused at the whole proceedings too.

'The cemetery was several miles from the church and by the time I had fetched my [motor]bike after the service and got it lined up behind the hearse I found all the other mourners had disappeared along a short cut. So just me and the hearse get off... The funeral car charged along at a rate of knots, and it was only by threading through the stationary traffic at the traffic lights – a very unpopular procedure! – that I was able to keep it in sight at all... Suddenly, in the middle of the main road, there was a shattering explosion and the cortege ground to a standstill. So did the rest of the traffic, and we had Kowloon paralysed in a matter of minutes. We eventually all put our shoulders to the back – but it's a bit inhibiting pushing against glass walls – and managed to get the hearse off the road, and the city mobile again.'

While the undertakers stayed with the broken-down hearse to await a replacement, Margaret was sent on to explain to the mourners, by now waiting at the cemetery, what had happened. Except that she didn't know the way, 'so the only man who did had to perch precariously on the pillion and yell instructions from the rear. He was so much taller than I that we swayed in the breeze, and so much heavier that I expected the front wheel to rise. My little Honda felt the strain and so did I.'

They arrived to find the mourners shivering: 'It was a cold winter's day with a biting wind, and there is a singular lack of distraction in cemeteries... Every funeral car here displays an outsized photograph of the deceased and we almost cheered at the sight of Uncle's cheery face twinkling down on us, when at last it rolled up, late for his own funeral, bless him.'

This is not quite the end of Alf's story. Revd Li Ping-kwong, president of the Methodist Church in Hong Kong, wrote to me saying he had known Alf since his adolescence and 'he was my guarantor when I applied for an overseas student visa to study theology abroad.' Some years after Alf's burial, he went on, 'the relatives of Revd Evans requested that his ashes be scattered into the sea. I was the one who conducted the ceremony.'

After that, it was decided to place his gravestone at the Methodist Conference Centre in Silver Mine Bay on Lantau Island, the biggest island in Hong Kong. The stone is designed to resemble an open book with, on the left-hand page, a photo of Bessie and Alf, beneath which he is described as 'Missionary to the Methodist Church in China and Hong Kong for 61 years.'

On the right-hand page is an inscription in Chinese. In translation it reads:
The Revd Alfred Evans
Born in England;
Dedicated to evangelism;
Travelled a long way to China and devoted himself there;
Worked with painstaking effort;
Built up solidarity with the Chinese;
The Gospel was widely spread;
Relieved people from pain and suffering;
Saved people's souls;
Worked diligently through day and night even without sleeping;
Husband and wife shouldered the same burden and heavy responsibilities;
Built their house by the lake side;
Lived happily without being homesick;
Since 1951, settled in Hong Kong;
Engaged in religious activities;
Worked to the best of his ability;

In 1967, Soul returned to heaven;
A great servant of God;
Honoured by men and God.

Born on 6 February 1879
Died on 4 February 1967

Alf and Bessie's memorial at the Methodist Conference Centre

54 PEARL AND JOHN

With Alf gone, Mildred had no one in Hong Kong through whom she could pass messages to Pearl. When a letter did come, there was no return address on it, and it was clearly not safe for Mildred to reply.

Pearl's final letter to Mildred and Les was sent on December 23 1967, and says very little, just: 'The weather is getting very cold now. I am keeping fairly well, doing my own cooking etc. A woman comes in half day a week to clean the room out and do some washing.

'My old arthritis, arteriosclerosis and high blood pressure keeps me from going out each day, but on the whole I am as well as one can expect with old age creeping on. I shall be sixty-three next year.' Mildred's son, Arnold, believes 'the Cultural Revolution made further letter writing too risky to contemplate.'

These were terrible years for Mildred for another reason. Her son Arnold says: 'The years of the Cultural Revolution were a time when Mildred had no contact at all with China, but when her thought and imagination were still much engaged by it. But she had much private grief to contend with, especially when her daughter, Catherine, died in tragic circumstances in 1964.' Mildred was also suffering once again from the debilitating dizziness that had led to her departure from China twenty-five years before.

I have an account of Pearl's life after Alf's death, from Dan Lu, son of her friend Mao Ming. Dan had worked in Canada for a while but was living in Hong Kong when he wrote to me, teaching at the Language Centre of the Hong Kong Baptist University.

He told me that Pearl's decision to move in with Norah was because she had been burgled while in her staff quarters at the Lester China Hospital. Dan was a child at the time, and remembers frequent visits to Pearl at Norah's, and of Pearl coming to his house. Although Pearl loved good food, he says, she was a poor cook and so 'my mother often asked us kids to take some well-cooked food to her or asked her to come over to our home to share'. Dan's family had a maid who was a good cook, and whose food Pearl liked. 'Pearl was full of loving care. Not only did she bring us kids candies, ice cream and chocolates from time to time, but also paid generously those who did her some service such as washing clothes, buying daily necessities.'

Dan remembers Pearl having few friends, and from 1980 onwards seeing virtually no one other than Norah and Mao Ming. Mao Ming was Pearl's successor as nursing director at the Lester Chinese Hospital, and 'when she was visiting my family, she spent most of the time talking with my mum about the hospital. She liked to listen to my mum telling her about her management of the whole hospital's nursing work.'

She also loved to speak in English with Dan's father, who was a doctor. Neither Dan nor his mother knew anything about Pearl's early life, nor that she had been refused permission to go to Hong Kong in 1967.

Apart from John's visit in the 1980s, Pearl seems to have lost touch with her friends and family. Dan wrote: 'She would have been overjoyed with any contact with her family. If she had received letters or phone calls from you people in the 1980s and 1990s, she would have responded quickly.'

I just wish I had known Pearl was then still alive!

I learn from Dan that Pearl died in 1994. My family thought she had died long before that. Pearl had been moved into a nursing home and, at the time of her death, Dan had returned from Canada on vacation. He and his mother visited Pearl, who was nearing the end, and did not recognise them. Norah visited daily and brought her food. John was told his step-sister did not have long to live, but he was ill at the time and unable to make the long trip. Norah arranged Pearl's burial at a Shanghai cemetery. She left her life's savings to the Nursing Society of Shanghai. Not long afterwards, Mildred also died. Pan-yan had outlived Chutney by just one year.

What of John? By the time of his second wife's death, he had become far more settled and successful in his teaching career. Eventually he remarried. Following his retirement from teaching he embarked on a kind of second career in promoting U.S. and China relations at the interpersonal and community levels. This was his personal calling, and through these efforts he became a prominent and respected member of the community based on his knowledge, unique perspectives and life experiences, including his time with Chennault and the Flying Tigers in Kunming.

Over the years, he garnered special recognition and various awards for his veteran status and his life's work. He was declared a "distinguished American" for his work with the Flying Tigers, fostering civic relations with China, and his long teaching career. He was also given the Dr Martin Luther King Jr Humanitarian Award and a Lifetime Achievement Award.

John died in 2019. I only wish Alf could have lived to see him declared an American hero and honoured by both the USA and China.

55 TO CHINA

I wanted to see Kunming, Chaotung and Stone Gateway for myself. As I did so, I was following in the footsteps of a number of those whose lives I have been exploring, and who had made their own nostalgic trips back to these places, among them John.

Apart from his visit to Hong Kong to visit Alf when he had his stroke in 1958, John did not return to China until 1983, having taken early retirement. It was nearly forty years since he left Kunming. His spur for returning was a fellow retiree saying he would like to see China, and John telling him if he could get a group of ten together, he would organise it.

From then on, John did a trip a year, and on one made a point of retracing Bessie's journey up the Yangtze to experience the rapids as she had done. I also took a cruise through the Three Gorges, in 2002.

My boat up the Yangtze was filled with American and Taiwanese tourists. Together with my husband Hugh, we boarded in the evening and almost immediately met up with a retired doctor and his wife from Toot Baldon, a small village about ten miles from our home in Oxfordshire.

We were up at 6.30am to see the boat go through the first gorge. The weather was hazy, but the scenery magnificent. Along with the timeless natural landscape, I saw the might and ambition of modern China. A great new dam was being built which was to provide a quarter of China's electricity. The 400km long lake created would mean three million people having to be rehoused, and whole cities rebuilt on higher ground.

In mid-morning we reached a side gorge and, wearing life jackets, got into sampans to be pulled up stream by trackers, four to each boat. They used bamboo ropes, like those used to pull Bessie, Alf and the other missionaries up the main river. The trackers waded through the shallow water, or ran along the shore for nearly an hour, while two men steered, using poles to fend us off from rocks and gravel banks. At the head of the gorge the water was very clear and we could see the bottom. It was much narrower than the main river, and the sides grew steeper as it wound its way through the hills.

It troubled me that the trackers were exerting so much effort just to entertain tourists, but I was told that the men hauling us were peasant farmers, and very poor. Working as trackers, they could earn more in an hour than in several days on the land. So the tracking work was sought after, and shared among all who wanted it. They would each haul only one or two boats a day, and for no more than ten days a month.

We disembarked on day three at Chongqing, as the missionaries did, but from there flew to Kunming, saving the many days of hard travelling that they endured. Ken Parsons had come this way in 1991. The airport had been a grass airfield in 1949 when he had been forced to evacuate here from Chaotung. As Ken wrote: 'Forty-two years before, I had landed in the St Paul, the old Dakota plane owned by the Lutheran Mission, after saying heart-rending goodbyes to all our Chinese and Miao friends.'

When John came to Kunming he found himself an object of curiosity: 'One thing that struck me as peculiar was how unusual we looked to the average Chinese person. While we were in town we stopped at a market. Some of us stayed on the bus. A small host of Chinese people stood near the bus and stared into the windows as if we were animals in a zoo. They especially gawked at the Americans. I asked why. Suddenly it dawned on me. Since Mao ordered all foreigners out of China in two weeks or face imprisonment, no white man had been there.'

When I visited, non-Chinese visitors were still comparatively rare, especially in the provinces. Hugh and I were also closely inspected: me for my 'yellow hair and long nose!' People came up to touch us, as if wondering whether we were real.

Like John and Ken Parsons, we sought out Alf and Bessie's mission house, and the Stinking Brook. Ken had found the spot, but it stank no more: 'the Communists had covered it over as soon as they took over the city.'

When John tried to find the house where he had grown up: 'I saw myself from the outside, a man standing in an empty lot, a barren place where I once lived. The house was gone, torn down, and the street was changed all around. The old pagoda was still there. I felt like a man standing in a dream.' The pagoda, that ancient landmark within 100yds of the compound, was the only clue for Ken 'that we had been walking up the street that had had so many memories and smells.'

I wanted to find the Zion church, the Methodists' main church in the city, built by Alf. During the cultural revolution it had been used as a factory, but when Ken Parsons came here 'the church gates were there but Zion wasn't. We had heard that one night an electrical fault had started a fire and the church had been completely gutted. Even so it was a nasty shock to be met with a huge pile of bricks instead of a church.'

Some key people were there to greet Ken, though. Among them Revd Chang

Hsien Chow, who had been ordained in Chaotung in 1947, and Professor and Mrs Henry Wu. Henry had been head of the Methodists' Tian Nan High School in the 1940s. They told Ken that they were going to rebuild Zion as a church for a congregation of 1,500, three times its original capacity, and add halls, public rooms and accommodation for staff. A plaque to Alf would be placed in the new porch. In 1980, restrictions on Christianity eased and the building was restored and allowed to operate as a non-denominational church.

By the time of my visit, the church was complete. As soon as we arrived at our hotel I telephoned Henry Wu, a good friend of Alf, and Zhu Aiguang, a member of the Miao tribe who had also known him. Mr Zhu had been a teenage pupil at the Tian Nan school when Alf was on the board of governors.

It was arranged that Zhu Aiguang would show us what was left of the Kunming the missionaries knew, and the new church, then take us to Henry's home for supper. A wedding was taking place when we arrived at the church, the hymns led by a good-sized choir. There was also a Sunday school in progress. The place was clearly thriving once again.

Like John and Ken, we travelled up the street where the mission compound was, and found nothing to see but the pagoda, then took the Burma Road to the original site of Tian Nan School, on a terrace cut into the red earth of a hillside. The site became a cement factory after the school was forced to close, but was now derelict. Mr Zhu told me he had come to Kunming in 1948 and spent three years at the school. The pupils and staff used to visit Uncle Alf's lakeside house at weekends and knew him well, so this visit was a trip down memory lane for him. There was, sadly, no time to try to find the house beside the lake.

John found his return to Kunming depressing: 'The Communists had changed so much. There were lots of changes in town. I felt out of place.' Many places he remembered had gone. 'There was a place where they used to sell fresh flowers each day. Countrymen and women brought all kinds of pretty flowers to sell in the mornings. That was gone. Kunming has such a sunny climate that you can grow any plant there, but it was all gone. It was painful to see... Kunming lake was there, but destroyed. One crazy leader wanted to fill in part of it to grow rice, but no rice would grow there. It ruined the lake. I hired a motorboat and toured a bit, tried to go back to places I'd known. I took some pictures. The mountains were still there, of course, and the temples, but the colours had faded, the life force. My vision of the beauty of Kunming and China had faded.'

From Kunming, Hugh and I flew to what was Chaotung to the missionaries, but is now known as Zhaotong, where we were given a royal welcome. A reception committee of five greeted us, and we learned that they had been expecting three couples, not just Hugh and me. Among the welcoming party was Ms Li Ke Rui, the granddaughter of John Li, who had been arrested by the Communists and died in prison. Mr Li was the first Chinese ordained by the Methodists, and a towering figure in the history of the missions to South West

China. Miss Li had come to arrange our visit to Shimenkan (Stone Gateway), and to invite us to dinner with her family.

Before dinner our hosts took us around the back streets in Zhaotong. It was like going back a century: the old houses were still standing and life seemed to be lived on the pavement, including tooth pulling and ear cleaning! A scribe was writing letters for the illiterate. The shops, which seemed to double as homes, were cramped and squalid and the people looked rather grubby, but had big open grins on their faces, at the sight of 'long noses' walking around together. I particularly liked the second-hand false-teeth stall!

Next day we were taken round the hospital, and shown the scanner which had been bought with money raised in England, and for which they were very grateful. Next we went to the church, where we were told the congregation was 200-to-300 on a normal Sunday, and 500-to-600 at Easter. We got a wonderful welcome, as Ken Parsons had a decade earlier, when John Li's granddaughter 'delighted everyone as she played her keyboard. There was singing, dancing and the generous giving of Miao costumes to each of the visitors.'

We were also offered Miao costumes, which we did not have room for in our suitcases, so they said they would post them. With my size I would fill about three of these outfits!

Alongside the church was an outbuilding they hoped to convert into a kitchen, and the now-derelict house formerly lived in by some of the missionaries, which they wanted to rebuild as a retirement home for members of the congregation with no family to care for them.

We thought our trip by Jeep to Stone Gateway would only take an hour, since it was around twenty miles away. In fact the roads were so bad that it took more than three hours of bone-shaking misery. The weather was quite cold and very foggy, so we saw little of the countryside. At one point the fog was so bad that the driver had to get out to see where the road went next. It was fortunate that he did, because he found we were heading towards the edge of a cliff.

Stone Gateway is, of course, a hugely significant place in the story of the Miao and the mission, and there is great poignancy in a visit today. The graves of Sam Pollard and Heber Goldsworthy – one killed by disease, the other murdered – are stark reminders of the dangers the missionaries faced.

The village had great resonance for Ken Parsons, who lived the first ten years of his life here. He was particularly affected by seeing that 'the house Heber Goldsworthy had started to build, using cut stone, before he was murdered by bandits in 1938, had been kept in repair. It was where I had often stayed during the endless months I was overseeing the building of the two new houses. Incidentally, it was where we had all slept together under the dining table, when the earthquake tremors were so frighteningly strong!'

The table was set for a meal, and 'on the table was a bowl of apples from one of the trees that father had planted years ago.'

Visitors are taken up to the graves of Pollard and Goldsworthy, as we were. Ken writes of a particularly significant visit, involving Heber Goldsworthy's children, and gives the background: 'In 1955 the Red Guards had desecrated the graves, scattering the large stones that had been so carefully chiselled over a wide area. Incredibly, the Communist authority had now reinstated both.

'The masonry was not quite identical with the original, but it was practically so. In front of these graves an explanatory stone tablet had been erected. The party, with a number of government officials and Chinese and Miao Christians, were invited to take part in a ceremony when it was decreed that the graves were to be preserved to mark the gratitude of the people for all that the missionaries had done to raise their standard of living.

'Goldsworthy's daughter and son were present and she was invited to lay a spray of six dahlias on the threshold of her father's grave, remembering the six decades since his death.' Eight dahlias were placed on Sam Pollard's grave, 'representing the eight decades since he died of typhoid.'

The graves were monumental, 10ft long, 8ft wide and 5ft high, with at the front an imitation stone door set in an elaborate surround. The flowers were placed before the door, high above which a large stone cross proclaimed this a Christian grave. The graves can be seen for miles around. The dahlias were very significant, says Ken, because 'unknown to the people there, they had been introduced from England by my father.'

Heber Goldsworthy's wife Ida had died a few months before the visit and the couple's son and daughter 'scattered her ashes on her husband's grave – a wonderful act of Christian faith and love.' She had been in England [and pregnant] when he was murdered, and their daughter Pat had never seen her father.'

On our visit, Ms Li had brought a huge picnic lunch consisting of bananas and rolls, plus spiced green beans in large sachets, which she had arranged for us to eat in the office/bedroom of the village bureaucrat. After lunch we walked along a dirt path, through the village, past thatched cottages and some derelict buildings to the basketball pitch, where children were playing.

At the end of the path was the original 'stone gateway', where the early missionaries, Sam Pollard and Harry Parsons, had laid rocks to make rough steps down the steep hillside so that horses could get in and out of the village. On the way there we stopped to see the market, which was in full swing. Several people came up to me, grinning, to shake hands; my yellow hair was again the subject of much interest.

After we arrived back from Shimenkan, we were taken to Mr Li's flat, where his wife and daughter had cooked us another enormous meal. Mr Li, who was about seventy, had been an artist and musician all his life, also a lay preacher. He said a prayer before the meal, in which he thanked us for coming so far to see them. Ms Li had a lovely contralto voice, so she and Hugh sang hymns together. From here we went on to Shanghai, and then home.

So that's my story, or rather the story of Pearl, Bessie, Alf and John. Four people, four remarkable lives.

56 AFTERWORD: THE MIAO CHURCH AFTER 1951

By the late 1940s the Church had become fully nationalised, with the missionaries there to provide specific support such as in medicine or education. When they left with the coming of the Communists the local people were well-prepared to take over the running of the churches, since a considerable number of Miao had been ordained.

However, life in the countryside soon became very difficult, during the disastrous agricultural and social 'reforms' of the Great Leap Forward, from 1958 to 1962, which led to the Great Chinese Famine and the death of between 15 and 55 million. This was followed soon after by the Cultural Revolution from 1966 to 1976, during which the Red Guards caused further upheaval and more deaths in the countryside.

As Christianity was seen as foreign and evil, Christians were persecuted. To have gone to a mission school was reason enough to be arrested and imprisoned. Families were divided, with husbands being sent to work as forced labour.

One of the places they attacked was Shimenkan (Stone Gateway). The Pollard script was banned. During this time the Miao Christians became an underground church. They hid their bibles and hymn books up the chimneys and were very careful about their security.

After the death of Mao in 1976, China gradually recovered from some of his worst policies and life in the countryside began to improve a little. The differences in dress and speech of the ethnic minorities was thought to be of interest to tourists and ethnic minority museums were created. Churches were repaired or rebuilt with the aid of government grants and the numbers of underground Christians began to grow, as they succeeded in passing on their faith to their children. Although the number of Christians increased, the structure of the individual denominations which had held churches together had disappeared, and so each church had its own hierarchy, usually one family.

Shimenkan, and the restored graves of Pollard and Goldsworth, became a centre for pilgrimage.

Prime Minister Margaret Thatcher had had a Methodist upbringing and was aware of the Pollard story, so when she went to China she asked to visit

Shimenkan and Zhaotong, much to the surprise of the Chinese authorities. Since they were some 1400 miles from Beijing, such a visit was impossible.

From the 1990s onwards the study of Miao culture and the Pollard story became increasingly popular. Pollard's books were translated and became the focus of academic study. Westerners were allowed to visit Shimenkan without a visa. Sam Pollard's grandson Stephen attended the celebrations for the eightieth anniversary of the great man's death. The Miao's creation and folklore stories, collected in 1940s by Keith and Ken Parsons, had been lost in the Cultural Revolution, but were now returned to the Miao, along with a computer programme to enable the Pollard script to be typed.

By 2004, estimates put the membership of underground churches in China between 15 and 90 million. This sparked a further crack-down.

John Parsons (Ken's son) visited Shimenkan in 2011. He writes: 'Then there was one loo but no drinking water! (As the Han spread across China the Miao were driven out of the valleys on to the hill tops – so their villages are often short of water). It took the headmaster of the school an hour or more to find water for a cup of tea. I found it very moving to stand where my parents and grandparents had stood. In the welcome service we sang hymns that my grandmother had taught both me and the Miao; I preached and it was translated straight into Miao. We were invited into the pastor's home for a meal and, in the gloom, it really was just as it had been in my grandfather's time, sitting in low stools around a coal oven – until the electric power came on and the TV burst into life!

'Everywhere we went in China we met Miao who treated us like royalty because of the Pollard story and what my grandparents had done. Incidentally, it was my grandmother who was held in highest regard. With her Devonshire burr you could not tell her speech from a Miao. The people loved her and she was held in profound esteem by the women – many copied her hairstyle, a bun – which you often see in the photos.

'In 2017 a film crew came to the UK to make an eight-part TV documentary on the life of Pollard. They were able to visit significant locations in Cornwall and the Isle of Wight and interview relatives of the key players. However, shortly after they returned to China the project was closed down for political reasons and is still in abeyance. This is but one sign of the present crack-down on Christians.' Another was the restriction on visiting Shimenkan.

One of John's contacts in China described the current state of the Miao church in Shimenkan like this: 'Old Shimenkan is still there, everything is the same except they rebuilt the memorial chapel with the ruins inside the new building. However, all the books and materials about missionaries are not allowed in the church, or even in family homes. We could not visit the church now, so people could not go to the graves from the path you went on. My friends and I went to the graves from another small path behind the hill. About ten days after we left, an iron door was put on that small path. But it's no use because they could not surround the whole hill, and many families still have missionaries' books secretly.' So the battle between the authorities and the Miao people goes on, and neither side gives way.

FOOTNOTES

Chapter 1
Page 1: **lying naked in the long grass** John Evans's description of Bessie's discovery of Pearl, based on his unpublished memoir.

Chapter 2
Page 4: **Riding the River Dragon** Chou Yentung, from a poem about a journey through the Yangtze gorges
Page 6: **they attacked the Savins' house and that of another missionary** as reported by Lewis Savin, *Driven from China, Bible Christian Magazine,* 1901
Page 7: **The narrowest escape was on the eighth day**, William Tremberth, *Six Weeks in a houseboat through the heart of China, Bible Christian Magazine,* July 1903
Page 9: **A sea of glass mingled with fire** Revelation 15:2
Page 9: **with a terrible vortex at the point** William Tremberth, *Six Weeks in a houseboat through the heart of China, Bible Christian Magazine,* July 1903. All subsequent quotes in this chapter from the same source.

Chapter 3
Page 11: **This is what Bessie wrote:** *Thoughts on Leaving for China* by Bessie A Bull, *Bible Christian Magazine,* July 1903
Page 12: **Love so amazing, so Divine** Isaac Watts, 1707, *When I Survey the Wondrous Cross*
Page 12: **And everyone that has forsaken homes** Matthew, xix. 29
Page 13: **On Sunday morning I went to East Cowes** Mary Toms, quoted in J. Woolcock's, *A History of the Bible Christian Churches on the Isle of Wight* 1897
Page 13: **were often in danger of losing their lives** J. Woolcock, *A History of the Bible Christian Churches on the Isle of Wight* 1897
Page 13: **Mary Toms was accused of making a riot** Joan Mills, *in The Female Itinerant Preachers of the Bible Christian Church* 1999
Page 13: **the pa'son couldn't praich a bit like her** J. Woolcock, *A History of the Bible Christian Churches on the Isle of Wight* 1897
Page 14: **I perceive the people are very ignorant** J. Woolcock, *A History of the*

Bible Christian Churches on the Isle of Wight 1897

Chapter 4
Page 15: **Given fine weather and strong chair bearers** Samuel Pollard *The Story of the Miao* 1919
Page 16: **It was an awkward fall** Harry Parsons *Overland to Chao Tong, 14 days' road life, Bible Christian Magazine*, October 1903. All subsequent quotes in this chapter from the same source.

Chapter 5
Page 20: **the massive stone walls of Chaotung city** R. Elliott Kendall *Beyond the Clouds, the story of Samuel Pollard in South West China* 1948
Page 20: **the city itself dwarfed by its setting** R. Elliott Kendall *Beyond the Clouds, the story of Samuel Pollard in South West China* 1948
Page 21: **Another missionary wrote home to say** Nancy Bryant in a letter to her brother Phil, Parsons family papers held by SOAs, 1905
Page 21: **We have been having some strange scenes here** Bessie Bull, *Some Encouraging Facts, Bible Christian Magazine* January 1904
Page 21: **I've had enough of being Miss Bull** Alfred Evans, from unpublished talks given in Hong Kong, August 1962
Page 22: **it was not the city in which above all others, one would choose to live** R. Elliott Kendall *Beyond the Clouds*, 1948
Page 22: **were taking a foolhardy risk** R. Elliott Kendall *Beyond the Clouds*, 1948
[page number to insert here] **During seventeen years of work** Samuel Pollard *The Story of the Miao* 1919
Page 24: **Having interviewed Brother A. Evans for China** Minutes of the annual Bible Christian Conference, 1903
Page 24: **Am getting ever so fat** Nancy Bryant in a Letter, Parsons family papers, held by SOAS, 1905
Page 24: **What is Mr Evans going to do** Nancy Bryant in a letter, 1905, Parsons family papers, held by SOAS

Chapter 6
Page 26: **Little did I dream** Samuel Pollard, *The Coming of the Miao* 1919
Page 27: **a strange, alluring doctrine** W. A. Grist *Samuel Pollard, pioneer missionary in China* 1920
Page 27: **The following Friday** Samuel Pollard, *The Coming of the Miao* 1919
Page 29: **One can never forget those days** Samuel Pollard, *The Coming of the Miao* 1919
Page 29: **a little man about five feet four** W. A. Grist *Samuel Pollard, pioneer missionary in China* 1920
Page 30: **They are so childlike** Nancy Parsons in a letter to her brother Phil, Parsons family papers held by SOAs, 1905

Chapter 7
Page 32: **The natives who are not used to us** Nancy Bryant, writing to Phil Bryant, Parsons family papers held by SOAs, 1905
Page 33: **The Chinese are strangers** Samuel Pollard, *The Coming of the Miao* 1919. All subsequent quotes in this chapter from the same source.

Chapter 8
Page 38: **On each side of the steps** Nancy Bryant in a letter to a niece or nephew, Parsons family papers held by SOAs, 1905
Page 38: **It is a pitiable sight to see** Nancy Bryant in a letter to a niece or nephew, Parsons family papers held by SOAs, 1905
Page 39: **Little girls do their hair into plaits** Nancy Bryant in a letter to a niece or nephew, Parsons family papers held by SOAs, 1905
Page 39: **How folk laughed when the current** Harry Parsons, in a letter Charles Stedeford, Foreign Secretary of the Missionary Society, 1905
Page 39: **How appreciative [they were]** Harry Parsons, in a letter to Charles Stedeford, Foreign Secretary of the Missionary Society, 1905
Page 40: **Whom do you want, Satan or Jesus?** Samuel Pollard, quoted by W. A. Grist in *Samuel Pollard, pioneer missionary in China* 1920
Page 40: **The people, as yet, understand but the barest elements of Christian truth** Harry Parsons, in a letter Charles Stedeford, Foreign Secretary of the Missionary Society, 1905
Page 40: **Thousands of people, mostly young men and maidens** Samuel Pollard, quoted by W. A. Grist in *Samuel Pollard, pioneer missionary in China* 1920
Page 40: **to leave scarcely a single virgin** Harry Parsons, in a letter to Phil Bryant, 1905
Page 40: **We realised at once that we must** Samuel Pollard, quoted by W. A. Grist in *Samuel Pollard, pioneer missionary in China* 1920
Page 41: **A pagan festival must either be absorbed** R. Elliott Kendall *Beyond the Clouds*, 1948

Chapter 9
Page 42: **When they were still a free people** R. Keith Parsons, *Our Providential Way,* unpublished memoir
Page 42: **As well as traditions regarding love and marriage** Traditional Songs and Stories of the Hua Miao of S. W. China, collected and translated by R. Keith Parsons, held in the Miao Archive at Southampton University
Page 47: **In the rapid and sudden changes** R. Elliott Kendall *Beyond the Clouds* 1948

Chapter 10
Page 48: **proved himself an able and faithful minister** Minutes of the annual conference of the Bible Christian Church, 1905
Page 48: **I shall not be at all sorry** Alfred Evans in a letter to Charles Stedeford,

Foreign Secretary of the Missionary Society, *Bible Christian Magazine* October 1906

Page 49: **A day to be long remembered** *A few pages from Dr Lillian Grandin's journal, Bible Christian Magazine*, August 1906.

Chapter 11

Page 51: **we are surprised to hear** Minutes of the China Mission committee annual meeting, April 1907

Page 51: **We are amused to receive** Letter from Nancy Bryant to Phil Bryant, October 1906

Page 52: **We cannot recommend the marriage** Minutes of the China Mission committee annual meeting, held in Exeter, April 1907

Chapter 12

Page 53: **His wife persecuted him terribly** Nancy Bryant writing to Phil Bryant, February 1906. All subsequent quotes in this chapter from the same source.

Chapter 13

Page 56: **At midnight the continuous barking of dogs** as reported by W. A. Grist *Samuel Pollard, pioneer missionary in China* 1920

Page 57: **Just as I expected eternity to dawn** from a letter Sam Pollard wrote to his wife, as reported by W. A. Grist *Samuel Pollard, pioneer missionary in China* 1920

Page 57: **Three men took me** from a letter from Samuel Pollard to Mr. Wilton at the consulate in Yunnan Fu, as reported by W. A. Grist *Samuel Pollard, pioneer missionary in China* 1920

Page 57: **I found Mr Pollard unable to** from Dr Savin's written report to the Consul, as reported by W. A. Grist *Samuel Pollard, pioneer missionary in China* 1920

Page 57: **Thank God I am a little better** Sam Pollard in a letter to his wife, dated April 18, as reported by W. A. Grist *Samuel Pollard, pioneer missionary in China* 1920

Page 58: **My dear son, I have been led to pray for you** from an account by Nancy Parsons, Parsons family papers held by SOAs, 1907

Chapter 14

Page 59: **Bessie was travelling through Yunnan** summarising an account from John Evans, in his unpublished memoir

Page 60: **She explained that she needed the medicine** Will Hudspeth, writing in *Kingdom Overseas*, journal of the Methodist Missionary Society, 1930

Page 60: **Last week outside the East Gate** Harry Parsons in a letter, Parsons family papers held by SOAs

Page 60: **Less than a month since I saw** Harry Parsons, writing to his sister and brother-in-law, Parsons family papers held by SOAs

Chapter 15

Page 62: **So far as I know, I am the only traveller** Edwin Dingle, *Across China on Foot* 1911. This and subsequent quotes in this chapter from the same source

Page 63: **My horse, fortunately, is well-accustomed** Alfred Evans, *Missionary Echo*, volume 4, 1909

Page 63: **The weather being fine** Alfred Evans, *Missionary Echo*, volume 4, 1909

Page 65: **she died four years later** *Dictionary of Methodism*, dmbi.online

Chapter 16

Page 67: **My wife and I were living in Tung Chuan** Alfred Evans, from a talk given in Hong Kong, October 1961

Page 67: **Thirty or forty heads were hung up** Harry Parsons, *Missionary Echo*, Volume 10, 1910

Page 67: **As the missionary in her sedan chair** *Missionary Echo*, Volume 6, 1911

Page 68: **The British Consul ordered Alf** adapted from R. Keith Parsons in *Our Providential Way,* unpublished memoir

Page 69: **We cleared out of Kunming** *Missionary Echo*, May 1912

Chapter 17

Page 70: **The cornet alarm was a false one** W. A. Grist, *Life of Samuel Pollard* 1920

Page 71: **It is ten years since the Miao first came** as quoted by W. A. Grist, *Life of Samuel Pollard* 1920

Page 71: **He heard the Miao praying** W. A. Grist, *Life of Samuel Pollard* 1920

Page 72: **I felt a thrill of joy**, Capt W. H. Hudspeth, *With the Chinese battalions in France, Kingdom Overseas*, April 1919

Chapter 18

Page 73: **Sam Pollard had foreseen the dangers** W. A. Grist, *Life of Samuel Pollard* 1920

Page 74: **Sam wrote pleading that a foreign missionary should be withdrawn** Emmie Pollard, as quoted by W. A. Grist, *Life of Samuel Pollard* 1920.

Page74: **Sam's scribbled notes to Frank Dymond have survived** W. A. Grist, *Life of Samuel Pollard* All subsequent quotes in this chapter from the same source

Chapter 19

Page 75: **All [elected] local authorities have been dismissed** Harry Parsons, *Missionary Echo* April 1916

Page 75: **REVOLT OF CHINESE PROVINCE** *The Times*, December 29, 1915

Page 76: **suffering severe haemorrhages** R. Keith Parsons, *Our Providential Way* unpublished memoir
Page 76: **has been ill a good deal** Nancy Parsons, writing to Phil Bryant, July 1916
Page 76: **One afternoon... I impressed upon them** Bessie Evans, *Missionary Echo*, February 1917

Chapter 20
Page 79: **I wish you were here** Nancy Parsons writing to her brother Phil Bryant, February 1919
Page 80: **We are having the most strenuous time of our lives** Harry Parsons writing to a Mr and Mrs W. J. Nichols 1919
Page 80: **From the commencement of the year** Alfred Evans annual report for 1919
Page 81: **The young mother took Bessie to the first wife's room** A. L. Austin *The Beckoning Hand* 1979

Chapter 21
Page 84: **Beyond the best there is a better** this and subsequent quotes in this chapter A. Mary Shaw *When you were there 1884-1984 Edgehill College* 1983
Page 87: **Alf was a great favourite** Joan Howie, quoted by Julia Bishop in *A History of the Bull Family*, unpublished

Chapter 22
Page 88: **in heaven, safe and secure in her arms** John Evans, unpublished journal. All subsequent quotes from John in this chapter from the same source
Page 88: **I learned that he was living in America** Dan Lu, letter to Julia Bishop

Chapter 23
Page 91: **Their leader asked father to take a letter** John Evans in his unpublished memoir
Page 92: **Harry and Annie Parsons had used their own savings** *Missionary Echo*, April 1924
Page 92: **Yesterday I was asked to take a girl and rear her** *Missionary Echo*, April 1924
Page 93: **One day Shuang Li took us to visit** John in his unpublished memoir

Chapter 24
Page 95: **After a short interval, to our surprise and dismay** Lettie Squire, *Missionary Echo*, October 1929
Page 96: **Since then we have had the Yunnan troops,** Alfred Evans, *Missionary Echo*, October 1929

Page 97: **Trenches were dug in several quarters** Frank Dymond, Annual Report for 1929

Page 97: **Not only were they a nuisance** Will Hudspeth, Annual Report for 1929

Page 98: **The year that has just closed** Alfred Evans, Annual Report for 1929

Page 98: **After the evacuation of 1927** Lettie Squire, Annual Report for 1929

Page 98: **The girl Li Shuang-mei** Nancy Parsons, letter to Phil Bryant, 1916

Chapter 25

Page 100: **Another sorrow has fallen upon Mrs Evans** *Missionary Echo,* 1932 [page number to insert here] **It would help us in connection** Alfred Evans, in a letter to William Grist, 1933

Page 101: **When I was eight** John Evans, from his unpublished memoir

Chapter 26

Page 103: **It is a very nice place to stay** Leslie Pacey, in a letter to his parents, from family papers held by Arnold Pacey, his son.

Page 105: **Leslie was asked to meet** this and subsequent references taken from the diaries and letters of Leslie Pacey and Muriel Button, held by Arnold Pacey

Page 107: **When Mildred stayed on in Kunming** Arnold Pacey, in a letter to Julia Bishop

Chapter 27

Page 108: **One day while we were eating** John Evans, from his unpublished memoir, this and all other quotes in this chapter

Chapter 28

Page 110: **Met by Mildred** this and subsequent references taken from the diaries and letters of Leslie Pacey and Muriel Button, held by Arnold Pacey

Page 111: **enables us to have Pearl in our home** letter from Alfred Evans to W. A. Grist, April 1935

Page 112: **The town was sixteen miles from the sea** Arnold Pacey in unpublished account of his father and mother's time in China

Page 112: **She has been doing too much** from the diaries and letters of Leslie Pacey and Muriel Button, held by Arnold Pacey

Page 113: **Pan-yan arrived** from the diaries and letters of Leslie Pacey and Muriel Button, held by Arnold Pacey

Chapter 29

Page 114: **After you left Beaman's** Pearl Evans in a letter to Mildred Button,1936. This and subsequent letter held by Arnold Pacey

PAGE 116: **I find these letters rather surprising** Arnold Pacey, in a letter to Julia Bishop

Chapter 30
Page 117: **One day they asked students** This and all subsequent references John Evans, from his unpublished memoir

Chapter 31
Page 121: **Last stage of the train journey to Kunming** Mildred Button, in her diary, held by Arnold Pacey
Page 122: **I am looking forward to the work** Alfred Evans, in a note held by Arnold Pacey
Page 122: **little more than a written declaration** Leslie Pacey, 1936, in his diary, held by Arnold Pacey
Page 122: **The most tragic thing of all** Mildred Pacey, 1936, in her diary, held by Arnold Pacey
Page 124: **When the Japs took over** Alfred Evans a letter to his sisters Lucy and Annie, February 1947
Page 124: **Our baby is expected** Mildred Pacey, 1936, in her diary, held by Arnold Pacey
Page 124: **Terrible news from the war zone** Mildred Button, 1937, in her diary, held by Arnold Pacey
Page 125: **They call it the Rape of Nanking** John Evans, in his unpublished memoir

Chapter 32
Page 126: **It was a most memorable trip** John Evans, in his unpublished memoir. All subsequent quotes in this chapter from the same source

Chapter 33
Page 130: **perhaps the most lonely and isolated mission** Kenneth May, Methodist Missionary Society annual report for South West China, 1936
Page 130: **On Saturday night March 5** Edward Moody, *Kingdom Overseas*, 1938
Page 132: **The repercussions of the Sino-Japanese war** from In *The tragedy of Stone Gateway, Kingdom Overseas*, 1938
Page 132: **With a great bodyguard** from In *The tragedy of Stone Gateway, Kingdom Overseas*, 1938
Page 132: **We had a military escort of four men** Heber Goldsworthy, quoted in In *The tragedy of Stone Gateway, Kingdom Overseas*, 1938
Page 133: **It may have been a turning point** Arnold Pacey, in a letter to Julia Bishop
Page 134: **Every journey involved Leslie in qualms** Arnold Pacey, in a letter to Julia Bishop
Page 135: **At length we came to a place** Richard Dobson *China Cycle*, 1946
Page 135: **Mildred may have left China** Arnold Pacey, in his unpublished account of his family's time in China.
Chapter 34

Page 136: **Each night after puffing its way** L. Constantine, *The Bitter Years*

Page 137: **Evans thinks that Kunming** Harold Rattenbury in his diary

Page 138: **Now we knew the aftermath of the Russo-German pact** L. Constantine, *The Bitter Years*

Page 139: **My inability to supply these returns** Alfred Evans, letter to Harold Rattenbury

Chapter 35

Page 140: **John returned from school in Hong Kong to a cool reception from Alf and Bessie** summarising the account from John Evans in his unpublished memoir. Subsequent quotes in this chapter attributed to John Evans come from the same source.

Page 140: **they simply told those close to them...** David Van Meter, Lester and Beatrice's son, in a letter to Julia Bishop

Chapter 36

Page 146: **These two were golden threads** Lester and Beatrice Van Meter, *If Only One*, 1974, this and subsequent quotes

Page 148: **Mrs Evans has her own rickshaw** Isobel Harrison in a letter home, 1940

Page 149: **To be in Kunming in the summer of 1940** L. Constantine, *The Bitter Years*

Chapter 37

Page 150: **The sky seemed full of these gleaming silver instruments of death** Lester and Beatrice Van Meter, *If Only One*, 1974

Page 151: **I shall never forget the date** Isobel Harrison in a letter home, 1940

Page 152: **The day after the first bombing** Alfred Evans, in a report, October 1940

Chapter 38

Page 154: **Chennault was a daredevil pilot** John Evans, in his unpublished memoir, this and subsequent quotes in this chapter

Page 155: **The astounding news was received with jubilation** L. Constantine, *The Bitter Years*

Chapter 39

Page 156: **When I entered the room** John Evans, in his unpublished memoir

Page 156: **You will have received my telegram** Alfred Evans in a letter to Harold Rattenbury, mission secretary, 1941.

Page 157: **Yes, it was a great shock to me** Letter from Pearl Evans to Mildred Pacey, 1941

Page 158: **confirms my suspicion** Arnold Pacey in a letter to Julia Bishop, 2001

Page 158: **I hope to serve the mission as best I can** Alfred Evans in a letter to Harold Rattenbury, 1940

Page 159: **It was a great blow to us** Isobel Harrison, in a letter to her parents, 1941

Chapter 40

Page 160: **The day after the AVG arrived** John Evans, in his unpublished memoir, this section drawn from his article in *Jing Bao Journal*, volume 61, number 367. Also subsequent quotes from John Evans in this chapter.

Page 161: **The storm has broken over us in the East** Kenneth May to Harold Rattenbury, December 1941

Chapter 41

Page 163: **The Japanese crossed** L. Constantine, *The Bitter Years*

Page 163: **all British and American influence must be eliminated** summarising The Methodist Missionary Annual Report, 1942

Page 164: **I protested that war was imminent** Kenneth Parsons, in his unpublished *China Diary*

Page 165: **Were I appointed to Kunming** Kenneth May to Harold Rattenbury, August 11, 1941.

Page 165: **You mentioned that Mrs Evans** Alfred Evans to Harold Rattenbury, July 1941

Page 165: **rented to a British military mission** Harold Rattenbury to Kenneth May, September 1943

Page 165: **he is a good deal upset** Harold Rattenbury to Kenneth May, June 1942

Page 166: **I have a feeling from what I have observed** James Heady to Harold Rattenbury, September 1943

Page 166: **Mr Evans is at present** James Heady to Harold Rattenbury, January 1944

Page 166: **It really begins a new epoch** Harold Rattenbury to Kenneth May, September 1943

Chapter 42

Page 167: **It was a two- to three-hour flight to Kunming** Jean Moore, *Daughter of China*, 1942. Also subsequent quotes in this chapter

Page 168: **This house has been a blessing to very may folk** Alfred Evans, writing to his sisters Lucy and Annie, 1947

Chapter 43

Page 170: **If there is one flag that deserves to fly** *Kingdom Overseas*, 1945

Page 170: **A Chinese Governor deposed, Fighting in Kunming** *The Times*, October 5, 1945

Page 171: **In the end the Kuomintang controlled the greater part** Geoffrey

R. Senior *The China Experience: A Study of the Methodist Mission in China,* 1994
Page 172: **The people left in Kunming were largely non-partisan** Methodist
Missionary Society annual report, 1945.

Chapter 44
Page 173: **that trouble passed and she was able to come** Alfred Evans in a
letter to his sisters Lucy and Annie, 1947. Subsequent quotes in this chapter
from the same source.
Page 174: **Very unfortunately my wife** Kenneth May to Harold Rattenbury,
1946

Chapter 45
Page 176: **Keith, hearing the truck** Kenneth Parsons, *China Diary* entry for
May 4 1947. All other quotes in this chapter from the same source

Chapter 46
Page 181: **If not specifically pro-Communist** *The Times,* September 4 1949
Page 182: **For several days there was a very strict curfew** Elliott Kendall in
*The coming of Communism to South West China and the Methodist Church. October 1949
to July 1951,* and subsequent quotes in this chapter
Page 185: **Mr Evans has become increasingly dissatisfied** Elliott Kendall,
in a letter to G Childe, July 1950

Chapter 47
Page 186: **To be quite honest, we knew** Ken Parsons, *China Diary,* 1949, this
and subsequent quotes
Page 187: **To be quite honest, a lot** Ken Parsons, quoted by Elliott Kendall
in *The coming of Communism to South West China and the Methodist Church. October
1949 to July 1951*
Page 188: **When your father and mother were here** Ken Parsons, *China Diary,*
1949

Chapter 48
Page 189: **they found an ex-army radio** Ken Parsons, *China Diary,* 1950
Page 190: **A distant relative raised a land dispute** Elliot Kendall, in a letter
written on August 13 1951 while he was sailing home on RMS Canton.
Page 190: **the vehicle arrived at the house** Elliott Kendall in *The coming of
Communism to South West China and the Methodist Church. October 1949 to July 1951*
Page 190: **kept in solitary confinement for four and a half months** Vernon
Stones, address to Missionary Society's General Committee, September 26 1951
Page 191: **It began to dawn on me** Elliott Kendall in *The coming of Communism
to South West China and the Methodist Church. October 1949 to July 1951*
Chapter 49
Page 191: **Around the time I first** Geoff Mauldon in a letter to Julia Bishop,

2001

Page 194: **For nearly two years** Geoffrey Jones in a letter to Julia Bishop, 2001

Page 194: **Vernon's particular experience** Elliott Kendall in a letter to G. Childe, July 1951

Page 194: **Freedom there is none** Elliott Kendall in a letter to G Childe, August 13, 1951

Chapter 50

Page 196: **When she came to greet me** John Evans in his unpublished memoir

Page 197: **Despite Communist claims** John Evans in his unpublished memoir

Page 197: **Pearl was a bosom friend of my mother's** Dan Lu, in a letter to Julia Bishop, 2001

Page 199: **Unfortunately it is still not wise** Alfred Evans in a letter to Mildred and Leslie Pacey, September 1960

Page 199: **It is not possible to send much** Alfred Evans in a letter to Mildred and Leslie Pacey, July 1961

Page 199: **This 77-year-old 'retired' missionary** *Methodist Recorder* 1956

Page 199: **he befriended two sisters, Jennie and Jane Fung** John Evans in his unpublished memoir

Page 200: **I am keeping remarkably well** Alfred Evans in a letter to Mildred and Leslie Pacey, September 1960

Page 201: **he is unable to go out as often as he once did** drawn from a letter written by Alfred Evans to Hilda and Walter Best, October 1961

Chapter 51

Page 202: **I am down here again for six months leave** Pearl Evans to Mildred and Leslie Pacey, May 1962

Page 203: **Since I was taken ill** Pearl Evans to Mildred and Leslie Pacey, May 1962

Page 204: **I am feeling much better** Pearl Evans to Mildred and Leslie Pacey, July 1962

Page 205: **Just a line to say goodbye** Pearl Evans to Mildred and Leslie Pacey, September 1962

Chapter 52

Page 206: **with new aircraft, to learn new skills** John Evans in his unpublished memoir. This and all subsequent quotes in this chapter

Chapter 53

Page 209: **to avoid my eighty-fifth birthday** Alfred Evans in a letter to Walter and Hilda Best, February 1964

Page 209: **Eyes are not too good** Alfred Evans in a letter to Walter and Hilda Best, November 1964

Page 210: **As according to our records** letter to Walter and Hilda Best from

W. M. Carter, Asia Field Assistant to the Methodist Missionary Society, January 1966

Page 210: **Uncle has not been too well** letter to Walter and Hilda Best from W. M. Carter, Asia Field Assistant to the Methodist Missionary Society, February 1967

Page 210: **He is still very seriously ill** letter to Walter and Hilda Best from W. M. Carter, February 1967

Page 211: **You will know how very weak and frail** letter to Walter and Hilda Best from J. Michael Franklin, February 1967

Page 211: **Pearl's request for permission to come to Alf's death bed** Ken Parsons, *My China Diary*

Page 211: **Something has always touched me strongly about his life** John Evans, in his unpublished memoir

Page 211: **His funeral ride was the most hilarious I have ever attended** Margaret Gardner, in an account sent to Julia Bishop

Chapter 54
Page 214: **The weather is getting very cold now** Pearl Evans to Mildred and Leslie Pacey, December 1967

Page 214: **the Cultural Revolution made further letter writing too risky** Arnold Pacey, in a letter to Julia Bishop, 2001

Page 214: **my mother often asked us kids** Dan Lu in a letter to Julia Bishop, 2001

Page 215: **John was told his step-sister did not have long to live** John Evans, in his unpublished memoir

Page 215: **Pan-yan had outlived Chutney by just one year** Arnold Pacey in a letter to Julia Bishop, 2001

Chapter 55
Page 216: **Forty-two years before, I had landed in the St Paul** Ken Parsons, *My China Diary*

Page 217: **One thing that struck me as peculiar** John Evans, in his unpublished memoir

Page 217: **the Communists had covered it over** Ken Parsons, *My China Diary*

Page 217: I saw myself from the outside John Evans in his unpublished memoir

Page 219: **the house Heber Goldsworthy had started to build** Ken Parsons, *My China Diary*

Afterword
Page 222: **Then there was one loo** John Parsons (Ken's son) in correspondence with Julia Bishop

ABOUT THE AUTHORS

Julia Bishop (née Bull) was born in 1945, read Politics and Economics at university and then went to work at the Atomic Energy Research Establishment, Harwell, as part of the executive staff, where she met her scientist husband, Hugh Bishop. After marriage and two children she worked in local government until she took early retirement in 2000. Her father had been researching the family history until his deteriorating sight made it impossible to continue, so he handed her a box-file full of bits of paper and notes. With the help of a genealogy computer program she continued the project and wrote it up in time for his eightieth birthday, but realised that her brief chapter on her great-uncle and great aunt, Alfred and Bessie Evans, could not do justice to the little she knew about them, so she decided to research them in more detail. It soon became apparent that they had lived extraordinary lives through extraordinary events in China. Quite a long time later, and with the help of her cousin Andy Bull, the result was this book. She lives with her husband in Oxfordshire.

Andy Bull is a journalist and author. He generally writes about travel, especially pilgrimage, and local history. When his cousin Julia Bishop called out of the blue and told him an amazing story about an ancestor he had never heard of, who rescued a one-day-old baby from a rubbish tip, and lived a life incredible in many other ways in China, in the first half of the last century, he was hooked. When she asked him to help turn her research into a book, he immediately said yes. You hold the result in your hands.

RWT.

Printed in Great Britain
by Amazon

49956247R00139